Contents

Acknowledgements

The publishers are grateful to the following for permission to reproduce copyright material:

Heinemann Educational Books Ltd and Heinemann Educational Books (East Africa) Ltd for extracts from *The Trial of Dedan Kimathi* by Ngugi wa Thiong'o and Micere Mugo; Longman Group Ltd for an extract from *Edufa* by E. T. Sutherland in Drumbeat Series; Oxford University Press for extracts from 'The Strong Breed' from *Collected Plays I* by Wole Soyinka © Wole Soyinka 1973.

The publishers are also grateful to the following for permission to reproduce photographs:

Contemporary Films for pages 66 and 68; Brian Crow for page 34; James Gibbs for pages 84, 86 and 89; John Haynes for pages 49 and 123; The Old Vic for page 141. The cover photograph was kindly supplied by Michael Etherton.
   The publishers regret that they have been unable to trace the copyright owner of the photograph that appears on page 100 and apologise for any infringement of copyright caused.

Studying Drama

Bri

wit
Da

🏛 **Longman**

The cover photograph shows a scene from *The Caucasian Chalk Circle* by Bertold Brecht, in a production given at Ahmadhu Bello University, Zaria.

Longman Group Limited,
Longman House, Burnt Mill,
Harlow, Essex, UK

Longman Nigeria Ltd.,
PMB 21036,
Ikeja,
Nigeria.

Longman Kenya Ltd.,
6th Floor,
Kenya Commercial Bank,
Industrial Area,
Nairobi,
Kenya.

Longman Zimbabwe (Pvt) Ltd.,
P.O. Box St 125,
Southerton,
Salisbury,
Zimbabwe.

First published 1983

British Library Cataloguing in Publication Data

Crow, Brian
   Studying drama.
   1. Drama – History and criticism
   I. Title
   809.2   PN1721

ISBN 0 582 64425 9

Printed in Singapore by
Selector Printing Co Pte Ltd.

Preface

This book is primarily concerned to help African students in their reading of plays by offering a practical guide to dramatic criticism. It is divided into two parts. Part One provides a guide to the craft of drama by discussing in separate chapters the basic elements common to dialogue plays, and by suggesting and exemplifying a method of reading which brings out the dramatic and theatrical nature of the text. Part Two extends the discussion to explore the characteristic features of the main kinds of drama, and ends with a chapter which examines the nature and problems of making value judgments of plays. Examples in both parts are drawn from a wide range of Western and African plays, though with African drama predominating. After each chapter in Part One there are exercises designed to test the reader's understanding of the chapter and his ability to apply the ideas to the practical criticism of a text or portion of a text, and also to stimulate further thought on relevant topics.

In most of the following chapters the discussion is tied to critical analyses of specific plays. It is therefore essential that readers should be familiar with the plays used as examples. The best approach would be for the reader to go through a chapter first, then to read the plays used in illustration of the points discussed, and then to return to the chapter, rereading it in the light of a fresh acquaintance with the plays. I give below a list of the principal plays discussed in each chapter, omitting those that are only briefly or incidentally referred to (details of the latter are given in the list of further reading at the end of the book).

Ch.2: Ola Rotimi, *Kurunmi*, Three Crowns Book, Oxford University Press, Ibadan, 1971; rptd. 1974.

Ch.3: William Shakespeare, *Hamlet*, ed. J. Dover Wilson, The New Shakespeare, Cambridge University Press, London, 1968; rptd. 1969.
Ama Ata Aidoo, *Anowa*, Longman Drumbeat Series 19, London, 1980.

Ch.4: Sophocles, *King Oedipus* in *The Theban Plays*, trans. E. F. Watling, Penguin Classics, Harmondsworth, Middlesex, 1947.
Athol Fugard, John Kani and Winston Ntshona, *Sizwe Bansi Is Dead*, in *Statements: Three Plays*, Oxford University Press, Oxford, 1947; 2nd impression, 1976.

Ch.5: Efua T. Sutherland, *Edufa*, Longman Drumbeat Series 11, London, 1979.

Athol Fugard, *Boesman and Lena*, Oxford University Press, London, 1973.
Ngugi wa Thiong'o and Micere Githae Mugo, *The Trial of Dedan Kimathi*, African Writers Series 191, Heinemann Educational Books, London, 1977.

Ch.6: Wole Soyinka, *The Strong Breed* in *Collected Plays 1*, Oxford University Press Paperback, London, 1973.

Ch.7: Efua T. Sutherland, *The Marriage of Anansewa*, Longman Drumbeat Series 19, London, 1975.
Aristophanes, *Lysistrata*, trans. Alan H. Sommerstein, Penguin Classics, Harmondsworth, Middlesex, 1973; rptd. 1975.
'Femi Osofisan, *Who's Afraid of Solarin*, Scholars Press, Nigeria, Ibadan, 1978.

Ch.8: Arthur Miller, *Death of a Salesman*, Penguin, Harmondsworth, Middlesex, 1961; rptd. 1967.
Aristotle, *Poetics*, trans. T. S. Dorsch, appears in *Classical Literary Criticism*, Penguin Classics, Harmondsworth, Middlesex, 1965; rptd. 1978.
J. P. Clark, *Ozidi*, Three Crowns Book, Oxford University Press, Oxford, 1966; rptd. 1977.
Aeschylus, *The Oresteian Trilogy*, trans. Philip Vellacott, Penguin Classics, Harmondsworth, Middlesex, 1956; rptd. 1968.
Samuel Beckett, *Waiting For Godot*, Faber and Faber, London, 1956.

Ch.9: Ngugi wa Thiong'o and Micere Githae Mugo, *The Trial of Dedan Kimathi* (see information under Ch.5).
'Zulu Sofola, *Wedlock of the Gods*, Evans Africa Plays, Evans Brothers, London and Ibadan, 1972; 4th impression, 1977.
Mukotani Rugyendo, *The Barbed Wire* in *The Barbed Wire and other plays*, African Writers Series 187, Heinemann Educational Books, London, 1977.

(The bibliographical information is to the edition used, to which the page references in the text refer).

I am grateful to Dapo Adelugba of the Theatre Arts Department of the University of Ibadan, and to Michael Etherton of the Department of English at Ahmadhu Bello University, for reading the whole book in draft and making helpful criticisms and suggestions. My thanks are also due to Tony Humphries for his help in compiling the photographs.

Introduction

By Dapo Adelugba

Brian Crow's book has come at an auspicious time when drama and theatre in Africa are beginning to gain official recognition as worthwhile fields of endeavour. School and college curricula have begun to include Drama and Theatre Arts. Educationists and the general public are now 'tuning in' to our 'station'.

Since my colleague's book speaks for itself, I wish in these introductory remarks to confine myself to general remarks on the place of educational institutions in the development of drama and theatre, the directions that drama and theatre in Africa are taking, and the role of the readers of this book.

The original position of academics, scholars and intellectuals was that drama had no place in universities or in higher educational institutions. That position is, of course no longer fashionable, but there is still the feeling in many academic quarters that only theorising about drama is valid in academia. Our own experience is that drama and theatre takes firm root when the young student is exposed to both the theory and the practice of the discipline. Brian Crow's analysis firmly establishes this point of view, and a careful study of it and of the exercises provided would be richly rewarding.

Ideally, drama and theatre should be introduced from a very early age. Due to the absence of theatre studies from school curricula at the primary and secondary levels in Africa, much basic introductory work, unfortunately, has often to be done at the university level where the student is being exposed to the subject in a curricular programme for the first time. There are signs that Nigeria will soon introduce theatre studies at all levels of education; it is hoped that other African countries would do likewise.

But the truth of the matter is that, in spite of the absence of an established school curriculum, there are many schools and colleges in Africa today whose enthusiastic and gifted staff have helped to develop and nourish drama and theatre. Unfortunately, however, when such devoted persons move away from a particular school or college and go elsewhere, the traditions they had built during their tenure soon wither into insignificance or disappear entirely. And enthusiasm, while it could go a long way, is not often enough. Misdirected and ill-informed enthusiasts could do damage to the nurture of the young in the fields of creative endeavour. The need for skilled teachers of drama has led to the development of programmes in Educational Drama and Educational Theatre.

There is, in my view, a need to develop unique educational drama and theatre traditions in Africa. At Ibadan, where I teach, I have attempted to encourage our students to consider the gradual development of a new dimension in creative arts instruction. While our students are fully briefed on the Anglo-American Drama-in-Education (D.I.E.) and Theatre-in-Education (T.I.E.) traditions, they are also encouraged to recognise the emergence of a new approach — Theatre-Arts-in-Education, which I wish to christen T.A.I.E.

A brief reflection on traditions of performing arts in Africa leads one inevitably to recognise the close relationship between dance, music, masks, design and oral performance in many contexts. The study of these traditions can produce novel results in the emerging educational drama and theatre efforts of teachers and arts educators in Africa. Some of the plays chosen for examination in this book will, we hope, lead the reader to a deeper reflection on the beauty and the richness of texture of the performing arts. Efua Sutherland's *The Marriage of Anansewa* is perhaps the classic in this regard.

When considering Efua Sutherland, one of the foremost leaders of theatre in Ghana, it is necessary to point out that her *Edufa*, another play used by Brian Crow in this book, is an adaptation of a Greek play. It is my firm belief that Africans, like all other citizens of the world, can be enriched by a knowledge of cultures and traditions outside of their own. The current fad in some misguided circles towards slogans — 'African plays for Africans', 'concentrate on your own culture', etc. — can only lead to a narrowing of the intellectual horizons of young Africans. Brian Crow's approach does not fall into this error: he has used plays from Africa and from other continents in a free and attractive manner.

This is not to reject the commonsensical theory that cultural education should begin at home. The reversal of the old unhealthy trend whereby Africans were educated in 'daffodil culture' while being blissfully ignorant of their indigenous cultures is most welcome. The increasing number of African plays in our bookshops is a good sign for the future.

Where, then, we may ask, is drama and theatre in Africa going? There was a time, in the not so far away colonial period, when educated African playwrights wanted their plays to be as near-British or as near-French as possible. Such plays are now, happily, few and far between. Drama in Africa, even when it uses an inherited European language, has become identifiably African.

Although we can assert that African drama in English and in French is now, for the most part, unmistakably African, there is no doubt that the use of a European language to express African thought and ideas raises interesting, sometimes unresolvable problems. How does the playwright create the appropriate register for the various classes or for the various age-groups? How will the different levels of fluency in the characters' own language be carried over into the language which the playwright has chosen as his medium of expression?

On account of the variety of ways in which African dramatists of English or French expression have approached these and other salient aesthetic questions, it is impossible to come forward with a simple formula. Even among the playwrights discussed in this book, as can be seen, there are differences in approaches to the language question. This is one of the side issues the reader may wish to consider as he goes along with Brian Crow on a worthy adventure.

There is also the wide and exciting field of drama and theatre in the indigenous languages of Africa. And, as educational policies in the continent insist more and more on the training of the young in their own languages, educated playwrights who can write fluently and expressively in their indigenous tongues will begin to emerge in larger numbers than hitherto. Training programmes in drama and theatre in Africa are already endeavouring to use indigenous languages and cultures with imagination, and the results of these will lead ultimately to the development of a methodology for arts pedagogy from which other countries may well, as time goes on, borrow. The time when curricular programmes could be blissfully imported from Europe or America and applied with tenacious exactitude can now be looked back at not in anger but with regret for the naivety of misdirected ardour.

And now, reader, what is your role? There is a widely held misconception that drama and theatre are for the wild ones, the way-out individuals, the eccentrics, the drop-outs. Nothing could be further from the truth. It is of course true for drama and theatre, as for all the arts, that a combination of intelligence and talent is needed to achieve success. But talent has been rightly described by an eminent wit as ninety-nine per cent perspiration and one per cent inspiration.

The reader of this book is enjoined, no matter how talented he is, to make the necessary effort to get the utmost out of it. While the majority of readers will emerge from the adventure as better analysts there will be some readers who will also emerge as stronger and more sure-footed creators. That is our fervent hope.

Drama and theatre belong not only in the world of the creative arts but also, to some degree, in the world of literature. Brian Crow's training in the latter world and his keen sensitivity to the former are richly harvested here.

So, reader, over to you.

Dapo Adelugba
Arts Director
Department of Theatre Arts
University of Ibadan

Part One

1 Drama and theatre

The words 'drama' and 'dramatic' are constantly used in everyday life without referring directly to the form of social recreation carried on in theatres. An airliner crashes, the passengers and crew are killed or seriously injured, and the newspapers will almost certainly refer to the incident as 'dramatic'; a government is overthrown and the former president disappears, and the headlines will announce 'Political drama in X-land'. Even when something less sensational happens, when for example we see a road accident, we are likely to say that we witnessed a 'drama', or a 'dramatic' event. What we really mean when we use 'drama' and 'dramatic' to describe events of this kind is that something sensational, or at least out of the ordinary, has occurred. The relatively dull routine of life has for a while been interrupted by something exciting, something that appeals to our imagination.

We know, of course, that when we describe such an exciting event as a 'drama' we are using the word differently from its use to describe a particular kind of theatrical representation, performed by actors for an audience. But the very fact that we use the same words to describe both sensational or exciting events and what happens in a theatre should alert us to certain connections between the two kinds of event. The most obvious similarity is that when we watch a drama in the theatre, or perhaps more likely nowadays at the cinema or on television, the events portrayed arouse excitement or curiosity similar to those evoked by certain incidents in real life, such as the fall of a government or an air crash. Not only is the excitement similar; often, the situations and happenings portrayed in drama are of the same kind as those real-life events that evoke newspaper headlines and stories which use the words 'drama' and 'dramatic'. Much drama, especially film drama, deals with political upheavals, with war, with spies and spying, with murder and assassinations, with disasters both natural and man-made — the very things that capture our imagination when we read about them really happening in our newspaper.

Drama does not always portray sensational happenings of this kind, or gain its grip on the audience in such an obvious way. Much drama does not feature particularly extraordinary people or incidents; and yet, if it is good, it contrives to capture our interest, to excite us imaginatively, to lay hold on our minds or hearts or both, at least for the time we are watching it. And in this, it has a similar, if not identical, appeal to exciting events in real life that we think of as 'dramatic'.

We are excited by watching, or hearing about, people being involved in events unlike the events of our own usually rather dull lives. The original meaning of the Greek word 'drama', 'to do', 'to act', suggests the nature of the excitement; most of us cannot help being interested in the doings or acts of others. At its most ordinary and least glorious level, this is the excitement of a 'nosey' person listening to a new bit of gossip. At its most elevated, at the level of dramatic art, it is the excitement we feel at being imaginatively involved in the significant imaginary lives of the characters on stage.

The theatre is the place we go to watch, and participate in, a kind of fantasy-life, to be 'nosey' about human beings in a special, organised way. The word 'theatre' also comes originally from a Greek word, *theatron*, which meant a 'seeing-place'. Of course, the word 'theatre' is used to describe more than just the building in which plays are performed: we talk of someone wanting 'to go into the theatre', meaning that he wants to join the theatrical profession, the people engaged in various ways in creating and performing plays. More important, we often use the words 'drama' and 'dramatic' and 'theatre' and 'theatrical' interchangeably; after seeing a play we might remark that 'it was a good piece of theatre', just as we might say 'it was a good piece of drama'. Even though we usually think of 'drama' and 'theatre' as being synonymous, and though there is no harm in using the two words to mean the same thing in conversation, it is possible, and critically useful, to distinguish between them.

What, then, is the difference?

The words 'theatre' and 'theatrical' can be applied to a wide variety of performances conducted for audiences. These are not necessarily plays. When an African leader decides to have himself crowned as emperor the word 'theatrical' seems an appropriate adjective to describe the 'performance' in which he is crowned, paid homage to, and his ascent to the imperial throne celebrated by state banquets and so forth. When a play is performed or a spectacular dance is executed by performers for an audience we naturally describe these occasions as being theatrical. If a masquerade or ritual is performed seasonally in the streets of a town or village we again think of this as being an example of theatre. When a brilliant orator makes a political speech to his supporters at an emotional party rally, 'theatrical' seems a suitable description. In fact, a whole range of quite different activities can be described as theatrical because they do have one thing in common — a 'larger than life', spectacular element in the performance, which is usually also connected with the arousal of emotion in the audience. In any happening that we feel deserves the description 'theatrical' we are confronted with a spectacle, a combination of — among other things — movement, gesture, voice, costume and physical objects in an impressive display.

The performance of a play is clearly an example of that wide range of activities we collectively describe as theatre. But it is only one example, one type of a large collection of activities some of which we would not think of calling 'dramatic'. What, then, distinguishes drama as a particular identifiable branch of the theatre? It is possible to answer this question in a number of different ways, at a number of different levels. But I offer this as a working definition of drama: a type of theatrical performance in which the active participants impersonate (that is, pretend to be people, beings or things other than they really are), and through a usually predetermined sequence of physical actions enact a story for the entertainment of an audience.

Drama could be defined in other, more complex, ways. We could, for example, try to describe it by identifying the particular kind of relationship that exists between the audience and a play in performance — by showing, that is, the peculiar nature of the dramatic response compared with our response to other kinds of literature. Or we could try to define drama at a sociological level by identifying its social nature and function — in other words, by describing as precisely as possible what kind of social activity it is and what effects it has on the audience's social behaviour generally. There are other directions, too, from which we could approach the task of saying what drama is, but let us proceed, at least for the time being, on the basis of the practical definition I have offered.

According to this definition, a variety of theatrical entertainments that are not dialogue plays must still be considered generally dramatic. A dance-drama, which may have no dialogue or speech, conforms to the definition given above, because the performers impersonate characters through the physical movements of their dancing, and a story is enacted through the sequence of dance movements. Similarly, the performer or performers of a mime-drama must by definition remain silent, but their performance is dramatic because they exploit movement and gesture to enact a story for the audience. Opera too is dramatic, even though the performers sing their words, usually to a musical accompaniment, instead of, or in addition to, speaking them. Thus, although speech is often thought of as being an essential ingredient of drama, it is actually quite common in Africa and elsewhere for impersonation to take place without a word being uttered, or for words to be uttered musically. Speech, then, is an essential feature of dialogue plays, but not of drama generally; and the same is true of stage-settings, costumes, stage properties and stage lighting, all of which are commonly used in theatrical entertainments but are not absolutely essential elements of drama. We can, in short, do without them, and yet still perform a dramatic entertainment.

If we apply our working definition of drama to a theatrical activity like ritual, we discover that what usually happens in a ritual ceremony does not quite conform to the definition. Ritual ceremonies differ among themselves, so it is dangerous to generalise. But it is probably true to say that most rituals do not involve true impersonation, the kind in which a performer consciously and deliberately seeks to represent someone other than himself. A Christian priest conducting a Mass, for example, does not impersonate anyone, and neither does an Islamic *imam* when he leads his fellow Muslims in prayer. The objection can be raised that in some ritual ceremonies the performers don costumes and masks and temporarily assume the identity of another being, usually a spirit. This of course is true, but is it, properly speaking, impersonation? My own feeling is that it is not, because in such ceremonies the performer usually enters a psychological state called 'possession', in which he believes that he actually *is* the spirit, that the spirit is actually inside him. The performer is not consciously and calculatingly imitating the behaviour of the spirit, which would be true impersonation; he is for a time actually *being* the spirit, or so he and his audience believe. It may of course happen that, as religious and cultural attitudes change, a particular ritual ceremony continues to be performed in a community but its significance for the performer and audience changes. It may be that the performer no longer becomes possessed, and the audience no longer believe that he embodies the spirit; and if this is so, we can say that the activity has changed from being a ritual to being drama, at least in as much as possession has been replaced by genuine impersonation.

Another reason why ritual ceremonies usually do not qualify as drama, according to my definition, is that they rarely, if ever, involve a sequence of physical actions the enactment of which communicates a coherent story to the audience. Physical actions they have in plenty, and usually the performers must do these actions in a strictly ordered sequence, otherwise the spiritual effectiveness of the ceremony is felt to be impaired. But what is communicated by this sequence of actions, though meaningful to the initiated spectators, is not what we usually think of as a story. It is possible, and quite likely, that the ritual ceremony is *based on* a story, perhaps a very old story about how the world, or mankind, or the tribe, came into being. But this does not mean that the story is immediately apparent or is being retold through the actions of the ritual. The ritual enactment is more likely to be an attempt to enter into direct contact with the spirit-world than an attempt to communicate a particular story through action. This is the case in the Christian Mass, as well as in African traditional ritual celebrations. The priestly celebrants of the Mass are trying to enter into spiritual communion with God, rather than telling the story of Christ, even though the story of Christ's life underlies the enactment of the Mass.

There is clearly a great deal of overlap between ritual celebration and true drama, and it is easy to see why people commonly think of ritual enactments as 'dramatic'. It is certainly true that performances which are undoubtedly dramatic have developed out of ritual enactments; Greek tragedy did so, and much of medieval European drama arose out of Christian religious observance. In contemporary Africa, dramatists have found traditional ritual occasions and ceremonies fruitful sources and subjects. Among African plays which in some way are based on or which dramatise ritual ceremonies are *The Contest* by the Ugandan Mukotani Rugyendo; *Ozidi* by J. P. Clark from Nigeria; and *Kongi's Harvest*, *The Road* and *Death and the King's Horseman* by Wole Soyinka. It may be that African cultures and attitudes will change so much that traditional ceremonies will come to be thought of as dramatic theatre rather than ritual theatre, and will be adapted to become fully dramatic in performance. In any case it is critically useful to make the distinction between ritual and drama, even though we should constantly recognise how closely related they are and accept that ritual may have dramatic elements in it even if it is not properly drama.

Before we leave the subject, it is worth mentioning another kind of theatrical performance common to African cultural traditions which is closely related to drama and often contains dramatic elements. This is the story-telling performance, in which an amateur or professional story-teller recounts tales, usually well-known traditional tales, for an audience. Often, the storyteller not only narrates his or her story, but 'performs' by acting out some at least of the characters and actions of the tale. For example, when the narrator tells the audience what a particular character said, he adopts the 'voice' of that person (or animal), and perhaps even suggests, through movement and gesture, the behaviour of the character. At such moments, when the narrator is impersonating the characters in the story, we are very close to drama, and we may even describe such moments as dramatic 'interludes' in the storytelling. But even though they may contain these moments when the story is conveyed through action and impersonation, story-telling performances cannot really be categorised as drama. The chief means for communicating the story to the audience remains words rather than actions, and generally the element of impersonation is not sustained for very long. It is easy to see how such an entertainment can become fully dramatic, and why it is that African dramatists can be influenced by traditional storytelling, both in the subject-matter of their plays and in their form. (See, for example, Efua Sutherland's *The Marriage of Anansewa*, which is based on the storytelling art of the Akan-speaking people of Ghana.)

Within our definition of drama, as I have said, must be included various types of theatrical entertainment that do not make use of speech or dialogue. In this book, however, we will be concerned only with the kind of drama that does make extensive use of words, in addition to the other resources of theatre. Moreover, we shall devote most of our attention to those dialogue plays which are the product of a writer's attempt to say something serious and genuinely interesting about our experience of life. The most popular drama of our time, the drama which attracts the largest audiences, is not usually, or even often, serious in this way. It is entertainment for its own sake, offering its audience amusement without the necessity of thought, thrills and sensation without too great a concern for probability — in general, escape from the routine of real life, with its often harsh realities, into an imaginary fantasy world.

Nowadays, plays are not confined to live performance on a stage for a relatively small audience. The introduction of technological media — such as film, television and radio — allows dramatic performances to be recorded on celluloid or tape or performed live in a television or radio studio and transmitted to thousands, even millions, of people at the same time. Clearly dramatists have had to adapt their dramatic craftsmanship to suit these contemporary media. In a filmed drama or telvision play, for example, all sorts of events and actions and settings can be realistically depicted in a way that they could not be on a stage in a theatre. Film-makers can simulate sensational events like the destruction of a skyscraper building by fire, or can reveal all the details of a normal physical environment in a way which the stage could never adequately do. Because so much can be shown or suggested through sophisticated photography of settings and action, the scriptwriters of film and television drama have to structure their plays differently from stage-plays. Similarly, a radio play depends entirely on aural communication: the writer of a radio play cannot show his audience anything at all, except through sounds; obviously, then, he must compose his drama in a quite different way from the stage-dramatist to allow for the absence of the visual dimension and the exclusive reliance on sound.

In spite of the technical differences in the way drama can be communicated, all drama — whether it be on the stage, film, television or radio — is characterised by the use of impersonation carried on through a sequence of actions which convey a story to the audience. When the actor impersonates he is creating a character, and when a number of characters are shown in interaction with each other there is produced that sequence of events and situations which we call the 'plot' or the 'action'. We must look more closely at character and plot since they are fundamental elements of drama and the terms most commonly used in describing and analysing plays. But before we do so a few more general remarks on drama are required, and we need also to think about how plays can be appreciated and enjoyed even when we can only read them, rather than watch them being performed in a theatre.

Exercises for Chapter 1: Drama and theatre

1 Describe (a) a *theatrical* performance you have personally witnessed (e.g. a ritual ceremony such as a wedding or initiation, a storytelling performance, a political rally) and (b) a fully *dramatic* performance (e.g. a dialogue play, dance-drama) that you have seen.

　　Compare the elements of impersonation and story told through actions in the performances. Suggest in what ways the two performances had different *effects* on you as a member of the audience.

2 Do you know of any traditional ceremony or performance which has changed considerably in recent years? If you do not know of one personally ask older people if they have noticed such changes. On the basis of the evidence you are able to collect write a brief description of the performance *as it used to be* compared with what it is now. Suggest the general nature and direction of the changes that have occurred. Suggest the possible social reasons for the changes.

2 Approaches

We begin our approach to the study of drama in this chapter by looking first at the nature and significance of dramatic *conventions*, those 'rules' which all dramatists must know and obey if they are to write dramatically successful plays. We will see how in the drama of the past and the present there are broadly speaking two basic conventions, the realistic and the non-realistic. The rest of the chapter introduces a method of reading plays *theatrically* so that, as the reader absorbs the words on the page, he is able to 'see' and 'hear' in his mind the action and dialogue.

Conventions

We talk of 'going to see a play', of the actors 'playing their parts'; but we also talk of children 'playing' in the street. Like the word 'drama', the word 'play' in English can obviously be used to refer both to activities that occur in normal, everyday life and to the more specific activity that goes on in theatres. Is this a coincidence, a mere verbal peculiarity in the English language? Apparently not, for in other languages too the ideas of playing a drama and playing a game are expressed through the same word. In French, a play and a game are both called *'jeu'*; in German the word is *'Spiel'*; in Hausa a children's game and a dramatic performance are both called *'wasa'*.

Clearly, the use of the same word in different languages to signify the playing of games on the one hand and the performance of plays on the other suggests that people see an underlying connection between both activities. The more we think about it, the more similarities we perceive between playing games and performing a play. In both, the players are required to use their imaginations, usually more than they normally have to do in their routine lives. Games often involve conflict, as does drama: the conflict between two teams in a football match can be as thrilling in its way as the conflict between characters in a play, and the suspense can be as great. A football match, like a stage play, arouses the emotions of the spectators, takes them out of themselves, captures their imaginations. Football matches, like plays, are artificial activities, in the sense that they are not a necessary and inevitable part of normal social life: and yet, for all their artificiality, they both involve intense and real feelings; the participants and audiences of both are very serious about their playing. In games and in drama the players and the audiences are free to be imaginative, but greater freedom of imagination is accompanied by more than usually strict adherence to rules. If the rules are broken in any serious way the game — football or play — is in jeopardy: it can no longer be taken as seriously as it was.

What are these rules that govern sports, games that children and adults play, and dramatic performances? They are agreements made between the players, and sometimes also between the players and the audience, about the object of the game, how things should be done and how the players (and perhaps the audience) should behave as this object is pursued. Another word for rules is conventions: in games we normally talk about the rules, but in drama they are termed *conventions*.

Dramatic conventions, then, are agreements made between the participants in the drama, including of course that very important participant the audience, about how the dramatic playing should be conducted. Some conventions are essential to drama, and they always have been and will be present in the performance of a play. We have already mentioned these in our working definition of drama in the previous chapter. There is the essential convention that the actors and audience accept the fiction that the actors will pretend to be people other than themselves. It is because audiences normally accept this convention that we are not outraged when a number of people appear before us with the express purpose of practising a kind of deception on us. We do not shout 'Liar!' or 'Cheat!', because we have agreed to be 'deceived'.

There is another essential convention, which is that the players should perform a sequence of actions (any combination of moving about the stage, gesturing, speaking or singing) which, taken together, add up to a coherent *story*. Although the stories which are enacted in drama differ greatly, yet there is a tacit agreement among all the participants that a story of some kind must be conveyed through the presentation of characters in action.

There are no other essential conventions in drama. Dialogue — the agreement that the actors will speak to each other as if they actually are the people they are pretending to be — is often taken to be a necessary dramatic convention It is certainly, and self-evidently, an essential convention of the dialogue play, but it is not a necessary feature of drama generally, as dance-drama and mime both prove. Dialogue, along with monologue and direct address to the audience, are speech conventions which can be found in some, but not all, drama. There are other conventions of this kind which are found in some drama from different cultures and over a long period of time, but which are not present in all drama all the time. For example, costume and make-up — to identify the characters and help to sustain their fictional personalities — are common conventions of drama; it is agreed that the actors should wear special clothes and cosmetics as part of the process of impersonation; but it is also accepted that it is not always essential for such costume and make-up to be used. Costume and make-up, like dialogue and the other speech conventions, are permanent but not essential and necessary features of drama: we agree to their use, but sometimes we also agree *not* to use them.

The drama of a particular culture at a particular point in its history is likely to favour certain conventions rather than others. For example, in Shakespeare's day the monologue and the aside were frequently employed, but nowadays they are rarely used. Why? Mainly because the majority of plays now being written and performed employ the conventions of realism, which was not the case in Shakespeare's day. It would be justifiably regarded as a complete breach of the 'rules' of realism if a character were suddenly to address the audience as though none of the other characters could hear him, or as if he had been aware of the audience's presence all along. What a character could once have said in a monologue or an aside must now be conveyed in other ways, most likely through the dialogue. Similarly, a modern realistic play could not employ, as Shakespeare occasionally did, a Chorus who could stand before the audience and ask them to imagine that many years had elapsed since the last scene. The passage of time would now have to be shown in other, more 'realistic', ways — for example, by alterations to the actors' appearance and acting, to suggest the ageing of the characters.

Realism and non-realism

The dominant convention in modern drama, then, is realism. What is meant by this term? Essentially, it means the representation of characters, actions and physical objects on stage in a strikingly lifelike manner. The dramatist does everything he can to make his characters behave *as if* they were real people in real-life situations and settings; and he is aided in this by the director, the designer and the actors. Another word which is sometimes used instead of realism, but which in this context means the same thing, is 'naturalism'. Virtually all film and television drama is in the realistic or naturalistic convention; and a great deal of stage drama, both in the West and in Africa, is either wholly realistic or deeply influenced by its conventions.

Most of us have become so familiar with realistic conventions that we do not even notice that they are conventions. We have become so accustomed to them that we take them for granted. The play begins: we see a room much like a room in our own home; we see people sitting or standing around, wearing the sort of clothes we wear, talking to each other in the language we ourselves use in everyday life, perhaps smoking cigarettes or drinking beer, just as we ourselves sometimes do. How could the portrayal of life be any different? This is 'real', an exact copy of real life. Sometimes, understandably, people forget that the portrayal of life *can* be different, that it does not necessarily have to follow the conventions of realism. When they forget this they complain that the drama is 'not true to life', not 'real'; it is 'unconvincing' or 'unbelievable'.

But most of us realise, after a moment's thought, that plays can portray life using conventions quite different from those employed in realistic drama. Indeed, most of the world's drama since the ancient Greeks has been 'non-realistic' in its conventions. (Note that we say 'non-realistic' and not 'unrealistic', which means something quite different!) Modern realism — the attempt to portray people, actions and material objects with photographic fidelity — is a very recent invention; interestingly, it came into vogue about the same time as photography began to develop, in the second half of the nineteenth century. Even today, much drama is non-realistic. Non-realistic plays can and do vary considerably among themselves, of course, but they do share a common feature: none makes a sustained attempt to portray life on the stage as if it were real life. This does *not* mean that non-realistic plays are less 'serious', less 'true to life' than realistic drama. It is possible to communicate something serious, something thoroughly true to life, without doing so as if the audience were watching real life itself.

That most Western drama has been — until recent times — non-realistic and yet also 'serious' is shown by the traditional use of verse. By virtue of the characters — or the major characters — speaking most of the time in verse, a play necessarily belongs to the non-realistic convention. It excludes the possibility that the dramatist is making a sustained attempt to present his characters in as lifelike a way as possible, since real people never spontaneously speak verse. When Shakespeare's Hamlet says:

> To be, or not to be, that is the question,
> Whether 'tis nobler in the mind to suffer
> The slings and arrows of outrageous fortune,
> Or to take arms against a sea of troubles,
> And by opposing, end them . . .   (p. 60)

he is speaking as no real person ever has or will. Shakespeare has granted Hamlet the expressive powers of a great poet, so that everything he says has the metaphorical richness found only in great poetry. The audience — both in Shakespeare's time and ours — knows that this is impossible; but the use of verse was, and is known to have been, a recognised convention of the drama when Shakespeare wrote, and is therefore accepted without question.

Although it is useful to divide drama into the two broad conventions of realism and non-realism, it must be borne in mind that plays within the same convention can differ widely, and that some plays successfully combine realistic and non-realistic elements. All drama, realistic or non-realistic, is a *stylisation* of life, an artificial selection and arrangement of certain aspects of life. Consequently, it is possible for a dramatist to vary the level of stylisation within a single play. Shakespeare, for example, often did this: his aristocratic characters normally speak in verse and behave quite differently from the 'low' characters, who speak in prose and whose behaviour is often clownish or comical. The characters in Shakespeare's plays are thus regularly *stylised* at different levels.

Of course, the variation in the level of stylisation at which characters can be presented is not restricted to the contrast between the 'upper' and 'lower' class characters. For example, in *The Good Woman of Setzuan*, by the modern German dramatist Bertolt Brecht, the basic idea around which the play is built allows for — indeed, virtually necessitates — a combination of the realistic and the fantastic. The play begins on a note of fantasy: three gods have come down to earth in search of a single human being whose virtue will redeem humanity and show that goodness is still possible in the world. They arrive at the Chinese city of Setzuan, still not having found such a person. In Setzuan they cannot even find accommodation until a kindly prostitute, Shen Te, agrees to give them shelter. In reward for this act of goodness — the first and only one the gods have witnessed during their stay on earth — they give Shen Te a sum of money, with which she is able to buy a small tobacco shop. The rest of the play deals with Shen Te's attempts to survive and remain her kind-hearted self in a ruthless, mercenary world where almost everyone is ready to live off or cheat the generous person.

Much of the play's action conforms to the realistic convention. Take, for example, this piece of dialogue:

MRS SHIN: How do you do, Miss Shen Te. You like your new home?
SHEN TE: Indeed yes. Did your children have a good night?
MRS SHIN: In that hovel? The youngest is coughing already.
SHEN TE: Oh, dear!
MRS SHIN: You're going to learn a thing or two in these slums.
SHEN TE: Slums? That's not what you said when you sold me the shop!
MRS SHIN: Now don't start nagging! Robbing me and my innocent children of their home and then calling it a slum! That's the limit! (*She weeps*)
SHEN TE: (*tactfully*) I'll get your rice.   (p. 29)

Shen Te and Mrs Shin, both in what they say and do, are recognisable as the lower-class inhabitants of a big city. Given a realistic stage setting, this piece of dialogue — and many others like it — would belong to the realm of realism or naturalism. But this does not make the play as a whole realistic; for there is the basically non-realistic event of the gods' occasional appearances, and at the end of the play their ascent into heaven on a cloud; and there is also the fact that in order to protect herself against those who would live off her Shen Te is forced to disguise herself as her (non-existent) male cousin, Shui Ta. In real life, we know that a woman cannot effectively disguise herself as a man and successfully deceive her closest acquaintances, as Shen Te does. Brecht employs other non-realistic devices in the play: for example, the characters sometimes directly address the audience; the action is regularly interrupted for songs; and there are dream sequences in which the gods appear to Wong the water-seller. Clearly, *The Good Woman of Setzuan* makes use of both realistic and non-realistic conventions, but the realism is framed by and contained within an essentially non-realistic style of presentation.

The dramatist is free to decide at what level he wishes to stylise his representation of life in any particular play, or — if he so decides — to combine different levels of stylisation. In other words, there is a wide range of conventions available to the dramatist; and for a few of the very best dramatists there is also the possibility of creating new conventions. This freedom is restricted only by the writer's own creative aims and limitations, and the need to communicate effectively with a particular audience.

To understand and appreciate all the possible conventions of drama would of course require a familiarity with a very wide range of plays from different periods of history and different cultures. Sometimes, even though a play is from a different time and place than our own, it is quite easy to recognise and imaginatively participate in the conventions it uses. On other occasions, a full response to the play depends on a knowledge of the culture, and especially the artistic culture, from which it emerged. The problem of not understanding some of the conventions employed in a play is more likely to occur, of course, with a play from an alien culture, or one from the remote past.

Sometimes even a play from our own time and place causes this difficulty. When Samuel Beckett's play *Waiting for Godot* was first performed in Europe in the 1950s audiences were generally mystified by it, and some were even indignant that such 'nonsensical' plays should be written and performed. Only gradually did audiences come to understand and appreciate the conventions operating in *Waiting for Godot*, and now it is regarded by many critics and theatregoers as one of the best and most important plays to have been written in Europe in recent times.

An African play which I suspect presents comparable difficulties, both for African and for non-African audiences, is *The Road* by Wole Soyinka. A convention much used in *The Road*, and on which much of its effectiveness depends, is that the characters 'move' into the past and re-enact the events of the past as if they could not control themselves, and as if time itself were totally fluid. When one reads the play, it is especially difficult to recognise this convention at work, and so it becomes inaccessible even for some Nigerian readers.

Visualising the play

As a difficult play like *The Road* demonstrates, it is crucial for the understanding and appreciation of any play to see what conventions are operating, and how and why they are at work. An audience which is able to watch a good performance of *The Road* will understand the time convention we have mentioned more easily than a reader of the play. In general, dramatic conventions are more apparent when we watch than when we read. The director, designer and actors have already done much of the work for us by identifying and understanding the conventions themselves and interpreting them appropriately in the performance. Plays are intended for performance, and their conventions are therefore conventions of performance — agreements between the performers and the audience which are only fully apparent, which only make complete sense, when the play is actually being performed. It is assumed, however, that the readership of this book will experience drama primarily through reading plays. We must therefore face the problem: how can we identify and appreciate conventions of performance when we do not see the plays performed? How do we even know that a particular convention is at work?

The text of a play is intended by the writer to be *a preparation for performance* rather than something which is complete in itself, like the text of a poem or novel. The script of a play is comparable with the notes written by a composer on a sheet of music paper: to achieve its completed form it needs performance, just as the music has to be played on musical instruments. Actually, it is not strictly accurate to say that a playscript is like musical notation: the notes in music are nothing until they are played; but words on a page can be read and enjoyed for their own sake. A play *can* be read as a purely literary work, like a novel or poem. If it is read in this way the pleasure of the play comes from the literary quality of the words, without any consideration being given to what the play would be like in performance. Most plays are in fact read in this way: not as drama but as literature. The problem arises when the reader either does not know how to read a play as drama, or when he confuses a dramatic reading with a literary reading: when he *thinks* he is reading a play as drama but is actually reading it as literature. When this happens, the reader lays himself open not only to an impoverished understanding of the play, but also perhaps to a distorted understanding, to misinterpretation.

The only way to read a play *dramatically* is to visualise it in the mind's eye as one reads. But to visualise a play as one reads, to turn the words into action scene by scene is easier said then done. How do we go about it?

The rest of our discussion in Part One will be aimed at answering this question as fully as possible. We can start by considering what we actually find when we open the text of a play, and by thinking particularly about an important feature of the text which readers often do not pay sufficient attention to — the stage directions.

When we open the book which contains the text of a play, we are confronted with only one thing — words. The first words in the text do not usually belong to the play itself. These words are normally given a page to themselves and comprise the list of the characters' names. (Sometimes, the list is headed with the words *dramatis personae*, 'the persons of the drama'.) In addition to the list of characters there is sometimes other prefatory material, the most common being a note by the dramatist about how he thinks the play could be or should be staged, or a note about the historical background of the events portrayed in the play.

Play readers are often tempted to pass an eye quickly over the list of characters and other introductory matter without taking real notice. But is is usually well worth spending a few moments carefully reading the list of characters and other notes. This is particularly necessary if a play has many characters. For instance, the historical epic *Kurunmi* by the Nigerian dramatist Ola Rotimi has 41 named characters. It is evidently going to be necessary to turn back to the list of characters quite frequently as we read the play to find out who they are. But our task is made easier by studying the list before we begin, especially as Rotimi gives us some assistance by dividing the characters into their different ethnic groups. Also, Rotimi gives us as part of the introductory material a brief 'Historical Note', which describes the historical circumstances on which the play is based. This, together with close reference to the list of characters, is a considerable help in identifying the characters and their relationships.

The usefulness of introductory material which many readers ignore is shown by the preliminary note to the text of *The Trial of Dedan Kimathi* by the Kenyan writers Ngugi wa Thiong'o and Micere Mugo. After the list of characters there is a note which reads:

The atmosphere is tense and saturated with sadness, as if the whole land is in mourning. Events move at a tremendous speed, people act with a general sense of urgency, as if to compete with time which is running ahead of them.

The play is in three movements which should be viewed as a single movement. The action should, on the whole be seen as breaking the barrier between formal and infinite time, so that past and future and present flow into one another. The scenes (street, cell, courtroom) should also flow into one another.

There is impersonation, merging of characters and reflection of history emphasising the complexity, duality and inter-relationships of people and events. A character like Shaw Henderson, for instance, can be played as a Judge-Prosecutor and member of the Special Branch. He is also the enemy-friend of the Africans.

(p. 2)

The dramatists have perhaps not said this as clearly as they might have, but their aims are nevertheless fairly evident. They want the performance to move along quickly (have 'pace'), reflecting the sense of historical urgency which is part of the content of the play. They also want scenes to merge with one another, even though they are set in different times and places. This is a practical suggestion as to how the play can be given in performance the pace which the dramatists have already recommended. It is also a way of expressing, through the staging, the play's concern with the relationship between past, present and future — showing how these are not separate and unconnected, but related points on a single line. Thus, the oppression of black people in the past (the slave trade) continues in the present, in a different but no less obnoxious form; and though the *way* in which white imperialists and their black collaborators exploit the black masses has changed from the days of slavery, the dramatists insist that exploitation and oppression have basically remained unchanged in essentials. Similarly, casting and the style of acting should reflect the relationships between people and events: several characters represent the whites in Kenya, but there is a sense in which they are merely aspects of one 'character' — British imperialism — and it is therefore appropriate for one actor to play several roles, thus bringing out for the audience the idea of their basic similarity politically.

When we read *The Trial of Dedan Kimathi* it is important to bear this production note in mind, and to try to 'see' the play being performed in the manner suggested by the writers. We have been given a useful hint about the conventions of performance envisaged by the dramatists, and we should make use of this hint to enrich our visualisation of the play.

Following the introductory matter is the text of the play itself. The texts of plays are composed of words, of two distinct types: words which are meant to be spoken by the characters, which are printed after their names; and words that belong to the stage directions which are usually scattered throughout the play (these words are usually in italics, to distinguish them from the rest).

The first words we are likely to read are the opening stage direction. This probably contains a more or less detailed description of the setting for the particular scene or Act, or even perhaps the entire play if there is only one setting. The first stage direction is thus often a crucial help in visualising the action of the play. The first stage direction in *Kurunmi* reads:

> *The play opens on Kurunmi's 'agbo'le', the closest English term for which is 'compound'. Even this term falls miserably short in portraying the sacred pictorial essence of what an 'agbo'le' really is. In this particular 'agbo'le', for instance, the gods of the tribe are present in varying images of earth, granite and wood. Here also exist, or are believed to exist, the spirits of departed ancestors: ethereal, invisible — eternal guardians of the bodies of the living, bodies that have warmth, and blood, and sweat. Agbo'le.*
>
> *Enter Abogunrin rattling a small gourd as he approaches the shrine of Ogun, the god of iron, in the centre of the compound. He stands before the shrine pouring libation on it from a keg of palm wine in his other hand.*

Rotimi is very concerned that the reader should understand the full meaning of the word *'agbo'le'*. It is important because Kurunmi's 'compound' is not just a dwelling-place but also a place of great spiritual significance. It is the 'home' of the tribal gods, of the ancestor's spirits, of all those invisible forces which oversee the world of the living. Dominating all is the shrine of Ogun, the Yoruba god of iron and war. By reading this stage direction carefully, the reader will not only be able to visualise the setting and thus have a clearer mental picture of the staging of the action, but will also have a richer understanding of the meaning of the play as a whole. For the stage-setting makes it clear that Kurunmi is not only the political and military leader of his people but also the guardian of its spiritual heritage. Kurunmi's home is the dwelling-place of the tribal gods and spirits, supreme among whom is Ogun, the god of war — war which is the subject of the play, and the cause of Kurunmi's eventual downfall.

Stage directions — especially the first stage direction of the play or of a new scene or Act — can give us information about the staging which may, in the hands of a skilful dramatist, contribute significantly to the total meaning of the play. An elaborate and brilliant use of staging in this way is found in Soyinka's *The Road*. The first stage direction begins:

> *Dawn is barely breaking on a road-side shack, a ragged fence and a corner of a church with a closed stained-glass window. Above this a cross-surmounted steeple tapers out of sight. Thrusting downstage from a corner of the shack is the back of a 'bolekaja' (mammy wagon), lop-sided and minus its wheels. It bears the inscription — AKSIDENT STORE—ALL PART AVAILEBUL. In the opposite corner, a few benches and empty beer-cases used as stools. Downstage to one side, a table and chair, placed in contrasting tidiness.* (p. 151)

The spectator is presented with a striking contrast between the shack and 'aksident store', on the one hand, and on the other, separated by a fence, the church. Both 'parts' of the setting are imagined to be by the side of a road which we do not see, but which will be continually talked about, and which gives the play its title.

As the play proceeds, we learn that Professor, the hero of *The Road*, is in search of the 'word' — the knowledge of death, which is also in his view the key to the meaning of life. There is of course no better place, at least in West Africa, to pursue the knowledge of death than by the side of a busy road, where death is such a familiar occurrence. (Professor is not beyond bringing the reality of death closer by deliberately interfering with road signs and forging licences.) Professor follows a daily ritual of preparing his followers — the drivers, touts and motor-park layabouts — for death by sharing out the palm-wine brought by Murano at a kind of communion service. Once, Professor had been a prominent member of the church which forms part of the setting, but he had sought the Word there in vain, finally being expelled for blasphemy from the congregation (and himself rejecting it). He has now, as it were, set up a rival 'church', and is following a different and as he believes more truthful road to the Word.

The Road is an extremely complex play, but we have said enough to see that the first stage direction indicates a physical setting which is itself an integral part of the meaning of the play. The contrast between the 'truth' to be found in the roadside shack and 'aksident store' and that of the church is part of the dramatic meaning, and it is physically presented in the contrast of the stage setting. The setting is thus symbolic as well as realistic, since the areas around the shack and the church and its graveyard are not just physical locations but stand for something more than themselves — for two ways to the Word. We will miss the important symbolism of the setting — which helps us to make sense of the play — unless we read the opening stage direction carefully and try to visualise the physical arrangement of the stage.

Sometimes, a stage direction is important not because it gives us visual images which complement the dialogue and action but because it describes a piece of action which does not involve dialogue — a purely visual piece of action. The first 'Movement' of The Trial of Dedan Kimathi begins with this lengthy stage direction:

> Darkness reigns. Distant drums that grow louder and louder until they culminate in a frantic, frenzied and intense climax, filling the entire stage and auditorium with their rhythm. The intensity of drumming eases up somewhat, to accommodate human voices. Twilight.
> Loud singing by a crowd of peasants. Their voices combine aggression with firm determination. Note that the peasants singing should also enact the flashback of Black people's History that follows the song.
> [There then follow the words of a Swahili song]
> A shot in the air. Overwhelming darkness. Drums and voices fall silent. Through the silence cuts the chilling scream of a person, followed by groans and more screams. Whiplashes are heard falling on human skins. Another loud, agonising scream. Abrupt silence.
> Vague twilight on part of the stage as drumbeats start a slow mournful movement. Sad music saturates the background as the enactment of the Black Man's History takes place on the stage. The phases re-capitulated flow into one another, without break or interruption.
> Phase I: An exchange between a rich-looking black chief and a white hungry-looking slave trader. Several strong black

men and a few women are given away for a long, posh piece of cloth and a heap of trinkets. Bereaved relations and children weep, throwing themselves onto the ground, while others raise closed fists in a threatening manner.

Phase II   *A chain of exhausted slaves, roped onto one another, drag themselves through the auditorium, carrying heavy burdens, ending up on the stage. They row a boat across the stage, under heavy whipping.*

Phase III: *A labour force of blacks, toiling on a plantation under the supervision of a cruel, ruthless fellow black overseer. A white master comes around and inspects the work.*

Phase IV: *An angry procession of defiant blacks, chanting anti-imperialist slogans through songs and thunderous shouts:*

[There then follows the shouts and song]
Staccato burst of machine gunfire.
The drums respond with a deafening, rhythmic intensity.
FEW VOICES: Uhuruuuuuuu-uu!
Silence.
Now definite dawn breaks over the full stage, catching figures running across. Some of the running figures are in underwear. For a time, action focuses on two retreating Mau Mau guerillas with machine guns on the ready. Note that a bush is just visible. Also a few boulders by the roadside. A few running figures escape through the auditorium.
Offstage we hear protesting voices and sounds of rough kicks, slaps and whiplashes.
Enter Waitina, with Gakunia-Gatotia, hooded.   (pp. 4–6)

It is absolutely essential to visualise this while reading it, otherwise its full meaning will not emerge. In the twilight there is enacted the story of how blacks were made slaves by the whites and their black collaborators, sent across the seas, and made to toil on plantations under the eyes of white masters and black overseers. The suffering and anger of oppressed blacks is emphasised, and their demand for freedom expressed in 'Phase IV'. The long history of slavery is linked with the modern African demand for independence through the sound of that very modern weapon, the machine gun, and through the long cry by several voices of 'Uhuru!', which is associated with the independence movement in East Africa. The twilight now changes into the full light of dawn, symbolic of the change from the long 'dark' history of black oppression to the 'dawn' of black liberation in the contemporary world; and the liberation struggle is embodied in the running, armed figures on stage, the fighters of the Mau Mau movement. The stage direction ends with a reminder that the oppression of blacks has not yet ended, despite the efforts of the liberation movement — a reminder expressed in performance by the sounds of violence which recur during the mime.

This enactment of the history of black suffering, in which — as the writers recommended in their preliminary production note — past, present and future time merge, sets the rest of the play in a particular historical and emotional perspective. It is therefore crucial that it be fully realised in the reader's visual imagination before he proceeds to the dialogue. It should be noted that unless this happens it will be difficult to appreciate the full significance of the final moments of the play, which are in fact a kind of delayed continuation of the mime at its beginning: again, there is darkness, the sound of violence (a shot and people's angry voices), but now the light comes up to reveal *'a mighty crowd of workers and peasants . . . singing a thunderous freedom song'*. At the end of the play the emphasis is on freedom and the ultimate victory of the black masses, rather than on the long history of exploitation and oppression.

Subsequent stage directions

The first stage direction of a play, then, is usually very important in that it tells us about the setting, which may often have symbolic meaning which contributes to the meaning of the play as a whole. It is thus vital that the reader, instead of passing over the stage direction quickly or ignoring it altogether, should use it to form as precise a visual image as possible of the setting. Sometimes, of course, the setting changes in the course of the play. If there is a major scene-change, this normally occurs between Acts. It is therefore wise to read the stage directions which begin each Act as carefully as one reads the first stage direction of the play, in case a new setting is indicated.

Stage directions do not occur only at the beginning of each Act. Most plays have stage directions scattered throughout the text, often a great many of them. Many are very short, only a word or two, and appear in brackets after a character's name. Let's look at a few examples from Ola Rotimi's *Kurunmi*:

OGUNKOROJU: (*unrushed*) Ehn . . . I know nothing . . .

LABUDANU: But Ogunmola, Ogunmola himself led them in attack. Ajaiyi too. And Osi Osundina — all of them. (*Silence*)

KURUNMI: Bring me the stew you cooked this morning. (*Tying a white cloth round his neck, dances*) The tortoise will say: 'Brother, not until . . .'

There is nothing special about these directions; they are fairly representative of the majority of stage directions to be found in play texts.

Sometimes, it is not so much what a character says as the way that he says it which is important. Or it may be that the same words can take on quite different meanings depending on the manner in which they are delivered. So, in the first example, the words which Ogunkoroju proceeds to speak take on a particular significance from the unrushed way he speaks them; if he had blurted them out, they could have meant something quite different, even though they were the same words. It is not only the way words are spoken that can affect their meaning: sometimes, silence can speak far louder than words. The second example calls on the actors to be silent for a few moments after Labudanu says 'And Osi Osundina — all of them'. What is the significance of the silence at this point? It occurs immediately after Kurunmi has been told of the defeat of his forces at Iwawun. The news is shattering, and it takes time for the implications to be fully grasped. (One implication, Kurunmi and the audience will soon discover, is that all Kurunmi's sons have been killed in the battle.) The silence called for in the stage direction is the silence of those who have heard terrible news and are trying to grasp its awful reality. It is a highly dramatic moment in performance, though if we read the play without visualising it the drama of this moment will probably be missed. Skilful playwrights often make use of pauses and silences in this way, and it is necessary to imagine the dramatic effectiveness of the stage direction as one reads.

In our third example, we have to visualise Kurunmi tying a white cloth around his neck and dancing; and as he dances he sings a song about a tortoise. (See p. 25.) The page of the text on which this occurs is littered with short stage directions (e.g. *'Takes bowl of stew'*, *'Mosadiwin hands him a ladle'*, etc.) and is difficult to read without losing the continuity of the dialogue and action. There is certainly a temptation at this point to skip over the stage directions quickly, so as to keep one's attention focused on the dialogue. Understandable as this temptation is, it is dangerous, for the business with the stew and the white cloth is not as insignificant as first appears. Kurunmi is about to receive the two messengers from Oyo, who want to know why Kurunmi did not come to the crowning of their new lord. Kurunmi has had Mosadiwin bring in the stew and ladle and then taken them out again, and now he again calls for them to be brought. When they arrive there is a stage direction which tells us that:

> *He leans back relaxedly in his chair, dips the ladle into the bowl of stew, scoops the contents: okro stew. He lifts the spoonful towards his mouth, repeatedly, letting much of the sauce slaver sloppily from his mouth down on to the white cloth, smirching it. The messengers are shocked.*

Kurunmi ends this pantomime by wiping his mouth with the unsoiled parts of the cloth and then holding it out to the messengers with the instruction to 'Salute your king for me'.

Between calling for the stew the first time and his words 'Salute the king for me' to the messengers there are no fewer than fifteen separate stage directions, some of them quite long, in only two pages of text. Difficult as these make the reading of the text, they are vital indications of a piece of stage business which powerfully conveys Kurunmi's feelings about the new Lord of Oyo, and which culminates in a shocking insult to him. The words of the dialogue are here only a part of the means by which the drama is conveyed; Kurunmi's pantomime with the stew, ladle and cloth are vital ingredients of the scene, and must be visualised even if it is physically rather difficult to follow the stage directions and the flow of the action and dialogue. It may simply be necessary to read these two pages again, to be sure of what is happening, before continuing with the play.

Conclusion

Reading a play, then, is not the same as reading a novel or a short story, however comparable the two activities may superficially seem. The final destination of prose fiction is to be read; but a play must be performed to be what it set out to be. We thus need a 'half-way house' between reading and performance; and this is provided by a kind of 'performance in the mind', a visualisation of the text in the process of reading it. A vital part of visualisation is the careful reading and imaginative mental rendering of the stage directions which usually constitute a large proportion of the words in any dramatic text. And this should be done even if it is sometimes difficult to read the stage directions carefully and follow the dialogue at the same time. Without the information and visual stimulus provided by the stage directions it will be more difficult, and sometimes impossible, to respond fully to the presentation of character, action and language in a play.

Exercises for Chapter 2: Approaches

Choose a short play you have particularly enjoyed reading. Read the first scene again carefully, trying to visualise at every moment the action being performed on the stage. Pay particular attention to the stage directions; you could, if you feel inclined, make a sketch of the stage-setting as you imagine it to be. Try to imagine the physical appearance of the characters, the ways they behave towards each other, and the tones of voice in which they speak to each other. Make notes as you read.

Write a brief (say, two-page) description of the scene as though you had just seen it performed. Imagining that you have been asked to direct the play in your school or college go through the rest of the play making notes about how you see the play being performed, the nature of the characters, their feelings towards each other, and so forth. At the end of this exercise you could write a couple of paragraphs on what you think the play is in general trying to communicate to its audience. How do you think the audience should feel, and how should they be thinking, as they leave the theatre after the performance?

If you do not know of a suitable play, try out this exercise on one of the following plays:
Yon Kon, by Pat Maddy;
Blind Cyclos, by Ime Ikeddeh;
Fusane's Trial, by Alfred Hutchinson.
These are all from Cosmo Pieterse (ed.) *Ten One-Act Plays*, Heinemann African Writers Series, 1968.

3   Character

Character in performance and in the text

Watching a play in a theatre, we see actors impersonating fictitious persons invented by the dramatist. If the acting is good we willingly 'suspend our disbelief' and accept the reality of the characters presented. We know we are not really watching a Danish prince called Hamlet, or his stepfather King Claudius, or his mother Queen Gertrude; but if the impersonators of these fictitious persons are skilful enough we are prepared to accept temporarily their reality as individuals, and to grant them an existence independent of the actors. We are, in short, prepared to think of them as real people rather than as actors.

So the reality of a character is established for us, in the theatre, by the actor or actress. It is established by what the actor says and does, by the *way* that he says and does them, and by the way other actors, playing other characters, respond to him. An actor lends the character his own physical substance for the duration of the performance. He uses his physical resources — his voice, speech mannerisms, facial expressions, ways of moving and gesturing — to create the character. And the reality of this character is further reinforced when we see and hear the other characters respond to him.

But when we read a play, as opposed to watching one in performance, the reality created by the physicality of the actors and such valuable incidentals as make-up, costume, lighting and scenery is absent. If the characters are to become real as we read a play we must establish that reality through our own unaided efforts. We must 'see' the characters, and 'hear' them speak their words, without actually witnessing their physical embodiments on stage. Characters exist in play texts only in the form of words: to transform these words into the realities of characters requires our imaginative effort.

We open a play text, we study the list of characters and any other introductory information the dramatist wishes us to have, and we get a sense of the setting by reading through the first stage direction. We are then ready to begin the process of visualising the characters and their relations with each other as these are revealed by what they say and do.

We are sometimes helped to begin this process by the words of the stage directions. Some dramatists describe the physical appearance and mannerisms of their characters in considerable detail in their stage directions. A notable example is George Bernard Shaw, who in plays like *Saint Joan* and *Major Barbara* wrote very lengthy stage directions describing his characters. Shaw was an exception, however; most dramatists offer only the briefest hints about the age and appearance of their characters, and others equally deliberately choose to say nothing at all about them.

The process of visualising the characters has of course already occurred. It occurred in the playwright's imagination as he composed his play. He had to imagine his characters, to 'see' them in his mind's eye as he wrote, to 'hear' them speak their words to each other. That process has now to be repeated; but instead of the dramatist doing the imagining, it must now be the reader. How is the reader to imagine exactly or even approximately the same characters that the dramatist originally imagined? How do the characters that begin in the dramatist's imagination come to be accepted as real by the playreader? Shakespeare, for example, imagined Hamlet and the other characters in that play. How is it that almost 400 years later a playreader can open the text of *Hamlet* and in the course of reading come to accept the reality of Hamlet, Claudius, Gertrude and the others?

We do not meet Hamlet or the other main characters until Act I, scene ii. The first scene takes place on the battlements of the royal castle and features two sentinels and Horatio. The sentinels have twice seen an apparition and they have brought Horatio, a friend of Prince Hamlet, to see it for himself since he is sceptical about their story. The ghost, which is in the form of the dead King Hamlet, appears twice during the scene. On both occasions Horatio speaks to it but each time it vanishes without replying. The scene ends with Horatio and the guards agreeing that the dead king's son, Prince Hamlet, should be told about the ghost.

The second scene, as the opening stage direction tells us*, takes place in the King's Council Chamber. The stage direction also informs us that the new King, Claudius, accompanied by the Queen, his councillors and others, are returning from Claudius's coronation. There is a 'flourish' of trumpets and the characters, 'all clad in gay apparel' (according to the stage direction), enter. Last of all comes Prince Hamlet, who is dressed 'in black, with downcast eyes'. As we visualise the scene in our own mind's eye we see a happy, brightly-dressed, group of people with the King and Queen at their centre. But we also see a solitary figure in black, who shares none of the others' happiness. (From the stage direction we know this is Hamlet, but of course if we are visualising the play as if it were being performed we do not yet know who this person is.) Not a word has yet been spoken and yet Shakespeare has caught our imaginations — at least if we are visualising the scene. For we already want to know who this young man is, why he is so different, in external appearance and mood, from all the others, and how he is related to the other characters, especially the King and Queen.

The King, Claudius, begins by speaking about his dead brother Hamlet. We already know that Hamlet is dead. We also know something that none of the characters before us knows — that his ghost is haunting the castle. If we are alert we will guess that the young man in black is

---

*Many of Shakespeare's plays, including *Hamlet*, involve very complex editorial problems concerning the origin and reliability of the texts that have come down to us, including the stage directions. Many of the stage directions in modern editions are the work of editors: in scholarly editions they have been carefully devised to reflect Shakespeare's probable intentions, and can therefore be treated as if they were the dramatist's own.

mourning for the dead king, though as yet we don't know what relation he was to the dead man, or why he should still be in mourning when no one else is. Claudius speaks lovingly, respectfully, of his late brother. He describes how he has married the dead man's widow and declares, apparently quite reasonably, that grief for the death must now be mixed with joy for the marriage. We are not told how long it has been since King Hamlet's death: we suspect that it has not been so very long; and of course there is the still unexplained presence of the young man in black.

Claudius makes a good impression in this first long speech. We 'see' a middle-aged man kingly in his speech and manner who speaks respectfully of his dead brother and lovingly of his new wife. When he turns his attention to affairs of state he is impressively strong in his attitude to the threat posed by young Fortinbras. He is clearly a man capable of acting swiftly and firmly, a man who understands and relishes power. We are not given any clue to Claudius's physical appearance but we can imagine him being as powerful in body and voice as he is politically. And yet he can exercise his power gently: he is tender towards his wife, and when he deals with Laertes's request to return to France he displays an attractive mixture of firmness, generosity and charm.

Having attended to the problem of Fortinbras and Laertes's request Claudius now turns his attention to the young man in black. He says, 'But now my cousin Hamlet, and my son —'; by doing so he satisfies some of our curiosity, which has surely been growing as the scene has progressed. In visualising the scene we have not known who the young man is. Now we learn that he is the son of the late King; that Claudius is his uncle but therefore now also his stepfather; and that Gertrude, being the dead king's widow, is presumably Hamlet's mother. We still do not know, of course, why Hamlet is still in mourning, or why he is so unhappy.

The Prince's first comment, which is spoken as an aside, is a play on the words 'kin' and 'kind' which suggests both that Hamlet is quite unlike Claudius in nature and that he is not kindly disposed to the new king. If we imagine Hamlet speaking these words, perhaps 'seeing' him turn away from Claudius and muttering them to himself, we are immediately made strikingly aware of Hamlet's hostility to his stepfather, and unconsciously we are probably asking ourselves why this young man should be so antagonistic to this apparently warm-hearted and generous man.

Claudius now asks the question that Shakespeare knows we have been waiting to have answered: 'How is it that the clouds still hang on you?' But if we expected, and hoped for, a straightforward reply, we are disappointed. Hamlet's response is a mysterious 'Not so, my lord, I am too much in the "son".' Again, Hamlet is playing on words, and doing so to express indirectly his dislike of Claudius. Hamlet doesn't like Claudius calling him his son, even though, as his stepfather, he has some justification for doing so; and his response to the King's question about the clouds is to point out that he is in the sun both in the sense of being called a son by Claudius, and because he is in the sun of Claudius's royal attention. (There is perhaps also the suggestion that he is in the dazzling 'sun' of the courtiers' 'gay apparel', while he himself is in black — a reproof to them, of course, for not continuing to wear mourning.) We can imagine the tension among the courtiers as Hamlet makes these hostile replies to Claudius's friendly overtures. We 'see' the courtiers standing around, alert and ill at ease, fearing what might next be said or done by Hamlet.

Gertrude herself is aware of the tension; and she speaks now in an attempt to relieve it. She asks her son to stop wearing his mourning clothes, to remove the memory of his dead father from the forefront of his mind, and to accept that 'all that lives must die'. We 'hear' Hamlet's sharp response, a brusque 'Ay, madam, it is common'. Shakespeare, very much aware of the questions that the audience is waiting to hear answered, makes Gertrude ask what we all want to know: why is he so obsessed with his father's death.

'Why seems it so particular with thee?' she asks. Hamlet's reply again involves an extended play on a word; this time an extended play on the word 'seems'. He points out that there is no 'seems' where he's concerned, and he makes a distinction between 'seeming', the exterior appearance, and what actually 'is', the inner reality. 'These', he says, referring to the outward forms of grief, 'indeed seem,

> For they are actions that a man might play,
> But I have that within which passes show,
> These but the trappings and the suits of woe.   (I,ii,83-6)

If we 'hear' Hamlet speaking the words of this reply to his mother's question we can't help but notice the passion with which he speaks. The repeated 'nay', 'Nor', 'No' express the emotional urgency of what he says, and suggest the violence of his feelings beneath the quiet, sombre exterior.

The violence of the language is related to what Hamlet is actually saying to his mother. Hamlet is concerned with the difference between 'play-acting' and the 'real thing'. He not only suggests that he is genuinely mourning his father's death ('But I have that within which passes show . . .') but he also implies that others are not, that their grief is mere show and not a true expression of their feelings. If we use our imagination as we read we are aware that this implication applies especially to Claudius and Gertrude. Hamlet is not saying so in as many words, but he is nevertheless telling the King and Queen that they are hypocrites, play-actors. Shakespeare could have let Hamlet answer his mother directly, or at least let him hint fairly obviously at the royal couple's hypocrisy. Instead, he makes Hamlet speak very indirectly, so that our attention is not so much drawn to Claudius and Getrude but to the abstract distinction between 'seeming' and 'being'. We have not been given a satisfactory answer to our question — which was also Getrude's question. We are still curious, probably even more so after Hamlet's mysteriously indirect reply. Unconsciously, we are asking: Why is Hamlet making this distinction? What is behind all this? What is wrong with him?

We can picture Claudius and Gertrude exchanging glances as Hamlet speaks. They are worried. Gertrude has tried to relieve the tension and has failed. The courtiers are waiting expectantly, embarrassed at the emotional antagonism between Hamlet and the royal couple, even more fearful than before that something awful is going to happen. Claudius now tries again. We have already seen that he is a clever, diplomatic man, and once more his cleverness is apparent. Instead of losing his temper with Hamlet, he diplomatically announces that it shows what a fine nature Hamlet has that he so devotedly mourns his father. But he also points out that it is nevertheless a fault to continue mourning too long, 'a fault to heaven, /A fault against the dead, a fault to nature . . .' Although Claudius speaks in an apparently kindly and fatherly way to Hamlet there is criticism in his words:

> But to persevere
> In obstinate condolement is a course
> Of impious stubbornness, 'tis unmanly grief,
> It shows a will most incorrect to heaven,
> A heart unfortified, a mind impatient,
> An understanding simple and unschooled.   (I,ii,92-97)

There is even a threat, for although Claudius asks Hamlet to think of him as a father he refuses the Prince's request to go back to the university at Wittenberg to continue his studies. If we remember that another young man, Laertes, had stood before Claudius a few moments earlier and had been warmly granted permission to leave the Court, the true nature of Hamlet's situation is made clearer. He is the heir to the throne, a very important person; in his present mood he is a danger to Claudius and Gertrude; and he is therefore told to stay at Court, so that he can be watched. The Queen softens the refusal with her motherly plea: 'I pray thee stay with us, go not to Wittenberg'. Hamlet — and everyone else — knows that he cannot refuse. He replies with a coldly formal 'I shall in all my best obey you, madam'.

Cleverly, Claudius chooses to interpret Hamlet's grudging words as 'a loving and a fair reply'. If proof were needed that Hamlet is right to see Claudius as a hypocrite, we now have it before our eyes. Claudius knows how Hamlet feels towards himself and Gertrude, and he knows that Hamlet only agrees to stay because he has no alternative. But the King needs to create the illusion that the hostility between Hamlet and himself and Gertrude is now at an end; and he simply misinterprets, deliberately, the tone of Hamlet's 'I shall in all my best obey you, madam' so as to create the illusion.

Visualising the exchange, we can 'see' Hamlet's stiff bow and 'hear' the cold formality of his voice as he replies to his mother's plea. There is a tense moment's silence, everyone waiting and watching, and then Claudius rises from his throne and smilingly announces that Hamlet's reply is loving and fair. With an expansive gesture he bids his Queen also rise and they move off, Claudius declaring that there will be a feast, the courtiers bowing as the royal couple pass. After the nervous stillness earlier in the scene, all is now movement, joviality and good humour — or to be more precise, the *appearance* of joviality and good humour. The King and Queen and their courtiers smile, laugh, behave generally as if all were well with the world; the tension has been broken, and we now watch a display of obvious relief. But this is play-acting of the kind Hamlet spoke of earlier, for we know that Hamlet has not really been reconciled with Claudius and his mother; and to remind us of this we 'see' the Prince, standing in unsmiling isolation as everyone else expresses a false joviality.

Hamlet is now alone to speak the first of his soliloquies. The soliloquy is a convention — more common in Shakespeare's day than our own — by which the audience is able to overhear a character speak his private thoughts. Hamlet says he wishes his flesh would melt away so that he could become as insubstantial as the dew, or that he would not be offending against divine law by committing suicide. He compares the world to 'an unweeded garden/That grows to seed'. We still do not know, of course, why Hamlet is so deeply unhappy. We know that his father has died, and that his mother has remarried her husband's brother: but the widow has ceased to mourn and so has everyone else. What exactly is wrong with Hamlet? Why is he not like everyone else? The sentiments he expresses in the first part of his soliloquy can only increase our curiosity. Why is Hamlet so weary of life that he wishes to end it? Shakespeare has manipulated our imaginative curiosity to the point where we really must have an answer to these questions. And that is precisely what the dramatist now gives us, in the remainder of Hamlet's speech:

> That it should come to this,
> But two months dead, nay not so much, not two,
> So excellent a king, that was to this
> Hyperion to a satyr, so loving to my mother,
> That he might not beteem the winds of heaven
> Visit her face too roughly — heaven and earth
> Must I remember? Why, she would hang on him
> As if increase of appetite had grown
> By what it fed on, and yet within a month,
> Let me not think on't ... frailty, thy name is woman!
>
> (I,ii,137–146)

And so the speech continues in the same vein for another thirteen lines.

What so deeply troubles Hamlet is the fact that his mother has remarried so soon — less than two months — after his father's death, and that she has married a man whom he regards as grossly inferior to his dead father. Hamlet knows that no genuinely grieving widow who loved her husband as much as Gertrude appeared to do could happily remarry less than two months after her bereavement. He knows that his mother and Claudius are hypocrites, that they do not sincerely feel what they say they feel. We can now understand, if we think back, what Hamlet meant when he said that there is that within him which passes show; and we can see why he made the distinction so forcefully between 'seeming' and the 'real thing'.

Shakespeare has subtly encouraged us to ask certain questions, and now he has equally subtly given us the information to answer them. The play moves forward, with new questions replacing the old ones. What is going to come of this antagonism between Hamlet on the one hand and Claudius and Gertrude on the other? Why did Claudius and Gertrude marry so soon after the former King's death? And why is King Hamlet's ghost stalking the ramparts of the castle, a fact of which Hamlet is still unaware?

Recreating character by visualisation

This analysis of part of a scene from *Hamlet* has been lengthy because I have tried to bring out several related points. First and foremost, I have been trying to illuminate the process by which the playreader establishes the reality of the characters as he reads. We normally, and correctly, think of the dramatist as the creator of the characters in a play. There is also a sense in which every reader of a play creates the characters. Characters only take on a reality to the extent that the reader is able to imagine them; and one can say that in imagining them the reader is creating them. A more precise way of saying the same thing is that although the dramatist *creates* the characters the reader must *recreate* them before they can become 'real'. The creation of the characters of Hamlet, Claudius and Gertrude is the product of an *interplay*, a kind of collaboration, between Shakespeare's imagination and ours.

In the scene we have examined, Shakespeare, like all skilful dramatists, encourages us to use our imagination. He does so by manipulating our curiosity, by attracting our attention to certain aspects of a situation, by encouraging us to ask questions, even if they are often unconscious ones, and then keeping us in suspense until they are answered. We gradually build up in our own minds the 'reality' of Hamlet as a fictional person by asking and answering our own questions: Who is he? What is the matter with him? What are his relations to the other characters? These are questions which Shakespeare wanted us to ask, and which he had in mind as he composed the scene.

We are not usually aware that we are even asking and answering questions, that we are following hints and clues provided by the dramatist, as we read a play. This is because the process is largely unconscious, and our conscious attention is directed elsewhere. One reason why my analysis of a part of Act I, scene ii of *Hamlet* was lengthy is that I was making conscious and explicit certain things that many readers would register unconsciously. I was also having to put into words a process of visualisation which would normally proceed without words. This process of visualisation is crucial, for it helps the reader to recreate as fully as possible what the dramatist originally created. In my analysis I was trying to show how, if one uses one's imagination as one reads, the characters and their situation assume a vivid, 'living' reality. Instead of merely reading words we 'hear' the characters speak them, and this 'hearing' can be accompanied by a 'seeing' of the characters' physical appearance, their movements and gestures, what they do as they say the words. By using our imaginations in this way we put ourselves, in one respect at least, in the position of a director, who must interpret the play as he reads so that he can 'see' the performance he will try to put on stage.

I am not suggesting that by visualising a play as one reads one is guaranteed a complete understanding of everything the play 'says'. The greatest plays — such as *Hamlet*, for instance — are inexhaustible in their meaning, and the characters in them never cease to exert a profound fascination. But by imagining the action in the mind's eye as one reads there is an increased receptiveness to the 'trail' of dramatic hints and clues which the dramatist lays for us. We allow ourselves to be manipulated imaginatively in the way the dramatist intended, and so we are better able to recreate what he first created. It is worth stressing again that a large part of this process is unconscious or only partly conscious; but it is nevertheless happening, and it finally produces a fuller and richer *conscious* appreciation of the play. One word of warning: the imaginative recreation of the text as one reads must always be on the basis of what the play itself offers us. It is no good, and it may be harmful, to use our imaginations in the wrong way — by reconstructing a scene without being guided by the dramatist's words. A 'free' use of the imagination in this way is likely to lead to a serious distortion of the characters' nature, their situation, and the meaning of the play as a whole.

There is another aspect of the presentation of character which I tried to bring out in my analysis of the scene from *Hamlet*. This has to do with the development of character. One of the commonest criteria for judging a dramatist's skill in characterisation is to ask whether he has successfully 'developed' his characters. By this we mean that a dramatist should present characters who 'grow' and become increasingly 'three-dimensional' in the course of the play. Shortly, I shall try to show why this idea of character 'development' is misguided in relation to certain kinds of drama. But now I want to look more closely at what we really mean when we say a character develops.

Clearly, for a character to develop as we read a play he or she must first take on a substantial reality in our imagination. We must 'believe' in the character, be convinced that in some sense he 'exists'. Only then, on the basis of this 'belief' in the reader's mind, can we come to feel that we are getting to know the character better as the play proceeds. The idea that a character develops is the result of a dramatist successfully creating the illusion for the reader that he is getting to know the character better. This is, of course, only an illusion, for it is impossible to get to know a character in the way that we do get to know people in real life. Becoming better acquainted with a real person involves a spontaneous exchange, a 'to-and-fro' of personalities which is impossible with a fictional person. If the idea that a character develops depends on this feeling that we're getting to know him better, and if this feeling is an illusion, how does the dramatist manage to create the illusion?

The so-called development of a character is primarily an illusion created by the real development of a *situation*. In other words, what we think of as the development of a character is really the development of a situation in which the character is involved. One could be even more precise and say that it is not only the situation which develops, it is also the reader's comprehension of that situation which develops, and thereby fosters the illusion of character-development.

For example, by the time Claudius and Gertrude rise and leave the stage with their retinue we feel that we have begun to know something about them and Hamlet. We could just as well say that Shakespeare has 'developed' their characters during the scene. Actually, what has been developed is the situation, and our understanding of it. We have learned that the wife of the man whose ghost we witnessed in the first scene has married her former brother-in-law less than two months after his death; and we now know how her son Hamlet feels about that. We also know that Claudius is at pains to be friendly with Hamlet but with little success, and that Hamlet is now going to be kept at court so that he can be watched. After the other characters have left the stage and Hamlet delivers his soliloquy, our understanding of the situation is primarily from Hamlet's position, which is another way of saying that we feel we know

Hamlet better than the others, which is the same as saying that Hamlet's character has 'developed' more than the others.

I have now used the word 'situation' several times; but what exactly is a 'situation'? Let's take an example of how we might use the word in real life. A man decides to climb a mountain; he gets halfway up and then gets stuck, so that he can go neither up nor down. We might well say of the man that 'he's in a difficult and dangerous situation'. We mean that he is in a certain physical relation to a piece of observable reality, namely the mountain. The man's dilemma could be reproduced on a stage, and it could be the basic 'situation' of a play, which could then be developed without the addition of any other characters.

But the phrase, 'he's in a difficult situation', could also be used of a man who has been foolish enough to accept a bribe, who is being investigated by the police. Again, we mean that the man stands in a certain relation to an observable reality, but now the reality and the man's relation to it are not so much physical as abstract and social. If the man is caught and found guilty he may be socially exiled by being sent to jail. If his crime became public knowledge he would damage his reputation and be publicly humiliated, even if he avoided a prison sentence. In other words, his relations with his family, his friends, his employer — in short, his society — are now in jeopardy. If we were to dramatise this situation its development would be much more complex than that of the man stuck on the mountain, and it would almost certainly involve showing the man's relations with a number of other characters. For example, the basic situation of the play could be developed by showing the man with the person who bribed him, with the policeman investigating the case, with his wife, with his employer, with his best friend, and so on.

A dramatic situation almost always involves showing the *relationships* between characters. The word situation can in fact be defined as the relationship between certain characters in relation to a particular event or observable reality. To say, then, that a character develops is — as we have seen — to say that a *situation* in which the character is involved develops; and this is the same as saying that the *relationships* between a number of characters develop. It is not so much that Hamlet's character develops in the excerpt we have looked at; it is that the relationship between Hamlet, Claudius and Gertrude develops. We feel we get to know Hamlet better; but what we are really getting to know better is Hamlet's relationship to his mother and his new stepfather. Our sense of getting to know a character, of his 'development', is thus primarily the product of our increasing knowledge, as the play proceeds, of how that character stands in relation to the others in the play. The 'others' can even include individuals with whom the character has no direct contact in the play. Fortinbras and Hamlet never meet in Shakespeare's play: and yet a part of what we know about Hamlet is defined by what we hear about Fortinbras, and vice versa. And of course we learn even more about Hamlet —his character develops, in common parlance — by observing the relationships between him and those he does meet — for example, Claudius, Gertrude and Ophelia.

Character and convention

The reality of a character, then, is always an imaginative reality, the result of a cooperative effort of imagination between the dramatist and the reader. Sometimes — indeed very often — we are inclined, however, to talk about characters as if they were real people rather than imaginary creations. Why? Partly, it is because some characters are so 'three-dimensional', so convincingly like real people, that it seems quite appropriate to think of them as if they are. Hamlet is such a character, and so too are Falstaff and Macbeth, among others by Shakespeare.

But there is another reason why we are often tempted to think of characters as real people. We saw in the previous chapter that there are, broadly speaking, two basic dramatic conventions: realism and non-realism. We also saw that almost all television and film drama, and a great deal of stage drama, belong to the realistic convention, in which the representation of characters, actions and physical objects is made to be strikingly lifelike. When dramatists are so much concerned with presenting characters and situations as if they are real people in real life it is natural that audiences get into the habit of perceiving the characters as real people. There is usually no harm in doing this: indeed, it is part of the 'willing suspension of disbelief' that we mentioned earlier which shows that the audience is using its imagination and entering into the spirit of the drama. But the temptation to think of the characters as real people occasionally leads to a more dangerous temptation, which is the tendency to lose sight of the *artificiality* of the characters.

It may, at first sight, seem a good thing to forget that the characters in a play are artificial: it suggests a capacity for entering into the imaginative world of the drama. The problem is that it can lead to distortion and lack of understanding, especially in two basic ways. First, it can prevent us from fully understanding, or even understanding at all, the *meaning* of the play. And secondly, it sometimes leads us into a wrong assumption or belief about what character should be in drama. I will deal with the first point in a moment. Let us now look more closely at the second point.

Audiences often think that it is somehow more 'right' for drama to present realistic characters rather than non-realistic figures. To put it another way, it is a common view that characters not only can but *should* be realistic — that all dramatic characters should give the impression of being real people in real situations. This prejudice is often apparent when a playgoer leaves the theatre complaining that the play was 'unbelievable' or 'not true to life', when what he really means is that the drama belonged to the non-realistic convention. In other words, a play which has deliberately *not* tried to present characters and situations *as if* they were real has been misinterpreted as a play which *did not know how* to present characters realistically. There is no reason why all drama should be realistic; as we've already seen, a great deal of the world's drama from the earliest times down to the present day has in fact been non-realistic in its conventions. There is also no reason why non-realistic drama should not be able to communicate serious and true insights into human experience. And it is just as possible for an audience willingly to suspend its disbelief

— to see a play, that is, as being imaginatively convincing — when it watches non-realistic drama as when the drama is in the convention of realism.

All characterisation in drama is artificial; it is always a product of the dramatist's artifice, his skill in creating the illusion of personality on the page and the stage. It is no less artificial when the dramatist creates a convincingly realistic figure, who behaves exactly as a person might do in real life, than when the product of his imagination is not immediately recognisable as an inhabitant of our normal everyday world. The only difference is that the same amount of artifice, the same degree of artificiality, has been expended on a different *style* of characterisation.

The notion of stylisation is very important in relation to characterisation, as well as to other features of drama. Characters can be stylised at different levels; or to put it another way, the illusion of personality can be created in different forms in drama. We can compare the stylisation of character with the different ways in which a mask-maker may represent the human face. At one extreme, the mask-maker could make an exact imitation of every feature of his model's head, so that the mask looks exactly like a real human face. On the other hand, he might choose to exaggerate certain features — for example, a long nose or a large mouth — so that, although the mask still bears a resemblance to a real face, it is no longer an exact imitation of one. Depending, then, on his selection of detail and the extent of exaggeration, the mask-maker is able to represent a face in many different ways, from the most lifelike (realistic) to the most abstract and fantastic (non-realistic). It is the same with the dramatist's creation of character, which may range from exact imitation of real life people to the portayal of characters who resemble people but are not 'lifelike'.

For example, in *Anowa*, by the Ghanaian dramatist Ama Ata Aidoo, the two main characters, Anowa and Kofi Ako, are lifelike — they are convincing as real people living in a real Ghanaian setting. We know, of course, that they are fictitious, inventions; but Miss Aidoo so successfully selects and arranges detail to create the illusion of real people that for the duration of the play we're prepared to regard them *as if* they were real. In the same play there are two characters who act as a chorus. The Old Man and Woman enter at the beginning of the play as a prologue, and at the end of each 'phase' (Act) they give us information and comment on the persons and events of the story. Sometimes they talk to each other, but usually they address their remarks to the audience. In one sense, both the Old Man and the Old Woman are realistic figures: they are like many old people everywhere with their 'nosiness' about other people's lives and their moralising remarks. And realism in this sense is increased by the way the dramatist characterises the old couple to represent strongly felt, but to some degree contradictory, views about Anowa and Kofi. But in another sense — the sense in which we are using the word 'realism' — the Old Man and Woman are not as realistically portrayed as Anowa and Kofi or the other characters. This is because Miss Aidoo has not been so concerned — deliberately, of course — to put them into an immediately recognisable setting — the road, a house — or to make them interact with the other characters. They never, for instance, speak to other characters; only to each other or the audience. They are, we might say, *in* the play but not *of* it. They are not realistic characters like the others; rather, they help to frame the main action, to place it in a certain perspective, and to comment upon it.

Within the same play, then, there are some characters who belong to the realistic convention and others who do not. Nevertheless, they are equally convincing *as characters*, despite the different levels at which they have been stylised. In some plays all the characters are non-realistic, in the sense that none is intended to give the illusion of being a real person. An example of such a play would be the fifteenth-century English play *Everyman*, in which God sends Death to punish Everyman for his sins but which ends with Everyman's salvation after Good Deeds has agreed to go with him to the grave. *Everyman* is an allegorical morality play in which the characters are personified abstractions, the embodiments of abstract qualities, and the action is designed to teach the audience a particular moral lesson. The anonymous author of *Everyman* was not concerned to present his characters *as if* they were people in real-life situations; rather, he has deliberately stylised them so that they speak and behave entirely in accordance with the idea or quality they represent — e.g. Good Deeds, Goods, Fellowship. (*Everyman* has been successfully adapted to a Nigerian, and more specifically Yoruba, social and religious setting by Obotunde Ijimere in his play of the same name.)

It is a mistake, then, to assume that dramatic characterisation must always belong to the realistic convention; it may be equally valid for it to be non-realistic, and sometimes — as in the case of the *Everyman* plays, for example — a non-realistic mode of characterisation is more effective in communicating the dramatist's meaning. I said earlier that there is a second reason why it is important always to bear in mind the artificiality of all characterisation, which has to do with the meaning of the play. A dramatist is unlike the writer of prose fiction in that he cannot speak for himself, he can only speak through the words and actions of his characters. The way in which a dramatist presents his characters is crucial for the play's meaning. We can go further than this and say that the meaning of a play as a whole is partly determined by *the particular meanings embodied in the characters*.

It is only by appreciating the artificiality of all dramatic characters — that is, by resisting the temptation to think of them entirely as if they were people — that we can appreciate their function as *meanings*. What do we mean when we say that a character is a meaning? In the medieval and the Nigerian *Everyman* plays the characters *stand for* or embody various abstract ideas or types of people. In these plays each character 'means' something definite which can be discovered not only from what he says and does but even from what he is called. In such plays it is easy to relate a character to a meaning; or to put it another way, to say what a character represents. Usually, however, it is not so straightforward to identify the meaning of a character because in most plays the element of typicality and abstraction is not so prominent as in allegorical drama. Nevertheless, a character in any serious play can be said to be a meaning in the sense that he or she embodies a particular attitude to life, a particular way of thinking and feeling. The attitude or attitudes which a character embodies — his ideas and feelings, his outlook on life — may be complex or simple, more or less easy to identify and understand. In either case, the attributes which a dramatist gives a character can be thought of as a spider's web, a tightly and often intricately drawn-together thread of human qualities; and this thread of qualities, considered as a whole, constitutes the meaning of the character.

Let us look more closely at Ama Ata Aidoo's *Anowa* to see how character functions as meaning.

We have seen that the 'development' of a character is really the development of the relationships between the characters: a character does not develop in isolation, but in relation to the other characters. In *Anowa* the relationship between Anowa and Kofi dominates our attention. The more powerful personality of the two is Anowa, a strange and beautiful girl. Before we actually see her we hear about her from her parents, Osam and Badua, and the choric figures, the Old Man and Woman. We are left in no doubt that she is out of the ordinary, a girl who has refused many suitors, who follows her own counsel and gives the impression of being proud and arrogant. When we see Anowa with her parents what we have heard about her exceptional nature is confirmed: she is fiercely independent ('Have I not told you that this is to be my marriage and not yours?'), and she is already determined what kind of marriage she wants with Kofi ('You will be surprised to know that I am going to help him do something with his life').

Having run off and married Kofi she appears next with her new husband on the highway, helping him to carry his load of skins and hides through the stormy night. Oddly, Kofi is more fearful of the storm and darkness than Anowa, who is physically fragile but spiritually strong. When Kofi suggests that they use medicines to protect themselves she refuses because she is confident that they can look after themselves. The only thing that does worry her is the fact that there is as yet no sign of a baby; but Kofi assures her that according to the doctor this is only because Anowa's soul is too restless. When she settles down the baby will come.

The scene on the highway shows Anowa and Kofi in love, working together in a true partnership. But it also hints at tensions in their relationship which are not yet fully apparent but which will become so later. Kofi knows how hard Anowa works, how much she helps him, and he loves her for it. But he assumes that she will stop working some day and will change: 'Anowa truly has a few strong ideas. But I know she will settle down'. When he suggests that she should stop coming on the roads she is alarmed: 'I like this work. I like being on the roads.' When he tells her that he is thinking of buying some slaves to do the work Anowa is horrified: 'Kofi, no man made a slave of his friend and came to much himself. It is wrong. It is evil'. Kofi in turn is angry and tells her: 'I like you and the way you are different. But Anowa, sometimes, you are too different. I know I could not have started without you, but after all, we all know you are a woman and I am the man'. The scene ends with them agreeing that they shouldn't quarrel but without having resolved this conflict.

Despite their love for each other it is becoming clear that Anowa's outlook is fundamentally different from Kofi's. Kofi adores his wife, at least partly because of her 'strangeness'. But he is himself a fairly conventional person who wants to be rich and who will use methods such as slavery to be so. He loves Anowa, but he assumes that a man's word

A moment in Anowa, *as the conflict between Anowa and Kofi begins to appear.*

must prevail over a woman's. Anowa, we are now discovering, is not just superficially different from most other people; she is profoundly exceptional. She doesn't want to stop work even though it is financially possible for her to do so: work for her is not a way of making money, but a way of life, a value in itself. She regards her marriage as an equal partnership built on shared labour; and she refuses to allow Kofi to dominate her. At the same time, it is she who suggests that Kofi should take another wife to help them, which shows that she is not at all possessive or domineering.

In the next scene between them towards the end of Phase Two the gap dividing them has grown wider. We see Kofi's slaves walking across the stage carrying their loads. Anowa has now been deprived of what she most wanted and enjoyed — tramping the roads with her load of skins alongside her husband. She insists that she cannot be happy is she cannot work, and that she has no interest in looking after the house for Kofi. She repeats that she is happy for Kofi to take another wife or even more than one; she merely wishes to remain his companion, 'your friend or your sister'. To Kofi's dismay, she identifies herself with his slaves: 'Mm, I am only a wayfarer, with no belongings either here or there'. And when Kofi objects that 'a wayfarer belongs to other people!' she replies: 'Oh no, not always. One can belong to oneself without belonging to a place. What is the difference between any of your men and me? Except that they are men and I'm a woman? None of us belongs'. She becomes almost hysterical when Kofi tells her that he has decided to buy some women slaves to keep her company; and she is not impressed by his argument for the 'kindly' use of slaves. Her response to his request to enjoy their wealth is scornful laughter.

Associated with Anowa is a complex idea of freedom. Anowa believes in and practises a kind of freedom which includes a deep abhorrence of slavery, even 'kind' slavery, and a conviction that all of us are and should be 'wayfarers', with no permanent home or possessions in this life. Connected with this sense of freedom is Anowa's belief in the value of labour, especially of a freely shared labour, which is her idea of the basis for a real and successful marriage. Anowa's refusal to modify her outlook guarantees her growing estrangement from Kofi, who is kind, loving and intelligent but in no way exceptional, and who is therefore unable to understand what Anowa is really like.

By Phase Three Kofi Ako is a very rich man — 'the richest man, probably, of the whole Guinea Coast', a stage direction says. Anowa, however, still wears her old clothes and goes barefoot, in spite of the big, richly-furnished house of which she is now the mistress. She is entirely uninterested in her husband's wealth and possessions: she wanders around talking to herself, remembering how she pestered her grandmother with questions about the white men's slaves and where they came from, and recalling her dream in which she was a woman giving birth to people who were torn apart by the lobster-men from the sea. She wishes that someone had 'taught me how to grow up to be a woman . . . in order for her man to be a man, she must not think, she must not talk'. We learn that Kofi has decided to send her away, back to her home village of Yebi: but Anowa refuses to go, partly because she swore that she would never return there, and partly because she does not concede Kofi the right to send her away. Kofi even threatens to brand her a witch if she continues to refuse to do his bidding. Their relationship has now reached a crisis point; and at this crucial moment Anowa exposes Kofi for what he is before the whole household:

> Kofi, are you dead? Kofi, is your manhood gone? I mean, you are like a woman. Kofi, there is not hope any more, is there? Kofi . . . tell me, is that why I must leave you? That you have exhausted your masculinity acquiring slaves and wealth? (p. 61)

Kofi goes off and a few moments later we hear the shot as he kills himself; and from the chorus we hear that Anowa also kills herself, by drowning.

The relationship between Anowa and Kofi, which is central to the action, spans a period in which they move from poverty to riches, partly at least through Kofi's decision to buy slaves. Their characters are defined in relation to this process of becoming wealthier; and it is also this process which defines them as meanings. To put it rather crudely, in the course of the play Anowa comes to 'mean' freedom, while Kofi comes to 'mean' unfreedom.

How does Anowa come to 'mean' freedom, and what kind of freedom is it? Anowa is first associated with *social* freedom in that she will not allow her parents to dictate to her whom she should marry. Her association with this kind of freedom is further reinforced when, having run away and married Kofi, she is highly unconventional in her interpretation of the social institution of marriage. Anowa's connection with the idea of social freedom is then widened and deepened by her outright opposition to Kofi's proposal to buy slaves. Anowa is not herself prepared to be subjected to social forms which she feels constrict her individual freedom, and she protests against the subjection of others. But Anowa's relation to the idea of freedom extends beyond the social. For her, freedom is the essential nature of life itself. From the beginning Anowa instinctively understands that all of us are 'wayfarers' on the road of life: we must all travel through life without ever having a real home or possessions. If we think that we have a home or that our material possessions are of any real value then we are deluding ourselves as a result of failing to understand the real nature of existence. We can say that Anowa has a *spiritual* conception of freedom which causes her to reject any form of materialism or any kind of social relationship which involves subjection of one person by another.

Anowa's reactions to work and wealth are determined by her passionate attachment to freedom. She works, not because work brings wealth, but because she sees labour as a value in itself, a satisfying way of expressing our human nature in action. Kofi, on the other hand, can only understand work as a means of acquiring wealth, after which he will cease to work. Similarly, Anowa is totally unpossessive, either about material things, money or people, for she sees the idea of possession as an illusion and an encumbrance to freedom. Kofi, on the contrary, thinks in terms of possessing things (money, a big house) and people (his slaves). The irony is that he becomes, in the process, not only a slave-owner but a kind of slave himself. He eventually enslaves himself to his desire for wealth, and by doing so he loses his vitality as a human being. The dramatist conveys this idea — that Kofi has destroyed his essential vitality — by showing him as impotent: his impotence is a kind of *symbol* of the harm he has done himself by acquiring slaves. By the end of the play Kofi 'means' unfreedom, sterility, the futility of a life lived for wealth, just as Anowa 'means' the opposite.

It must be emphasised that freedom, the rights and wrongs of acquiring wealth, the need for equality between men and women, and the rest, have not been discussed as debating points between Anowa and Kofi. Rather, these themes emerge from the dramatist's presentation of the relationship between the two main characters. We become aware (if we are alert readers) that the characters and their relationships have been stylised very artfully to be associated with certain ideas, feelings and attitudes — in short, to function effectively as meanings. And unless we perceive the characters as meanings we cannot grasp the overall meaning of the play.

Let's conclude with a summary. It is essential when reading a play to aid our imaginative perception of the characters, their relationships and situations by visualising the scene in our mind's eye. By doing so we are better able to identify and appreciate the conventions of characterisation operating in a particular play — whether, that is, the presentation of character is essentially realistic or non-realistic. In either case, however, it is vital to bear in mind that all dramatic characterisation is artificial, in the sense that any good dramatist stylises his characters — selects and arranges the details of their personalities and relationships — so that they embody certain 'meanings'. As the characters interact so the characters-as-meanings interact, thus contributing to the total meaning of the play.

Exercises for Chapter 3: Character

1   Think about a person you know in real life who is by nature 'awkward' and argumentative. Note particularly those features of his behaviour which most clearly exhibit his nature. (He or she may, for example, have a habit of interrupting other people when they are speaking; or the person may characteristically use certain facial and/or hand gestures.) Imagine this person waiting with, say, two or three other people in a queue for a bus or in the post-office. Write a play that will last no more than five minutes in performance about the argument or arguments that this person gets into with the other people. Try to bring out, as vividly and fully as possible, the person's character, and the feelings he or she provokes in the others. Try to make something *happen* rather than have a play which is all talk. Pay special attention to the need for *selecting* a few features of the real-life person's behaviour and giving them special prominence in the play. (Do not try to give a complete picture of the person as he or she actually is in real life.) Develop character by developing the *situation* in which the characters are involved; or, to put it another way, by developing the *relationships* between the characters.

2   Read Act I of Shakespeare's *Hamlet.* When you come to the scene discussed in this chapter read it in conjunction with my visualised analysis of it. As you read the following scenes make notes which express your response to the different characters and their relationships. Try all the time to 'see' the characters and to 'hear' what they say. Then write a short essay (four or five pages) offering a dramatic reading of the whole of Act I.

   As a further exercise, you could read the rest of the play in the same way.

4 Plot

Dramatic storytelling

In the previous chapter I suggested that when we say that a character develops we really mean that a *situation* develops in which that character is involved. The technical term we use to refer to the development of a situation, or sequence of connected situations, is the 'plot'. We think of the plot of a play as the totality of situations that occur from beginning to end. A word that we commonly substitute for 'plot' is 'story': to describe the plot of a play is to tell its story. Later, I will suggest that we can make a useful distinction between 'plot' and 'story'; but for the time being we can assume they mean the same thing and look more closely at how stories are told in drama.

In a play a story is told through action, including that most important dramatic action, speech. Dramatic storytelling is in this respect different from storytelling in novels and prose fiction generally. For whereas the prose writer tells us about his characters and the situations in which they are involved mainly through description, the dramatist can only let us know about his characters and their lives by showing them *in action*. We know them by what they do (including that form of doing called speech) and by what is done to them, rather than by what we are told about them. Let us now look in more detail at how one of the greatest dramatists, Sophocles, who lived and worked in the Greek city-state of Athens in the fifth century B.C., went about telling the story of King Oedipus.

King Oedipus opens with an exchange of speeches between Oedipus and the Priest. We hear of a terrible plague ravaging Thebes, and of the hopes of its people that their king, who once before saved the town, will again be able to do so. The exchange ends with the approach of Creon, who has been sent by Oedipus to the god Apollo's temple to try to discover how he should act. The playwright has plunged us straight into an intensely dramatic situation: a city menaced by a mysterious and deadly plague, the hopes of its people pinned on one man. There is nothing leisurely about this opening scene: Sophocles 'grabs' the audience's interest from the very beginning, and cleverly gives us necessary background information — for example, about Oedipus once before having saved the city — in the process of presenting the immediate drama of the plague-ridden city.

Our interest has been stimulated; it must now be maintained. We wait expectantly to hear what word Creon has brought back from the oracle. What he says heightens the dramatic tension of the original situation: the plague has come because Thebes has been morally polluted. Somewhere in the city the murderer of the previous king, Laius, is still at large. Oedipus justifiably asks: 'Where shall we hope to uncover / The faded traces of that far-distant crime?' (p. 28). The suspense Sophocles is creating is similar to that of the popular detective or murder story, in which a clue is needed so that the murderer can be apprehended. We wait for the moment when the first clue is discovered, a process which Oedipus himself tries to hasten by proclaiming that anyone who knows the identity of the murderer should come forward, and by cursing anyone who remains silent to protect the killer.

The Chorus suggests that Oedipus should seek the help of the seer Teiresias, and we are told that he is already awaited. We, the audience, share with the characters on stage the desire to know more than we do, and the expectation of everyone in the theatre is raised as Teiresias enters. Will he be able to throw light on the circumstances of the murder and the identity of the murderer? But his response to the King's request surprises us: he refuses to tell Oedipus who the criminal is, even though he clearly knows. Finally, after Oedipus has accused him of having himself been involved in the crime, the seer makes the astonishing declaration that Oedipus himself is the polluter: 'I say that the killer you are seeking is yourself' (p. 36).

The story has taken a remarkable turn: the main 'detective' now stands accused of the crime; the saviour-king is said to be himself the source of the plague ravaging his kingdom. Of course, we only have old Teiresias's word for this, and as Oedipus is quick to point out, when Thebes was menaced by the monster called the Sphinx it was he, and not the seer, who was able to solve its riddle and save the city. Oedipus angrily accuses Teiresias of being in league with Creon to overthrow him by making a false accusation. We realise that Oedipus's words, though spoken in anger and shock, may be true. Consciously or unconsciously, we are asking ourselves: what is behind all this? Can there be any truth at all in what Teiresias says? And where is it going to end?

The dramatist has prepared us for a tense confrontation between Oedipus and Creon. This is what we now see. Creon defends himself against the King's accusations, and the arrival of Jocasta, who is Laius's ex-wife and now Oedipus's (as well as Creon's sister), ends the quarrel. The two men part, still on bad terms. Jocasta tries to persuade her husband not to take the seer's words seriously. 'No man,' she says, 'possesses the secret of divination' (p. 45). As proof of this she tells Oedipus about the falseness of the prophecy made about her son by Laius, that he would kill his father and marry his mother. But her words disturb Oedipus rather than comfort him for Jocasta mentions that her late husband was killed at a place where three roads meet. Oedipus begins to fear that he may indeed be Laius's killer. He tells Jocasta the story of how, to escape the prophecy that he would kill his father and marry his mother, he left home for ever. In his travels, however, he killed a man fitting the description of Laius at a crossroads. It begins to seem that there might after all be a basis in fact for Teiresias's accusation. Like Oedipus and the other characters we must now await the arrival of the sole survivor of the incident in which Laius was murdered. As the King points out, if this man sticks to his original story — that Laius was killed by a band of robbers — then Oedipus cannot be guilty of the crime. And as Jocasta is quick to note, there is still no reason for her husband to pay any attention to prophecies for, however Laius died, it was not by the hand of his own son, who had perished as an infant.

Sophocles has succeeded in creating suspense as to whether or not Oedipus is, as Teiresias declared, the murderer of King Laius. The resolution of this suspense depends on the testimony of the shepherd who witnessed Laius's death, and who is now being fetched. But this is not the only suspense we experience. Though it has not been discussed by the characters we are aware that the dialogue has established a strange coincidence — that the prophecy that the child of Laius and Jocasta would kill his father matches a similar curse associated with Oedipus, which drove him to leave his home town so that he would never see his parents again. There is as yet no reason to believe that the two prophecies are connected, though it is ominous that there should be the coincidence, that Oedipus should apparently have unknowingly killed Laius, and that Teiresias should have declared: 'This day brings you your birth; and brings you death' (p. 38).

The possibility that Oedipus will ever fulfil the fate predicted for him seems to disappear once and for all as a result of what happens next. A messenger arrives from Corinth, Oedipus's home town, to announce that King Polybus, his father, has died a natural death. Paradoxically, Oedipus and Jocasta are joyful for it seems that he can never now commit the horrible crime of parricide. Oedipus does not forget, however, that his mother still lives and so the curse that he will commit incest with her is still possible. The messenger, on hearing this, tells Oedipus that 'your fears are groundless, vain' (p. 53). The reason is that neither Polybus nor his wife were kin of Oedipus. For the first time he hears that Polybus was his adoptive father, given to him by the very messenger who now stands before Oedipus.

Let us pause for a moment and consider the psychology of the audience at this moment. Remember that we have been entertaining a gnawing suspicion that the two curses, the one on Laius and Jocasta and the other on Oedipus, may be in some, as yet unknown, way connected. The news that Oedipus's father has died apparently removes this suspicion. All seems well, at least as far as the curse on Oedipus is concerned. And then, suddenly, and ironically thinking that he is giving the King good news, the messenger tells us something that makes our fearful suspicion return. Polybus was not, after all, Oedipus's father; and so the possibility returns that the two curses may yet be linked. Tension has been removed only for it to re-assert itself even more strongly than before. The obvious question, upon which everything depends, is now: if Oedipus did not come from Corinth, then where did he come from?

Sophocles now has the King asking this question himself, and he learns that he was found 'in a wooded hollow of Cithaeron', that his ankles were rivetted, and that he was given to the messenger by a shepherd. When Oedipus urgently asks: 'And who was he? Can you tell us who he was?' (p. 54) we know there can be only one reply, which we are expecting and yet dreading: 'I think he was said to be one of Laius' men' (p. 54). The direct connection, with its terrible implications, between Oedipus's infancy and Laius and Jocasta has at last been made. Terror-stricken, Jocasta pleads with Oedipus not to continue this quest for knowledge of his origins. But Oedipus must speak to the shepherd, who is the same man as the survivor of Laius's murder — a man who is already on his way.

Sophocles has shaped his story so that everything now depends on the words of one man. We know, as we see the old shepherd approaching, that the whole truth will now be revealed. 'It was,' says the shepherd, 'a child of Laius' house' (p. 58). Oedipus asks: 'A slave? / Or of his own begetting?' And the quest for the truth moves to its inevitable conclusion:

SHEPHERD: Must I tell?
OEDIPUS: You must. And I must hear.
SHEPHERD: It was his child,
             They said. Your lady could tell the truth of it.
OEDIPUS: *She* gave it you?
SHEPHERD: Yes, master.
OEDIPUS: To what purpose?
SHEPHERD: To be destroyed.
OEDIPUS: The child she bore!
SHEPHERD: Yes, master.
             They said 'twas on account of some wicked spell.
OEDIPUS: What spell?
SHEPHERD: Saying the child should kill its father.

(p. 58)

Teiresias's prophecy has come true: this day has indeed revealed Oedipus's birth and thus destroyed him. The King leaves the stage, and after a speech from the Chorus an attendant arrives from the palace to announce that Jocasta has hanged herself and that Oedipus has plucked out his eyes. Sophocles' play ends with the blind Oedipus being led away, a man utterly destroyed, about to be separated from his children by his mother-wife Jocasta, and cast out from the city of Thebes.

King Oedipus is a masterpiece of dramatic storytelling. This does not necessarily mean that it is a play which thrills us by its exciting happenings. In fact, very little *happens* in it, in the sense of seeing violent verbal clashes, or murder, or suicide being enacted on the stage. It is true that, for example, we see Oedipus raging against Teiresias and arguing with Creon. But most of the dialogue is not of this obviously 'dramatic' kind; and though we hear of such things as the murder of Laius and the plague sweeping through the city we do not see them. Even when Jocasta commits suicide and Oedipus blinds himself we are told about these events rather than actually witnessing them with our own eyes. And yet, despite the relative lack of overt actions, *King Oedipus* leaves us with a sense of a profoundly dramatic *action* having been unfolded and completed before us. We have been made to care about Oedipus's fate, and to wait expectantly to see how it will be decided. Sophocles has done this, in accordance with the theatrical convention of his time and place, primarily through that form of action called speech. He has arranged the encounters between his characters and devised their verbal exchanges so that we become imaginatively involved in what is happening and how it will work out. He has, in other words, told his story through action, even if that action is primarily speech, and at the same time has involved us in the developing action.

We will look more closely in the next chapter at how good

dramatists make dialogue into a kind of action. For the time being we will concentrate on how Sophocles unfolds a complete action before us, the development and resolution of which commands our imaginative engagement. In other words we shall ask: what is it, from the point of view of plot, that all good dramatic storytelling has in common?

Suspense

Like all skilful playwrights, Sophocles presents us at the beginning of *King Oedipus* with a situation which is interesting in itself and which promises the development of further situations which will intensify and eventually satisfy our initial curiosity. We don't know, in the first scene of his play, what is going to happen next, but the interest of the initial situation — a king trying to discover why his city is plague-ridden and how to save it — is such that we are filled with a strong desire to know how the problem will be resolved. It is not until the end of the play that this resolution occurs, and that is only after the most hideous facts have come to light.

The psychological state Sophocles has induced in us, the audience, is what we commonly call *suspense*. And suspense is created, in the first place, by the stimulation of the audience's interest in a situation. In *King Oedipus* it is a particularly 'strong' situation, the drama of a city afflicted by a deadly plague. But interest may also be attracted by an opening scene which has nothing so obviously dramatic about it — which is, in fact, populated by characters, incidents and conversation reminiscent of normal everyday life.

Take, for example, the opening of Soyinka's comedy, *The Lion and the Jewel*. The setting is a clearing on the edge of a market in the centre of a typical African village. There is nothing remarkable about the two characters who appear in this first scene: Lakunle is a young, poor schoolteacher, Sidi is a good-looking village girl, dressed in traditional costume. Nor is there anything very extraordinary in their conversation. Lakunle is courting Sidi but not very successfully since he is unwilling, or unable, to pay the bride-price which she insists is a necessary condition for marriage. He is scornful about the inferior 'savages' with whom he has to live in the village and he accuses Sidi, when she fails to respond to his romantic rhetoric, of being hopelessly 'bush' herself. She, in return, ridicules his high-flown language and makes him aware, with some pleasure, of what a laughing-stock he is in the village. It is clear that these two are no Romeo and Juliet: when the other young people enter, we are already wondering, consciously or unconsciously, whether their relationship is likely to last. This seems to depend, at least partly, on the outcome of Lakunle's resolution to turn the village inside out, and especially to punish, in ways unspecified and for reasons we don't yet understand, the village Bale (chief), Baroka. By the end of this scene Soyinka has us looking forward to seeing and hearing more about Baroka and the courtship of Lakunle and Sidi.

There is nothing like the intense, momentous suspense of the first scene of *King Oedipus* in Soyinka's comedy. When we speak of suspense in relation to the opening of *The Lion and the Jewel* we mean something much more low-key, the desire to know more about the relationships and actions of characters whose lives are recognisably of the everyday world. It is still suspense — the stimulation of interest in character and situation, the arousal of a desire to know more, and the expectation that 'more' will happen: but it is a different kind of suspense, the kind normally associated with comedy rather than tragedy.

Whatever the kind of suspense the opening of a play offers, the dramatist must sustain and intensify the initial interest in the subsequent scenes. He must, in short, keep his implicit 'promise' that the opening situation will lead on to other situations worthy of our first interest. The sustaining of suspense is not, however, a simple matter of manipulating the audience into wondering what is going to happen next, though a successful play will always do this in some form. For example, it may be quite clear how the story is going to develop, and even what its final outcome will be. This was certainly the case for the Athenian audience which watched *King Oedipus*, for all Greek tragedy was based on stories already well known to the spectators. They knew, from the moment they entered the theatre, that Oedipus would be revealed as the murderer of his father and the husband of his mother. Does this mean that there was no suspense for the Athenian audience as it watched Sophocles' play?

It is hard to believe that the Greek dramatists and audiences could have had a conception of drama that placed no importance on suspense. And in fact we know from our own experience that it is perfectly possible to know the story of a play before we enter the theatre or of a film before we go into the cinema and yet still be gripped by the drama as we watch. For example, members of a Yoruba audience watching Duro Ladipo's *Moremi* or of a Tanzanian audience watching Ebrahim Hussein's *Kinjeketile* are likely to know at least the most important of the historical facts dramatised in these plays. Or a keen film-goer who has already seen one of his favourite movies several times can still be enthralled by it, gripped by its suspense, even when he goes to see it for perhaps the fourth or fifth time. The reason why we can know the story of a play or film, including its outcome, and yet still feel suspense as we watch has to do with our enjoyment of the tension between our sense of a developing action and its possible ending(s) on the one hand and our sense of what is happening at any particular moment on the other.

The easiest way to explain this is by using an example. Let us say that we are watching an adventure film. There is an exciting car-chase in which the hero is being pursued by several carloads of villains armed with guns. It looks as if our hero will on this occasion meet a violent end at the hands of his enemies. Or does it? For we know that the death of the hero in a film of this kind is extremely unlikely, even impossible. Things like that simply don't happen to heroes in films like this. In other words, we know in our own minds that the hero will escape, and yet we feel suspense as we watch the pursuit and wonder how our hero will avoid apparently certain death and triumph over his enemies. The suspense is the tension we experience between our knowledge that our hero will eventually overcome his present difficulties and the apparent certainty that on this occasion he is in such terrible trouble that he cannot possibly escape. The suspense of *King Oedipus* is essentially of the same kind, only in reverse.

Assuming that, like the original Greek audience, we already know the legend, the suspense generated by Sophocles' play derives from the tension between knowing what the terrible outcome will be and yet still hoping that it can somehow be averted. Like Oedipus himself — and no doubt because to some extent we identify ourselves with him — we hope that the arrival of Laius's man and the story he tells about the circumstances of his master's death will exonerate the King of murder. Similarly, when word arrives that Polybus has died of natural causes, we feel, like Oedipus and Jocasta, a great relief of tension because it now seems that he cannot fulfil the prophecy. And we feel this relief of tension *even though we know the happy turn of events is in fact illusory*.

It should now be clear why there is more to the successful sustaining of suspense than the dramatist merely making us wonder what will happen next. Rather, he must create and sustain a continuing, though varying, tension between our knowledge or expectation of what the completed action will be and our perceptions and feelings at any particular moment. This being so, the tension may be generated not so much by the 'simple' means of making us eager to know what the next happening will be, but by making us want to know *how* that happening, which we can perhaps already foresee, will actually come about. Or the dramatist may even encourage us to anticipate both what will happen and how it will do so and concentrate on directing our psychological tension to the matter of how a particular character (or characters) will be affected by it and how he will react to it. Another kind of suspense, often practised by the so-called 'Absurdist' dramatists, is produced by creating a tension in the spectator's mind about the very nature of what he is seeing. When you cannot 'believe your own eyes', when you are in serious doubt about what is actually happening, a special kind of tension, of suspense, may be induced. (An African play which has an 'Absurdist' quality about it, and in which the suspense is partly of this kind, is *The Invisible Bond* by the Ugandan dramatist Nuwa Sentongo.)

In the opening scene or scenes of a play, then, the playwright's task in respect of plot is to create a situation or situations which capture our interest and arouse our expectations of further interesting situations arising. In what we may roughly think of as the 'middle' of his play, he creates such situations, which follow from the first and which are linked to each other by virtue of telling a coherent, unified story. The dramatist must now preserve and intensify our interest by manipulating the tension we feel between what we sense to be the action as a whole and the particular situation at any given moment. What, then, is the playwright's task at the end of the play? Or to put it another way, what must he have accomplished before his play can be satisfactorily concluded?

It is easiest perhaps to answer this in a somewhat roundabout way. Most of us have at one time or another been aware of the sensation of being disappointed, 'let down', by the ending of a story. We feel that it was in some way inappropriate or inadequately prepared for. We then experience the feeling of 'anti-climax', the sense of being cheated out of complete satisfaction with the narrative's overall effect. The dramatist, like other storytellers, must at all costs avoid creating a sense of anti-climax in his audience. He must be sure to fulfil the expectations he has aroused in the spectators, satisfy the curiosity he has himself provoked, even if he does so in a way the audience did not quite expect. (For example, he may provide a 'twist' at the end which takes the audience by surprise but which satisfies their expectations about how this kind of play should end.) How, in principle, does he do this? Essentially, it is by finally resolving the tension he has throughout been manipulating between our sense of what the action as a whole may or could be and our sense of what has happened and is happening at any given moment in the course of the play. He must, so to speak, 'close' the electrical circuit, ensuring that there is no mental 'electricity' (tension) left unaccounted for.

Sophocles, for example, does this by manipulating situations so that our darkest suspicions are finally confirmed and Oedipus revealed as the polluter of Thebes. Our deepest expectation — that Oedipus cannot escape the fate predicted for him by the oracle and confirmed early in the play by Teiresias — is at last fulfilled. Tension gives way to a sense of tragic inevitability. The conclusion of *King Oedipus* is profoundly satisfying, in spite of the horror it reveals, because we are aware that all along there has been a *logic* to the working-out of the story which has reached its proper culmination. Logic may seem a strange word to use in relation to the unfolding of a story in a play. Certainly, it is not the rigorous mathematical logic of a problem in algebra; but it is a kind of logic nevertheless, the sense that the ending has brought to its fullest, final development the potential meaning already present in the very first situation of the play. All good plays have this kind of logical 'feel' to them, a sense of the inevitability of things ending as they have done. This is true even though the range of ways in which stories are structured in drama is enormous — for example, from the most loosely connected episodes to the most tightly-knit: and even though a play might end by deliberately denying that there is any inevitability in human affairs — as in Brecht's *The Good Woman of Setzuan*, for instance, which has an epilogue in which the audience is asked how the world is to be saved.

Plot versus story

Earlier in this chapter I said that a useful distinction can be made between plot and story. The distinction is useful because it helps us to understand how a carefully-wrought plot contributes to the *meaning(s)* of a play.

A single story can be told in many different ways, depending on the particular overall effect or impression the story-teller wishes to achieve. By telling it in one way rather than another the narrator is able to create a particular emphasis, direct our attention to certain aspects of experience rather than others. Sophocles, for instance, didn't have to dramatise the story of Oedipus as he did: he was free to present it in other ways. Instead of beginning the play as he did, with Oedipus already king of Thebes and married to Jocasta, he could have begun by showing us Laius and Jocasta casting out their child after the oracle had predicted the crimes he would commit. Or he could have presented a first scene which dramatised Oedipus's decision to leave Corinth because of the same prophecy. In either case he could then have shown Oedipus's adventures before he reached Thebes, including the murder of Laius on the road and his encounter with the Sphinx, rather than telling us about them in the dialogue.

Why, then, did Sophocles choose to tell his story as he did, when he had so many options open to him? One possible answer would be that it was conventional on the Athenian stage to report violent actions rather than showing them, so that Sophocles found it easier to conform to the expectations of his audience by beginning his story where he did. Another answer has to do with the play's impact upon us, the audience. Each individual no doubt receives a slightly different impression from his neighbour, but I think most readers or viewers of *King Oedipus* would agree that it leaves us with an especially powerful sense of the way in which Oedipus, in trying to escape the prophecy, has actually fulfilled it. The dramatist thus seems to emphasise the idea that men, however lofty their status, however heroic their actions, are powerless to oppose a destiny which has been obscurely marked out as theirs.

King Oedipus creates other powerful impressions related to this conception of destiny but I think enough has been said to bring out the main point, which is that *a plot is a story which has been carefully and deliberately arranged to produce a certain effect on the audience.* Incidents and situations are invented, or selected from an existing story or from historical reality, and arranged in a certain order to evoke certain emotions in the audience, or to make it think about certain ideas, or a combination of both. By these means the audience's attention is directed from the very beginning to some central concern(s) which emerge, however indistinctly at first, from the initial situation. The subsequent scenes develop our awareness of these concerns, presenting them in increasing complexity. Just as the portrayal of characters and their relationships in serious, skilful drama is contrived to make them the embodiments of meaning, so the ordering of the plot contributes to the communication of a total effect, which is the full meaning of the play.

We can observe how a dramatic plot creates meaning by looking at a South African play, *Sizwe Bansi Is Dead*, devised by Athol Fugard, John Kani and Winston Ntshona. As well as our immediate interest in its plot the play is worth attention for at least three other reasons. It is a fine example of a work created not by a single author sitting at his desk but by the collaborative effort of several people who have built up the drama through improvisation. Secondly, it shows what can be achieved using minimal resources — in this case, only two actors and the simplest settings and stage properties. And thirdly, it demonstrates how effective the convention of direct audience address can be in involving the spectators in the action.

The first scene is set in Styles's photographic studio in the township of New Brighton, in the South African city of Port Elizabeth. Styles enters reading a newspaper from which he reads out headlines, together with his own comments, to the audience. One of the newspaper stories, about a planned expansion to a car plant, sets him off reminiscing about his days working at Ford, and the visit of Henry Ford II to the factory. He begins to act out his story, taking the parts of Mr 'Baas' Bradley, Mr Ford, the workers and himself. His account of the ludicrous preparations for Mr Ford's extremely brief visit (according to Styles he took three enormous strides into the factory, looked around and then took three equally enormous strides out!) is graphic and very funny, even though the point of the story is to bring home to us the economic oppression and degrading working conditions of black South Africans.

He returns to his newspaper saying: 'Six years there. Six years a bloody fool' (p. 9). An advertisement for an insecticide called Doom gets him reminiscing once again in a way that continues his previous story. After his years at Ford Styles decided to set up a small business as a photographer. We hear of his endless waiting for permission to use the room he'd found as a studio, and he tells — and acts out — the amusing tale of how he finally defeated the giant cockroaches that infested his studio, not with Doom but with a little cat called Blackie.

Having told us something about himself Styles now 'introduces' us to his studio, with its name-board advertising 'Reference Books; Passports; Weddings; Engagements; Birthday Parties and Parties'. The room may look like just another photographic studio but, according to Styles, it's really much more than that:

> This is a strong-room of dreams. The dreamers? My people. The simple people, who you never find mentioned in the history books, who never get statues erected to them, or monuments commemorating their great deeds. People who would be forgotten, and their dreams with them, if it wasn't for Styles. That's what I do, friends. Put down, in my way, on paper the dreams and hopes of my people . . . .
>
> (pp. 12–13)

To illustrate this idea Styles acts out more stories of the work he does and its significance for the dreams and ambitions of his customers. Again, humour is associated with pathos, especially in the story of the huge family which came to be photographed just before the grandfather's death. As he finishes acting out this episode Styles speaks to the audience with what we recognise as a special urgency in his voice:

> You must understand one thing. We own nothing except ourselves. This world and its laws, allows us nothing, except ourselves. There is nothing we can leave behind when we die, except the memory of ourselves.
>
> (p. 16)

He is about to embark on yet another story when there is a knock at the door and a man walks nervously into the studio in an ill-fitting new suit. Styles looks at him, breaks into a smile and announces to the audience: 'A Dream!'

Thus far in the play a character has delivered a lengthy monologue and acted out stories from his own experience. Nothing has really 'happened' in the sense that situations have been changed and developed by the characters' decisions and actions. It is only when we analyse the structure of Styles's monologue that we realise a development has taken place. Styles's account of Henry Ford's visit to his South African factory has humorously but powerfully highlighted the wretched oppression of black South Africans. His description of how he went into business, conquering the cockroaches to do so, concentrates our attention on one ordinary black South African's attempt to make a decent life for himself in his miserable society: it is the story of a dream come true. Dreams are the subject of the next and final part of his monologue. Here, in his very ordinary studio, people come to live out for a few moments their hopes and dreams and to establish on film their identities, the proof of their existence, before they die and are forgotten. When the Man enters, Styles's comment to the audience ('A Dream!'), taken in conjunction with what he has been saying about the significance of his studio for his people, suggests that we are about to witness a representative example of the hopes and aspirations of black South Africans.

We now see what Styles meant when he said earlier that his studio is 'a strong-room of dreams.' Encouraged by Styles and stimulated by his own fantasies, the Man gets over his initial nervousness, which seems to make it difficult for him even to give his own name and address, and poses stylishly for the 'card' which he will send to his wife in King William's Town. Styles even persuades the Man, who's called Robert Zwelinzima, to pose for another shot, this time a 'movie' in which he appears to be walking through the City of the Future. The camera flash goes off, and there is a blackout except for a light on Robert in his pose. The 'photograph' comes to life and Robert begins dictating the letter that will go with the photo to his wife Nowetu.

He tells of how his problems may have been solved because someone called Sizwe Bansi is, in a manner of speaking, dead. He describes his first week in Port Elizabeth, the order to leave the city, and his move to the house of a man called Buntu. Without any break in the action there is now a 'flashback' to Buntu's house, with the actor who has been playing Styles now doubling as Buntu. Their dialogue gives us more information about Sizwe's arrest and the endorsement in his passbook to return to King William's Town. Buntu, who is much more knowledgeable in these matters than Sizwe, informs him of the full implications of his endorsed book, the near-impossibility of his finding work or remaining undetected. His advice is to catch the train back to King William's Town.

The scene ends with Buntu offering to treat Sizwe to a drink at a bar called Sky's place. The device of Sizwe dictating the letter to his wife is used again to change the scene, in a 'flashback within a flashback', to the street outside Sky's bar. Sizwe and Buntu are happily drunk, but they both sober up very quickly when Buntu, who has disappeared into the dark to relieve himself, runs back to report that a dead man covered in blood is lying in the shadows. Buntu wants to make off immediately but Sizwe at least wants to carry the corpse home. The man's passbook tells them that he is Robert Zwelinzima and that he has a valid work-seeker's permit. Buntu refuses to take the body to the dangerous area where he lived; he is about to return the passbook to the man's pocket when Sizwe asks: 'Would you do that to me, friend? If the Tsotsis [armed robbers] had stabbed Sizwe, and left him lying there, would you walk away from him as well?' (p. 34). Sizwe addresses the audience, overcome by despair at the injustice of life and man's inhumanity to man. He starts to tear off his clothes, asking 'What's wrong with me?' (p. 35) and asserting his manhood. Buntu meanwhile tells Sizwe to give him his passbook and he stands studying the two books.

The next scene takes us back to Buntu's house. Sizwe is getting back

Sizwe Bansi, in his new identity as Robert Zwelinzima, in Styles's photographic studio.

into his clothes while Buntu transfers the photograph from Sizwe's book into Robert's and vice versa. Buntu explains that this is Sizwe's only chance of being able to remain in Port Elizabeth and find work. Sizwe is horrified: he refuses to lose his name, his identity, to 'die' voluntarily as Sizwe Bansi. How can he simply become a ghost? Is he not a ghost already, asks Buntu:

> When the white man sees you walk down the street and calls out, 'Hey, John! Come here' ... to you, *Sizwe Bansi* ... isn't that a

ghost? Or when his little child calls you 'Boy' ... you a man, circumcised with a wife and four children ... isn't that a ghost?'
(p. 38)

Eventually Buntu persuades Sizwe of the necessity of becoming Robert Zwelinzima, of the insignificance of a name when one's survival as a human being is at stake. Buntu goes off and Sizwe picks up the passbook, looks at it for a long time and then, putting it in his pocket, moves downstage into the light where he was when he began dictating the letter to his wife. He now concludes it, returning as he does to the pose of the 'movie' photograph. We are once again in Styles's studio, with Styles behind the camera: 'Hold it, Robert. Hold it just like that. Just one more. Now smile, Robert ... Smile ... Smile ...' (p. 44); and with a camera flash and blackout the play ends.

We can now look back over *Sizwe Bansi Is Dead* and see how its plot structure has directed us to experience and think about certain crucial problems in black South African life; in other words, how its plot has been shaped to create meaning. Styles's long monologue, as well as entertaining us with its humour, has functioned as a kind of introduction. It has established, first of all, the general economic and social oppression of black workers and their families; but it has also, both in Styles's story of the establishment of his little photographic business and in his descriptions of his clients, brought out the blacks' struggle to preserve some sense of their human dignity, to keep alive dreams which their daily reality threatens to crush. With the entrance of the Man into Styles's studio we embark on a story which is specific to one individual but which, as Styles clearly hints, is also representative of the common lot of black people in South Africa. The scene between Sizwe and Buntu establishes the personal details of Sizwe's dilemma. There is no solution to it: the only consolation Buntu can offer is a few drinks and a good time in Sky's place.

The discovery of Robert Zwelinzima's body is not at first associated with Sizwe's problem. Rather, it presents in an immediate, inescapable way the issue of the dignity owing to every man, even in death. Styles has been concerned with this in his monologue, and that is what his studio is all about — the place where black people can momentarily assert their dignity. Sizwe cannot at first bring himself to leave the body where it is. He is horrified that it can be so devoid of even the most basic dignity, and he despairs for himself and everyone like him, who are regarded as less than men solely because of their skin colour. His action in tearing off his clothes to show the audience that he is a man like any other is very appropriate at this point. It makes a simple but crucial point in a particularly powerful way; and it also anticipates the moment of change in Sizwe's own identity. When he dresses again, it will be as Robert Zwelinzima, at first reluctantly but then with increasing hope. For the discovery of the body not only brings to the fore the problem of human dignity in South Africa, it presents Sizwe with a chance to escape his specific dilemma by altering his identity. As a plot device it concentrates attention on what has already been established by Styles's monologue and studio as a central concern of the play — the issue of *identity*.

Blacks come to Styles's studio to assert their identities with pride, however oppressed they may be. Sizwe Bansi asserts his identity, gives himself and his family some hope of a future, by 'dying' and being 'reborn' as someone else. He is at first horrified by the idea because he associates it with a complete loss of his dignity. But he is finally won over by Buntu's argument, which is that names are of no importance in a society like South Africa, and neither is pride of any value if it is based on self-delusion. What *is* important is to survive, and perhaps, by becoming 'a real ghost' (i.e. a man who understands without delusions that he cannot have a true identity while he is so oppressed), to 'Spook them [the whites] into hell. . . .' (p. 38).

If we had to paraphrase the meaning which emerges from the structure of the play's plot it might be this: that in a situation of such intense oppression as that experienced by many black people in South Africa the struggle to preserve a sense of identity and dignity must take extreme and paradoxical forms. It may even involve appearing to be someone else so that one's true identity can be retained. For the black South African to try to be himself in a false, self-deluded way — by caring about the 'form' of his dignity while having none in substance — is in fact to lose the last remnant of his authentic existence. Black South Africans must find and use any stratagem that allows them to survive and, by truly understanding their situation, fight back against their oppressors. The play ends, in the present, with a visual restatement of the theme of identity as the camera flashes on a smiling Sizwe Bansi who is now Robert Zwelinzima.

The authors of *Sizwe Bansi Is Dead* have thus carefully shaped the plot of their play to bring out certain crucial aspects of South African experience.They dramatise the issue of identity — not in an abstract, generalised way, but as it is encountered by black South Africans who are denied their social identities — and hence their dignity as human beings — in their own country. The play demonstrates how the structuring of the story determines the meanings it can convey to the audience. At the same time, it reveals how rich a dramatic experience can be generated using the minimum resources of cast and staging.

Conclusion

Before we conclude this chapter with a summary of its main points let us remind ourselves once more that in reality, as we watch or read a play, we do not separate one aspect or element of the drama from the others. We don't normally think of plot as a separate entity, distinct from characterisation; on the contrary, there is usually a fusion of our interest in the plot of a play with our absorption in the characters. This is because, as we actually experience a play, the situations and events of its plot are only felt to be significant because of the people involved, and the significance of the people involved depends on what they do and what is done to them.

In drama, then, we only know about characters and their lives by witnessing them in action, and this is true even if the action is primarily speech. Stories are structured in many different ways in drama (as in the novel and, for that matter, the short story), but all good dramatic storytelling is concerned with the unfolding of a complete action in which our interest is captured at the beginning and held until the end. This careful, deliberate manipulation of our interest and curiosity by the dramatist is suspense. It is more than the encouragement to ask ourselves what will happen next, though this is part of suspense: we may still experience suspense even though we know what will happen next. Suspense is created by the tension between our sense of a developing action (the outcome of which we may even know or be able to guess correctly) and our sense of what is happening, and has happened, at any given moment. The dramatist concludes his play only when this tension is finally resolved and our sense of suspense satisfied.

Though we often think of them as being the same thing, a useful distinction can be made in critical discussion between plot and story. A plot is a story which the dramatist has fashioned in a particular way (rather than in one of the other ways equally open to him) so as to produce a particular impression on the spectators. The ordering of a story in a particular way directs the audience's attention to certain issues and areas of experience rather than others, and by analysing the structure of the plot we are helped towards an understanding of the dramatist's overall meaning(s).

Exercises for Chapter 4: Plot

1 Take a story that you know and which interests you, and which you feel has potential for dramatisation. (It may be a story you have read, or that is well known among your people, or even one that has happened to you or to a friend.) As briefly as possible make a summary of the story, noting only its *essential* features and omitting details. Make a 'plan' of a short play (to last no more than thirty minutes). To do this you need to decide what situations and characters you will show and the order in which you will show them. As you do so, you must bear in mind the modest resources that would probably be available to you if you were to stage the play: e.g. you'll probably only be able to have one, or at most, two settings, and you will probably have only a small cast of three or four actors. When you have settled on what you will show and the order in which you will show it — i.e. when you've made a *plot* out of a *story* — look again at your plan and see if you can cut it down even further while retaining the essence of your story. (You'll probably find that you can, though you may not want to!)

Think of other ways in which the same story could be told dramatically, remembering that you can create different impressions and meanings for your audience depending on the way you select and arrange your plot. (Bear in mind, also, that you do not always need to start your play at the 'beginning' of the story, as *Sizwe Bansi Is Dead* and *King Oedipus* both show.) Having worked out three or four possible plot-outlines ('scenarios') choose the one that most appeals to you and write a short play on the basis of it. Try to create suspense in your first scene and to maintain and intensify it until the end of your play.

(An alternative way of working on this exercise, if there are several of you in a drama group, is for each of you to make your own scenario of a story independently of the others and then come together to compare the different versions. The one best liked by the group, or each in turn, can then be improvised into a short play.)

2   Re-read a play that you especially enjoyed reading the first time, or that you enjoyed when it was performed. As you read, make notes describing the impressions the play makes on you and suggesting what you think are the issues or problems or areas of experience that it deals with. Working from your notes, write a brief statement (of one or two paragraphs) saying what you consider to be the essential meaning of the play. Going back over the text, think about how its impact and meaning are related to the ordering of the plot. Try to reinforce your interpretation of the play by considering how different impressions and meanings would have been produced had the dramatist told his story differently.

5 Dramatic speech and imagery

Words in action

I said earlier that we don't need to have words at all to have drama. But dialogue plays, with which this book is concerned, are nothing else but words. At least, in their printed form they are nothing else but words — the words of the prefatory material and stage directions, and the words of the characters' speeches, which are usually by far the majority. It is possible, and a very common practice, to read the words of a play exactly as we would those of a novel or poem — that is, in a purely *literary* way. But we are concerned here with the dramatic and theatrical qualities of plays, and this means that we want to make the text of a play into something more than words on a page such as we find in a prose story. We want to make the words given to each character into truly *dramatic* words, and that means understanding them as *words in action*.

What is the difference between 'words in action' and the prose language we find in a short story or a newspaper report? There is a sense in which the words of any well-written passage are 'in action', if by this we simply mean that they have been given a life of their own, the capacity to 'enact' an idea or emotion or state of mind, through the writer's skill in selecting and arranging them. But in drama words are in action in another sense, for to have their full, intended life they must be *spoken* by the actors — that is, they must become *verbal actions*. A good dramatist will have this fact constantly in mind as he writes, and he will try to put together the words so that the actors can make their fullest contribution in characterising their roles. A speech, if skilfully composed, will naturally suggest to the actor a particular speech rhythm or rhythms, and evoke a particular tone or tones of voice which in turn will tell us about the character and his response to a particular situation. It helps us as readers to get the full dramatic value of the words if we 'speak' them in character in our minds as we read. Of course, we need to do this very cautiously at first, feeling our way gradually into the character's ways of speaking until we eventually feel confident that we 'know' his or her 'voice'. (The danger here is that we may accidentally endow a character with the wrong 'voice' through our misguided imaginative zeal.) And it helps also to bear in mind that actors not only speak words, they also accompany them with expressive bodily and facial gestures and movements, just as we do — in less stylised and self-conscious ways — in real life. In good dramatic writing the rhythms of the characters' speeches very often evoke these expressive actions for us.

But there is yet another, more profound sense in which the words in drama are 'in action'. The meaning of what is said by a dramatic character is not limited to the semantic meaning of his words. It embraces what the words *do* as well as what they *say*; or, to put it another way, it includes not only the surface meaning of the words but their value as *actions*.

Words are never spoken in a vacuum, either in drama or in real life. They always belong within a context, a situation of some kind, which produces them and which helps to give them their full meaning. A straightforward example of this in real life is the use of sarcastic irony. Let's say that a young man A has been waiting for the arrival of his girl-friend B, who eventually turns up, without apologising, thirty minutes late. A says to B: 'Oh, I'm so glad you could make it. It's very kind of you', and as he speaks he looks meaningfully at his watch. If we weren't aware of the context of the remark it would seem to be a statement of genuine pleasure and gratitude to B for having come. When we refer it to the situation, however, we recognise it as an ironical comment of a very common kind. The real meaning is the reverse of the 'surface' meaning: it is a forceful, if subtle, way of pointing out to B her failure to be punctual and of chiding her for her rudeness in not even apologising.

It's clear from this example that it is sometimes not the apparent meaning of the words that counts but what they *do* in the context of a particular situation. A play is a succession of situations, of varying dramatic contexts, and the words spoken by the characters must be understood in relation to them; understood, that is, as dramatic *happenings* and not just as things said.

A good dramatist, then, must think on at least two levels simultaneously as he writes dialogue. He must consider not only the 'surface' meaning of the words — their overt, substantial meaning — but also what they are *doing* in terms of the characters, their relationships, and the overall action.

We will illustrate this and some other points about dramatic speech by looking in some detail at Act I, scene i of *Edufa*, by the Ghanaian playwright Efua T. Sutherland. The setting is the courtyard of Edufa's compound. The scene reads as follows:

[*EDUFA'S hands reach out and pick up the pots. He is heard issuing instructions urgently to someone inside.*]

EDUFA: Pour first the dew water, and then the stream water, over the herbs in the bathroom. Quickly. Then bring out fire for the incense.

[*Outside the courtyard walls, a chorus of women is heard performing.*]

CHORUS: [*Chanting to the rhythm of wooden clappers.*]
Our mother's dead,
Ei! Ei – Ei!
We the orphans cry,
Our mother's dead,
O! O – O!
We the orphans cry.

[*The chanting repeats. As the voices, the clack-clack accompaniment and the thudding of running feet recede,* SEGUWA *comes hurriedly out of* EDUFA's *rooms. She listens as she crosses to the kitchen, and is clearly disturbed by the performance. Her brief absence from the court is filled in by the chanting which becomes dominant once again as the* CHORUS *return past the house. She comes back, carrying a brazier in which charcoal fire is burning in a small earthen pot. She hesitates by the kitchen door, still preoccupied with the performance outside. At the same time* EDUFA *rushes out in pyjamas and dressing gown. He carries a box of incense, and has the air of a man under considerable mental strain.*]

EDUFA: Why are they doing a funeral chant? They are not coming towards this house? [*To* SEGUWA] You've spoken to no one?

SEGUWA: [*With some resentment*] To no one. My tongue is silenced. [*Pause*] It must be for someone else's soul they clamour. [*The chanting fades.*]

EDUFA: [*Composing himself*] No, they are not coming here. [*Pause*] Put the fire down.

[SEGUWA *places the fire close to the central seat.* EDUFA *rips the box open, and flings incense nervously on the fire.*]

Keep the incense burning while Ampoma and I bathe in the herbs.

SEGUWA: It seems to me that the time has come now to seek some other help. All this bathing in herbs and incense burning; I don't see it bringing much relief to your wife Ampoma in there.

EDUFA: Doubting?

SEGUWA: I'm not saying I doubt anything. You have chosen me to share this present burden with you, and I'm letting my mouth speak so that my mind can have some ease. It is I myself who say I'm hardy, but how can I help having a woman's bowels?

EDUFA: Calm yourself. I cannot give in to any thoughts of hopelessness. Where is your faith? I thought I could trust it.

SEGUWA: You can trust my secrecy; that I have sworn; though what I have sworn to keep secret, now frets against the closed walls of my skull. I haven't sworn to have faith against all reason. No, not in the face of your wife's condition in that bedroom there. Let's call for help.

EDUFA: [*With indications of despair*] From whom? We are doing everything we can. Also, it is Ampoma's wish that no one should be allowed to see her.

SEGUWA: And is she dead that we should be bound to honour her wishes? She is not herself. In her present state we can expect her to say childish things. The sick are like children. Let me call for help.

It is most unnatural that even the mother who bore her should be kept ignorant of her sickness, serious as it now is. Ah, poor mother; if we could but see her now.

> She is probably pampering the children you've sent to
> her, keeping them happy, thinking she is relieving her
> daughter for rest and fun with you, her husband.
> [*Bitterly*] How you are deceived, mother.

EDUFA: Don't fret so much. Calm yourself, will you?

SEGUWA: It is your wife who needs calming, if I may say so.

EDUFA: You've promised to stand with me in this trouble. You
will, won't you? Your service and your courage these last
few days have given me strength and consolation. Don't
despair now. Ampoma is getting better.

SEGUWA: Better? Ho, ho. After fainting twice last night? [*Shrugs*]
Ah, well, just as you say. I promised to stand with you
and will. But may God help us all, for the bridge we are
now crossing is between the banks of life and the banks
of death. And I do not know which way we're facing.
[*Pause*] Where is the incense? I'll keep it burning.

EDUFA: [*Relieved*] Your kindness will not be forgotten, believe
me, when we can smile again in this house. [*He gives her
the box. She sprinkles more incense on the fire.*] See that
the gate is barred.

The scene has been preceded by a 'Prologue' in which Abena has
told us of the illness of Edufa's wife, Ampoma, and of his insistence that
the gate of the compound should be locked against visitors. We now hear
a man's voice — we would guess that it is Edufa's, even if we didn't have
the playtext before us — giving an urgent instruction to prepare a herbal
bath and bring fire for the incense. His words prepare us for a ceremony
and make us curious to know of what sort it will be and for what purpose.
As his orders are being carried out, we hear a chorus of unseen women
chanting a mourning dirge in the street outside. We are invited to wonder
if there is a connection between the two activities, if the ceremony and the
dirge are both for the same person. The chanting recedes; there seems to
be no connection: but then it returns and with it the possibility that there
has been a death in the house. Abena has told us that Ampoma is not
mortally ill, but there is now a temptation to wonder if she has not
suddenly died, especially as Abena left the stage saying: 'I don't know
why I should be so sad' (p. 3). A woman (Seguwa) crosses the stage, and
as the stage direction indicates, we are meant to notice how disturbed she
is by the sound of the dirge. The man now rushes out onto the stage,
carrying a box of incense. The sense of urgency in his first, off-stage words
is matched by his physical movements, which are hurried and strained.

When the man speaks it is to voice the suspicion that the audience
itself has been entertaining: 'Why are they doing a funeral chant? They
are not coming towards this house?' (p. 5). His questions are linked to his
specific enquiry of the woman: 'You've spoken to no one?' (p. 5). The
man's mental 'leap' is baffling. Why should the mourners be coming to his
house if no one has died or is dying? And why should he be so concerned
about the woman having said something that would have brought the
mourners to the house? His words tell us, indirectly, that there is
something seriously wrong in this household, something more than
Abena has told us about in the 'Prologue', and that, whatever it is, the
man wishes to keep it secret. The woman assures him that she has spoken

to no one. There is a pause, which has the effect of adding weight to the words she now speaks: 'It must be for someone else's soul they clamour' (p. 5). It is the 'someone else's' that is disquieting: it makes us ask: 'who is the *someone* she has in mind?' From what Abena has already told us it is clearly Ampoma, Edufa's wife, though we have been given to believe that she is not mortally ill. The chanting now fades and the man relaxes and composes himself. 'No,' he says, 'they are not coming here' (p. 5). Again, a strange and revealing remark, for it implicitly suggests that he was more than half expecting them to come here, that it would somehow have been appropriate for the mourning women to have come to his house.

We've had only a few seconds of dialogue and yet we've already learnt a lot from it. Even if we did not already know about Ampoma from Abena's speech in the 'Prologue', we would by now be sure that someone in the compound is either very ill or even dead. We have also become aware that there is great tension in both the man and the woman. We know that related to this tension is the man's desperate wish to keep what has happened or is happening a complete secret. For some reason, which we do not yet comprehend, he is deeply fearful. The woman's words have also betrayed her real feelings, which have to do with her association of the women's mourning with someone in her own household. With this information, and with the powerful evocation of tension and fear to which the dialogue has contributed, we've already been convinced of the 'reality' of the characters and their situation; and the dramatist has already established a sense of suspense, the desire to know what is going on, what has caused the fear and tension, and how the situation will develop.

The man tells the woman to keep the incense burning while Ampoma and he bathe. (Recreating the characters and action in our 'mental theatre' we have to wait for the characters to be identified by what is said and done: the man's words now make it certain that he is Edufa.) We know now that Ampoma is at least still alive. The woman's response, however, suggests — though it does not directly say — that her life is in danger, and that the effectiveness of this form of treatment is dubious. Edufa is quick to note her reservations, and there is clearly an accusatory tone in his 'Doubting?' (p. 5). And yet, of course, Edufa was himself doubting only a few moments ago, when he thought that the mourning women were coming to his house. He assures her: 'I cannot give in to any thoughts of hopelessness' (p. 5). These may sound like the words of a strong, determined person, but we catch the hint of desperation in Edufa's assertion; indeed, the mere fact that he can say this suggests that the 'thoughts of hopelessness' are pressing in upon him.

The woman emphasises that she has kept the whole affair a secret, which intensifies our awareness that Edufa is for some reason fearful of his wife's condition being publicly known. But she also insists that it is now time for that secrecy to be dispensed with and help sought. Edufa's reply — 'From whom? We are doing everything we can. Also, it is Ampoma's wish that no one be allowed to see her' — simultaneously brings out his sense of hopelessness, despite his having just said that they must not despair, and his persistent refusal to let the illness become common knowledge. The woman points out that Ampoma is too ill to make rational decisions and that it is 'most unnatural that even the mother who bore her should be kept ignorant of her sickness, serious as it now is' (p. 6). Her words point up the conflict she is experiencing within herself about whether to keep silent or to seek help for Ampoma, even against Edufa's wishes. At the same time they emphasise the deception that Edufa is practising and to which she is a now unwilling party.

Edufa recognises that she is under stress. He reminds her of her promise to stand with him and tells her how much her support has helped. He tries to be optimistic: 'Don't despair now. Ampoma is getting better' (p. 6). But it doesn't work: 'Better?' asks the woman ironically, and laughs: 'After fainting twice last night?' (p. 6). Her response awakens us once again to Edufa's self-deception and the real desperation it conceals. But she agrees to keep her promise, though her warning ('But may God help us all . . .') only serves to raise the tension further. Edufa is relieved when she says that she will keep the incense burning: 'Your kindness will not be forgotten, believe me, when we can smile again in this house' (p. 6). Perhaps, though from what has been said we are by no means convinced that such a happy time is certain, or even likely. And the final words of the scene — 'See that the gate is barred' —bring us back harshly to the threatening present, and to Edufa's obsession with a secrecy which seems to preclude the possibility of help from outside.

This is a short scene, with relatively little dialogue. And yet it conveys a great deal — far more than might appear at first glance. Efua Sutherland's dialogue functions here, like all good dramatic speech, at several distinct but related levels simultaneously. It establishes plot facts — the gravity of Ampoma's illness, Edufa's refusal to allow outsiders into his compound. But it does more than give us vital plot information for it is also used by the playwright to convey character. The dramatist, unlike the novelist, cannot tell us in so many words that Edufa is practising a desperate self-deception on himself by insisting that Ampoma is getting better, or that Seguwa experiences an inner conflict between her pledge to Edufa to keep the illness secret and her desire to seek help from outside before it is too late. But we learn these things about the characters through their own words, in which their inmost feelings are revealed — even, perhaps, in spite of themselves. The dialogue in this brief scene has thus vividly established the 'reality' of Edufa and Seguwa; it has made us believe in them, made us feel their fear and tension. Their dialogue even helps to establish the 'reality' of Ampoma, even though we don't yet see her but only hear about her illness.

In establishing the reality of the characters, the dialogue of this scene also engages us imaginatively in their situation, and in this way it helps to create suspense. What Edufa and Seguwa say arouses our curiosity. What lies behind Edufa's obsession, made so evident by his words, with keeping his wife's illness a secret, even if this means rejecting the possibility of external help? The dialogue makes us forcefully aware that something is being left *unsaid* in this scene, that something fearful is happening or has happened which neither Edufa nor Seguwa speak of but which is preying on their minds. We want our curiosity to be satisfied; in other words, we want to know how the tension established in this initial scene will be developed and ultimately resolved, and how this will affect the characters involved.

We can now see, then, that the words of the dialogue in this scene are 'in action' in a number of ways. They not only give us important factual information but also convey character, establish relationships and create suspense. The dialogue between Edufa and Seguwa is thus not only a matter of things being *said*; it is also a form of *action, of things being done*, in the sense that a number of important dramatic functions are being fulfilled. This being so, we may observe finally that the dialogue in this scene works at the level of advancing the action of the play as a whole. Not a single speech is irrelevant or too wordy. Everything that is said serves to focus our interest on certain matters — Ampoma's dangerous illness, Edufa's secrecy about it — and to make us curious about what will follow.

The principle of economy in dialogue is of fundamental importance, especially in modern realistic drama. It was summed up in a phrase by the Italian dramatist, Luigi Pirandello, one of the finest modern writers for the European stage: he called it *'l'azione parlata'*, which translates as 'the action spoken', or 'the action in words'. If, in drama, words are in action, there is also a sense in which action is in words. What is meant by this is that in much modern drama of realistic speech the characters do very little else but talk, so that the words often *are* the action, the drama. When this is the case it is clearly essential that the dialogue should be written with precision and economy, every word contributing to the overall dramatic effect.

Dialogue and convention

In *Edufa*, as in most contemporary plays, the characters speak to each other in very much the same way as people converse in real life. But this has not been true of most plays written in the past, nor is it so even of many plays of our own time. A large part of the world's drama has traditionally had, and still has, dialogue which is intentionally different from the talk of real life. Sometimes, this non-realistic dialogue consists of highly stylised prose, but more often non-realism in dialogue means verse.

The predominance of realistic prose speech in modern drama no doubt has much to do with the unprecedented democracy of modern societies — the idea, and to some extent the reality, that every individual is essentially equal, at least in terms of basic rights and opportunities, with every other individual. This democratic impulse in modern life has by no means, however, killed the urge among dramatists to write poetic drama, whether the poetry be in verse or in highly stylised prose. And in African societies, even more so than in the West, dramatists and audiences alike seem to remain strongly disposed towards the effects that poetic language can achieve.

There is an understandable temptation for people interested in drama to take sides on the issue of whether prose or verse is the 'superior' form of language for the stage. Those who favour verse drama are sometimes heard to argue that dramatic poetry allows for the more subtle and intense expression of ideas and emotions than is possible in realistic prose. The 'advocates' of realistic stage language, on the other hand, are likely to suggest that the use of verse in contemporary drama is unacceptably artificial and may even signal an evasion of the realities of modern life. Useful as such a debate may be in focusing attention on the relative merits of the different kinds of language that can be used on the stage, it is misconceived to think in terms of 'taking sides' on the matter. Some confusion about the relative merits of verse and rhetorical prose on the one hand and realistic prose dialogue on the other may be dispelled by an understanding of the word 'artificiality' in relation to each. The use of poetic language is sometimes thought to be 'superior' to realistic speech because the latter is held to be no more than a transcription of real, everyday speech. According to this view, the dramatist is little more than a living tape-recorder who faithfully writes down the kinds of things that real people would actually say in such a situation. Conversely, realistic dramatic speech is sometimes praised for being less artificial and more 'true to life' than verse.

It is important to realise that, in good drama, speech, like character, is equally artificial whether it be in the realistic or non-realistic convention. What varies is not the artificiality, but the *level* of stylisation of the language created by the dramatist's artifice.

This is a difficult point to grasp because realistic prose speech in drama so evidently *seems* less artificial than verse. Take this exchange between Edufa and Seguwa in the scene we have already discussed:

EDUFA: Why are they doing a funeral chant? They are not coming towards this house? [*To* SEGUWA] You've spoken to no one?

SEGUWA: [*With some resentment*] To no one. My tongue is silenced. [*Pause*] It must be for someone else's soul they clamour. [*The chanting fades.*]

EDUFA: [*Composing himself*] No, they are not coming here. [*Pause*] Put the fire down.

One is tempted to say that there is nothing here which is different from ordinary conversation. The sentences are short and simple, and follow the rhythms of everyday speech. What may escape us, until we analyse the excerpt more closely, is the dramatist's selection and arrangement of the words to be spoken, and their integration with other dramatic elements, to create a deliberate effect —namely, the raising of tension and then its relaxation. Even the pauses have meaning, being more effective at the two points they are indicated than words would have been. Movement and gesture have also been fully coordinated with the spoken word to create a total effect: in her tension Seguwa stands holding the brazier; it's only when the mourners have passed that Edufa reminds her that she is still holding it and can put it down. Her movement in doing so signals a physical relaxation of her mental tension, just as her holding of it complemented the tension of the dialogue. What we get, in this brief exchange, is a carefully shaped *rhythm* compounded of spoken words, chanting, silence and movement. It *seems* natural but it is really quite different from real-life conversation. It doesn't waste a word, and it has none of the repetitions, unplanned pauses and general verbal 'interference' of everyday speech.

Realistic prose speech in drama is just as artificial, then, as speech in the non-realistic convention. It is simply that it has been stylised to sound like real-life conversation, even as it performs a number of dramatic functions that genuine real-life conversation does not, and cannot, normally fulfil. (A simple test would be to imagine a play written as people really do speak: the result would be boring and perhaps incoherent, or at least very difficult to follow.) There is nothing less contrived, less deliberately artificial, about realistic dramatic speech than about verse or rhetorical prose. What *is* different is the level of stylisation. Verse speech is language at its most stylised, and thus at its most removed from ordinary speech. One very important effect of this difference is that verse is able to bear a heavy weight of imagery, while the requirement of life-likeness denies a similar capacity for imagery to realistic prose speech.

Verbal imagery

We must look at this last point more closely because it is the chief way in which verse dialogue differs from realistic speech in the drama. We can begin to do so by looking at one of the most famous speeches in drama, spoken by Jaques in Shakespeare's *As You Like It*:

> All the world's a stage,
> And all the men and women merely players.
> They have their exits and their entrances,
> And one man in his time plays many parts,
> His acts being seven ages. At first the infant,
> Mewling and puking in the nurse's arms.
> Then, the whining school-boy with his satchel
> And shining morning face, creeping like snail
> Unwillingly to school. And then the lover,
> Sighing like furnace, with a woeful ballad
> Made to his mistress' eyebrow. Then, a soldier,
> Full of strange oaths, and bearded like the pard,
> Jealous in honour, sudden, and quick in quarrel,
> Seeking the bubble reputation
> Even in the cannon's mouth. And then, the justice,
> In fair round belly, with good capon lin'd,
> With eyes severe, and beard of formal cut,
> Full of wise saws, and modern instances,
> And so he plays his part. The sixth age shifts
> Into the lean and slipper'd pantaloon,
> With spectacles on nose, and pouch on side,
> His youthful hose well sav'd, a world too wide
> For his shrunk shank, and his big manly voice,
> Turning again toward childish treble, pipes
> And whistles in his sound. Last scene of all,
> That ends this strange eventful history,
> Is second childishness and mere oblivion,
> Sans teeth, sans eyes, sans taste, sans everything.

> (II,vii,139–66)

The entire speech is based on a very old idea, popular long before Shakespeare's time, that the world can be likened to a theatre and man's life to the performance of a play in it. In terms of this extended comparison a person's birth and death are like the first entrance and final exit of an actor in the performance of a play. Similarly, an individual life can be seen as having several phases, ranging from helpless infancy to equally helpless senility, which can be compared to the way in which a single actor may be called upon to play several different roles in the course of a performance.

The language of Jaques' speech is clearly quite different from what we'd expect to find in a play whose dialogue is in the realistic convention. What Jaques is saying is said through images, which we may think of as pictures in the imagination created, in this case, through words. The entire speech is a succession of images, all constructed on the basic image of man as actor on the great stage of life. We have the 'picture' of infancy, a baby 'Mewling and puking in the nurse's arms'; of the schoolboy, with his satchel and his shiningly scrubbed face, dawdling on his reluctant way to school; and so the pictures follow one another until we reach the final one of man in the last performance of his life, when, lacking teeth, sight, taste and everything else, he is once again as helpless as he was in infancy. Jaques, like many of Shakespeare's characters, expresses himself in language which constantly embodies thoughts and feelings in a stream of imaginative pictures. The result is dramatic speech of great range, depth and vividness, spoken by characters who have the expressive powers of great poets.

It is obvious that a character who speaks like a real-life person cannot plausibly use imagery as Shakespeare has Jaques do, in a highly concentrated, continuous way. For one thing, it is hard to imagine a character in a realistic modern play being given a long speech to himself in which he makes such an elaborate comparison between life and the theatre. In most modern plays this simply wouldn't fit in with the prevailing realism of the characterisation, action and dialogue. It would probably sound false, contrived. Even if a modern, realistic play contained an 'equivalent' of Jaques' speech — and this is not impossible — what would it be like? Something like this, perhaps:

We are all actors on the stage of the world.
We all make our entrances and exits, and each
of us plays many parts in a single lifetime.
The first is infancy, which we spend puking
in our nurse's arms. Then there's the
reluctant schoolboy, with his scrubbed face,
going at a snail's pace to school. And then
there's the lover, sighing and composing silly
love poetry to his mistress. The next part is
that of the soldier, swearing away, trying to
be as manly as possible, seeking to make a big
reputation for himself even at the risk of death.
And then there's the judge, with his big belly,
severe eyes and learned speech. The next part
we play is the skinny old man, with spectacles
on the end of his nose, his trousers too large

for his scraggy legs and his voice breaking
once again, this time from manliness to a
childish squeaking. To finish off the performance
there is the last role, when we return to
second childhood, our memory gone, our teeth gone, our
eyes and sense of taste no longer working.

There is a great deal of difference between Shakespeare's original speech and this modern version of it. Apart from the problem mentioned above of such a speech probably being out of place in a modern realistic play, it clearly loses a great deal in 'translation'. Although it follows the basic structure of imagery of Jaques' original speech, it lacks the vividly particularised detail that we find in Shakespeare. There is all the difference in the world between 'the whining schoolboy with his satchel /And shining morning face, creeping like snail / Unwillingly to school' and the modern version above, with its 'reluctant schoolboy, with his scrubbed face, going at a snail's pace to school'. And it is very hard for modern dramatists to bridge this divide, for the simple reason that in a realistic play the characters must speak in at least approximately the same way as real people, and if they do so there is a definite limit as to how 'poetic' their language can be.

I say it is difficult for modern playwrights to reconcile the impulse towards employing poetic imagery and the constraints of realism, but I'm not saying that it is impossible. Some dramatists are able to give their characters 'poetic' speech, rich in imagery, which is nevertheless based on the way people actually do speak in a particular dialect or language. This is an especially important fact in relation to African drama, for it has to do with a distinctive quality of dramatic speech in many African plays in English, irrespective of whether they are written in verse, rhetorical prose or in the realistic convention.

For virtually all African writers in countries which were formerly British colonies, English is a second or in some cases a third language. Sometimes, of course, African dramatists choose not to write in English, though their plays may subsequently be translated into that language to reach a wider audience. (For example, Ebrahim Hussein's *Kinjeketile* was written and first performed in Swahili, and such popular Nigerian dramatists as Hubert Ogunde and Duro Ladipo wrote and performed their plays in Yoruba.) The richness and subtlety of their native tongues are at the disposal of these writers, and the advantage exists of being able to communicate with their audiences exploiting the deep relationship between indigenous language and indigenous culture. On the other hand, the English-language African dramatist faces the disadvantage of having to communicate in a language which is ultimately alien both to himself and his audience, however fluently it may be spoken and understood. (An important exception here is Pidgin, which uses English-derived elements of language in a way that does not have this 'alien' quality.) But the situation isn't a simple one of disadvantage, for the African dramatist also has the possibility of infusing his English with influences drawn from his mother tongue, and thereby enriching it in a way that may be denied the writer whose first language is English.

The most distinctive feature of this pervasive influence in English-language African drama is the idiomatic richness of much of its dialogue, and especially the effective use made of proverbial or quasi-proverbial sayings. Take this exchange between Utisi, a village girl, and her boyfriend Muindi in *Utisi*, by the Kenyan playwright John Mike Kibwana:

MUINDI: It's this ripeness of your head which makes me speak to you. Could it be that when your mother was carrying you she ate some soil from the footprints of my parents? Utisi, lengthy words don't make one wiser. I'll not keep you for a long time. May I hear then that you'll wait for me?

UTISI: Perhaps.

MUINDI: Girl, don't play about with a breakable branch. Besides, I have a desire to dance with you. Do you hear?

(p. 7)

This piece of dialogue, and that of the play as a whole, belongs to the realistic convention, but it is a realism which, where language is concerned, owes much to the rhythms and idioms of one or more of the indigenous languages of Kenya. The result is a vividness of expression which can be used for humorous effect or to heighten emotion, both of which are the case in *Utisi*. This enrichment of English by another language or a dialect is not, of course, restricted to African writing. A notable example of a European play whose linguistic beauty owes much to the author's use of dialect is *The Playboy of the Western World* by the Irish dramatist J. M. Synge. The characters of this play, who are Irish peasants, speak in a dialect of English based on Synge's close acquaintance with what he called the 'folk-imagination' and speech rhythms and idioms of Irish country people. A similar linguistic richness has also been available to, and been exploited by, some contemporary Black American dramatists, notably in a play like Ossie Davis's comedy about race relations in the deep South of the U.S.A., *Purlie Victorious*.

The poetic resources of language are accessible, then, to some dramatists writing in prose and in the realistic convention when their dramatic speech is drawn from a vernacular which retains highly coloured idioms, and distinctive vocabulary and speech rhythms. Does this mean that for other realist prose playwrights there is no possibility of employing verbal imagery, pictures in the mind created through the words of the dialogue? On the contrary, verbal imagery remains a most important resource for realist dramatists generally, even if — unlike Synge or Soyinka — they do not have access to a form of English enriched by a dialect or another language. How, then, may dramatists whose characters speak like real people employ verbal imagery which is both convincing and effective?

To answer this question let us look at Athol Fugard's *Boesman and Lena* which — like *Sizwe Bansi is Dead* — is set in South Africa. There are only three characters, one of whom never speaks. Boesman and Lena are a Coloured couple who have spent most of their lives tramping the roads. As the play opens they walk onto the stage heavily burdened with all that they have in the world, their *pondok* (little shack) having been bulldozed to the ground by the White authorities that morning. Not a great deal happens in the play: Boesman and Lena argue and reminisce; an old African appears, 'an image of age and decrepitude', and Lena talks to him

Boesman and Lena, carrying their worldly possessions, on their endless journey.

though he can't understand her or she him; the old man dies, quietly in the darkness, of natural causes, and Boesman and Lena once again pick up their loads and resume their endless tramping of the roads.

The language of *Boesman and Lena* is firmly rooted in the vocabulary and speech patterns of South African Coloureds. What the characters say to each other, and the words and rhythms in which it is said, reflect the unrelievedly harsh and comfortless realities of their lives. There is nothing remotely 'poetic' about these lives, and it would be absurd to expect Boesman or Lena to speak in a poetic way, with a deliberate use of verbal imagery for poetic effect. And yet there is imagery in the language of the play, the effect of which may be reasonably described as poetic, even if it is of a very different kind from the poetry of Jaques' speech in *As You Like It*.

As they enter, Boesman and Lena are visibly carrying their lives around with them, in the form of their material possessions. Their lives have been lived on the roads; as Lena says: 'Boesman's back. That's the scenery in my world' (p. 5). Lena remembers what happened that morning, what she asked Boesman and his response:

> Where we going, Boesman? Don't ask questions. Walk! *Ja*, don't ask questions. Because you didn't know the answers. Where to go, what to do. I remember now. Down this street, up the next one, look down that one, then turn around and go the other way. Not lost? Which way takes you past Berry's Corner twice, then back to where you started from?
>
> (p. 4)

We begin to hear the names of the small towns and villages between which they constantly wander: Redhouse, Veeplaas, Bethelsdorp, Missionvale, Swartkops, Coega, Korsten. Lena is confused about the sequence of their travels:

> Wasn't it after Redhouse? Our last time here. Remember that *boer* chased us off his land. Then we came here. Is that right?
> [*Boesman ignores her.*]
> Then we went to Korsten
> BOESMAN: After here we went to Korsten?
> LENA: *Ja*. [*Boesman laughs at her derisively.*] How was it then? [*Pause.*] You won't tell me. (p. 7)

She continues worrying over the correct order (p. 8) until she believes she has it right:

> It's coming! Korsten. Empties, and the dog. *Hond*! How was it now? Redhouse — Swartkops — Veeplaas — Korsten. Then this morning the bulldozers . . . and then . . . [*Pause.*] Here! I've got there!
>
> (p. 9)

She is so concerned to establish the sequence that she evens plans to work it out as far back as it's possible to go, 'back and back until I reach Coega Kop' (p. 10). But her elation is short-lived: Boesman takes pleasure in making her aware that she has it wrong, or at least that she can't be sure whether it's right or wrong. Lena becomes desperate, and in her growing confusion she forgets the sequence altogether. She struggles physically to re-establish her sense of direction, without success (pp. 11–12), and Boesman takes advantage of her angry disorientation to suggest that one day she'll even have to ask him who she is:

> BOESMAN: What about Rosie? Nice name Rose. Maria. Anna. Or Sannie! Sannie who? *Sommer* [Just] Sannie Somebody.
>
> (p. 12)

And so the play continues, Boesman and Lena picking over the bare bones of their lives, which continue to be intimately intertwined in the dialogue with places they have stayed in or passed through. As Lena puts it:

> I meet the memory of myself on the old roads. Sometimes young. Sometimes old. Is she coming or going? From where to where? All

mixed-up. The right time on the wrong road, the right road leading to the wrong place.

(p. 22)

In the final moments of the play we see Boesman and Lena pick up their belongings and prepare to take to the road again. Lena asks:

> Where we going? Better be far. Coegakop. That's our farthest. That's where we started.
>
> BOESMAN: Coega to Veeplaas.
>
> LENA: [*slowly loading up the rest of her share*]. First walk. I always remember that one. It's the others.
>
> BOESMAN: [*as Lena loads*].Veeplass to Redhouse. On *baas* [boss] Robbie's place.
>
> LENA: My God! *Ou* [Old] *baas* Robbie.
>
> BOESMAN: Redhouse to Missionvale . . . I worked on the saltpans. Missionvale to Bethelsdorp. Back again to Redhouse . . . that's where the child died. Then to Kleinskool. Kleinskool to Veeplaas. Veeplaas to here. First time. After that, Redhouse, *baas* Robbie was dead, Bethelsdorp, Korsten, Veeplaas, back here the second time. Then Missionvale again, Veeplaas, Korsten and then here, now.
>
> LENA: [*Pause . . . she is loaded.*] Is that the way it was? How I got here?

Athol Fugard, the author, in the role of Boesman.

BOESMAN: Yes.
LENA: Truly?
BOESMAN: Yes.
         [*Pause.*]
LENA: It doesn't explain anything.
BOESMAN: I know.

(p. 45)

Why has Fugard, in inventing the dialogue, chosen to devote so much of it to references to these places, and the order in which they were visited? A careful, imaginatively-engaged reading of the play allows us to perceive that the significance of these places is not merely geographical but has to do with the very nature of Boesman's and Lena's existence. For this Coloured couple, whose lives have been spent on the road, the overall shape and meaning of life is closely bound up with the sequence of their travels and with what happened where. For Lena especially, it is crucial to put life into some sort of order; to establish her identity, the fact that she has existed, by knowing the exact order of their wanderings. The climax of this process is when Lena discovers that even though she now knows the correct order of their travels it doesn't explain anything, it doesn't suddenly give a new meaning to life. So the recurrent concern with place and its ordering in the dialogue constitutes a sustained verbal image of Boesman's and Lena's lives as oppressed wanderers, the 'wretched of the earth' with no fixed home or identity. The final effect of this (and other recurrent verbal images in the dialogue) is 'poetic', in the sense that language has been artistically employed to achieve richly evocative meaning; and this is true even though the language itself is consistently realistic and devoid of obvious poetry.

Spectacle and visual imagery

It is often assumed that imagery in drama is restricted to language, to the words spoken by the characters. This widespread misconception is the consequence of plays being studied as *literature* rather than for their dramatic and theatrical qualities. When plays are understood as theatre it is not only verbal imagery which is appreciated but also images which are communicated visually, through what the audience sees. In the theatre, sitting watching a play in performance, it is usually fairly easy to perceive the presence of a visual image and to understand its significance for the play as a whole. When we read a play, however, it is usually much more difficult to become aware of these visual elements, or at least to give them the appreciation they deserve. To do so, we have to recreate the scene mentally from the evidence of the text in a way that has already been discussed.

A play is a sustained sequence of things seen (and heard), a lengthy series of stage-pictures which change and flow into each other. For much of the time — perhaps even through the entire performance of a play — these stage-pictures may neither create any spectacular effect nor function as visual images. A spectacular effect would be achieved if and when the visual element on stage became so predominant and impressive that the audience's attention was focused on it for its own sake. An example would be the inclusion in a play of an elaborate dance with musical accompaniment which for its duration absorbs the spectators' entire attention. Spectacle is an important feature of many African plays, and it is usually based on traditional forms of spectacular display in festival and ritual celebration. The combination of dance, music and, often, incantation or song constitutes a kind of 'language' in much traditional performance in Africa, and it offers a rich source of expressive possibilities to the contemporary African dramatist.

Take, for instance, this moment from Duro Ladipo's *Moremi* (adapted into English by Ulli Beier) where speech, dance, music and incantation have been blended under the influence of Yoruba performance and poetic tradition:

> *The Oni* [traditional ruler] *sits in state. He greets them* [the crowd].
>
> ONI: The owner of heaven will protect this town. Oduduwa
>   your father will be at your side. Oramfe's thunder will
>   come to your aid.
>
> ILARIS: Aaaa-seeee! So let it be.
>
> CROWD: May all of us live long.
>   Head heavy with beaded crown
>   Oranmiyan reborn!
>   Huge fellow
>   who must force his way through the palace doors.
>   Hero in the town.
>   Hero in the battlefield.
>   Hero with open ears:
>   nothing escapes your knowledge!
>   Divine father!
>
> *They dance to the music of the iron gongs.*
>
>   *Laoko laoko*
>   *Laoko o larute*
>   *Laoko laoko*
>   *Laoko o larute . . .*
>
> ONI: May you all live long!
> CROWD: Head heavy with beaded crown!
>   Oranmiyan reborn!
>
>   (p. 8)

It would be easy to overlook, in reading the text, how impressive this could be on the stage, and how powerful an emotional response it could arouse in a Yoruba audience. We need, as readers, to recreate imaginatively the visual and aural dimensions of the scene; and we also have to bear in mind that a dance and its musical accompaniment, or a piece of ritual action presented on stage, may carry specific and intense meanings drawn from the traditional context upon which they are based. When the audience is also aware of the traditional associations, stage spectacle can function as a most effective medium for conveying meaning.

The use of what the audience sees to convey 'poetic' meaning need not, however, be restricted to spectacular display based on traditional performances. Everyday objects can function as visual images or symbols, and they often do so in conjunction with dialogue and action, which reinforce the meaning of the image. We'll conclude our discussion of imagery by looking at how this is done in *The Trial of Dedan Kimathi* by the Kenyan writers Ngugi wa Thiong'o and Micere Githae Mugo.

Dedan Kimathi, a leader of Mau Mau fighting against the British colonising power in Kenya, has been captured and put on trial. There is an attempt by guerrillas loyal to Kimathi to rescue him from the courtroom. This involves a gun being hidden in a loaf of bread which is intended eventually to reach Kimathi. But the plan goes wrong. The guerilla posing as a fruit-seller, to whom the woman is to hand the bread, is arrested during a roundup by the authorities, and the warder sympathetic to Mau Mau who would in turn have taken the loaf from the fruit-seller is suddenly transferred to another place. The woman meets a boy and girl, street-urchins fighting over some money given to the boy as a tip by an American tourist. She begins to educate the boy about the political struggle going on in Kenya. Despite the setbacks, the woman, boy and girl plan to free Kimathi themselves. The woman will go into the courtroom first and 'speak' to Kimathi with her eyes; when she coughs the boy and girl will break the bread, bring out the gun and start shooting. The Judge sentences Kimathi to death and the court rises. The boy and girl move swiftly towards Kimathi, breaking the bread and holding the gun: a loud shot is heard, there is darkness and then the lights come up again to reveal the stage filled with workers and peasants, led by the boy and girl, singing a freedom song.

The loaf of bread is a very important item (more properly, stage property) in the play. The audience's attention is first drawn to it when the woman is being searched and questioned by a white soldier. He empties out the contents of her basket, among which is a parcel wrapped in paper. Searching for weapons, he unwraps it and finds the loaf inside. He is about to take a bite from it when the woman, reacting strongly, pleads with him not to take the last piece of food she has for her family. The soldier is fooled but the audience is not: we recognise that there is something special about the loaf, and we have clues as to what it might be in the soldier's comment about how it might have been a grenade or home-made gun, and in his observation that it is heavy.

The next time our eyes are directed towards the bread is when we see the boy looking at it hungrily, after the woman has stopped the fight between him and the girl (p. 17). When the boy, in gratitude to the woman for giving him money to buy food, offers to help her in some way, she gives him the task of handing over the loaf to the orange-seller outside the courtroom where Dedan is being tried. The boy is disappointed by the apparent triviality of the job; but the woman replies with 'Bread is life!' and makes it clear that the loaf is somehow 'worth a life' (p. 22). When he can't find the orange-seller he decides that he is being tested, to see if he will eat the bread. He breaks off a piece but then remembers that 'she would be watching me all the time' (p. 31), and tries to patch it back on the loaf. He is interrupted by the arrival of the girl, who still has his money. Later, when he catches up with her, they fight and the stage direction reads:

> *They roll struggling toward where the knife and the bread are. Boy gets to the knife; throws it away. Girl rolls him over. She gets the*

> *Bread and throws it, smashing it on the floor. Gun falls out of the loaf. Both see it . . . (pp. 42—3)*

What we have been suspecting is now clearly revealed: the loaf contains the gun that is intended to rescue Dedan Kimathi. The boy's first instinct is to report it to the police, but the girl realises that if he does so he will himself be arrested as a 'terrorist' (p. 43). To their surprise they find the fruit-seller, who turns out to be the woman in disguise. Together, they enter the courtroom, and for the last time our attention is focused on the loaf as it is broken by the girl and the gun taken out.

The loaf is thus at the centre of the audience's attention at several crucial moments during the play. This in itself, however, does not make it a visual image. For it to be an image *it has to mean something more than itself*, it has to convey some kind of emotional and/or intellectual meaning to the audience. Another way of putting it would be to say that for the loaf to be a visual image it has to have a *symbolic* dimension, which means that while being itself it also suggests other qualities or properties in the minds of the audience. In what possible way, we might justifiably ask, can so ordinary a thing as a loaf of bread convey a symbolic meaning?

Even without any other clues an alert reader or spectator may have been reminded of something when the woman, referring to the loaf, says 'Bread is life!', and also when the bread is finally broken in two to reveal the gun. The reminder would have been of how, for Christians, the bread taken by the communicant at Mass is the bread of life, the symbol of Christ's body which was voluntarily sacrificed for man's redemption. The breaking of the bread is a moment of great symbolic significance in Christian worship, being the ritual prelude to the act of eating the bread which is the means to spiritual redemption.

Bread, then, is a very ordinary thing but for many people it is, or can be, a powerful symbol: the symbol of redemption or salvation. *The Trial of Dedan Kimathi* is not a Christian play, nor do its authors expect us to endow the bread with a symbolic significance on this evidence alone. Let's take this last point first. The association of the loaf with the Christian symbol of salvation develops in relation to the dramatists' use of a range of references to Christianity in the play.

For example, there are religious allusions in the dialogue. The woman makes an explicit parallel between the 'call' of Jesus and the 'call of our people' (p. 19): the boy implicitly compares Dedan Kimathi with Christ ('They say . . . they say he used to talk with God' (p. 20)); and the woman affirms that 'Faith in a cause can work miracles' in the context of Dedan as the Christ-like miracle-worker on behalf of the Kenyan peoples (p. 21). The structure of the plot also has Christian associations, for the capture and trial of Dedan is strikingly similar to the story of the arrest and trial of Jesus. Note especially how Dedan was betrayed by those closest to him, as Christ was, and his cry to the traitors in the courtroom: 'Thirty pieces of silver./ Judases. Traitors' (p. 79). And, like Christ, Dedan undergoes a series of 'temptations' by those forces of evil which would like to divert him from his redemptive role — temptations which he, like his illustrious predecessor, successfully overcomes.

Through dialogue, plot and actions which allude to Christ's life we are thus invited to compare Dedan Kimathi in his role as saviour of the oppressed Kenyan people to Christ in his role as redeemer. The loaf, understood in this pattern of allusion and parallel to Christianity, becomes something more than bread: it becomes associated with the bread of the communion as a means to salvation. It becomes, in other words, a visual image.

It is important to realise, however, that these Christian references do not make *The Trial of Dedan Kimathi* a Christian play. On the contrary, it is made very clear by the woman that the 'call' she has heard is not that of Christ but the 'call' to national liberation. Salvation is viewed here in social and political terms, and it is achieved through means which include violence. Orthodox religion, in the person of the priest who is one of Kimathi's tempters, is attacked on the grounds that it is being used as an instrument of ideological coercion and oppression by the colonialists and their black collaborators. When the bread is broken to reveal the gun we are being offered, deliberately and ironically, an idea of salvation which is very different from that associated with Christianity.

We'll conclude with a summary. In drama words are 'in action', both in the sense that they are written (and should therefore be read) to be spoken, and — even more importantly — in the sense that the words of drama not only convey meaning by what they 'say' but also by what they 'do'. As readers, and as aspiring dramatists, we have to bear in mind that dialogue operates on several levels: there is the obvious semantic meaning of the words, but there is also the level of what the words are *doing* in presenting character and character relationships, in creating the 'reality' of situations, and in developing suspense and the action generally.

A great deal of the world's drama, in the past and in the present, has been written and performed in the form of verse dialogue, or of rhetorical prose. The predominant modern form of drama is realism, in which the characters speak *as if* they are real-life people. This does not mean, however, that realistic dramatic dialogue is the same as the conversation of everyday life. Realistic dialogue has been carefully devised and arranged to give the impression of real-life speech, though in fact it is highly artificial. In fact, realistic prose speech is just as artificial as verse or rhetorical prose, the difference being that it is stylised at a different level. One of the consequences of this difference is that verse dialogue is able to carry a great deal of imagery of an explicit, poetic kind, while this is largely denied to most realistic dramatic dialogue. Some playwrights, however, including many in Africa, are able to combine an essentially realistic mode of speech with considerable use of imagery because the everyday language on which their dialogue is based is itself rich in the 'popular' imagery of idiomatic usage, and — in Africa especially — of proverbial and semi-proverbial sayings. But even when this is not the case, realist dramatists can still employ verbal imagery, for example — as in *Boesman and Lena* — by creating a sustained, recurrent pattern of reference in the words of the dialogue which gradually acquires a special symbolic significance for the audience.

There is the potential for visual, as well as verbal, imagery in drama, since plays are created to be seen as well as heard. The symbolic dimension of a visual image may be conveyed through spectacle; and in Africa stage spectacle is usually associated with the display of traditional festivity and ritual, which often includes not only a powerful visual element but also dance, song, music and incantation. But everyday objects can also be visual images, provided that in the course of the play they acquire a 'more than everyday' symbolic significance, as for example the loaf of bread does in *The Trial of Dedan Kimathi*. In this process the visual element is often conjoined with a deliberate use of the other dramatic elements, such as dialogue and action, to create the imagery.

Exercises for Chapter 5: Dramatic speech and imagery

1   Consider one of the following ideas for a play:
   a) A man, now in his mid thirties, left the village many years ago for a distant town. He gives the impression, in letters and on occasional visits back to the village, that he has been successful in the town and has become wealthy and powerful. The villagers come to think of him as their most successful son. One day, unexpectedly, he arrives back, announcing that he has come to stay. (He has not been seen, or even heard from, for a very long time, which increases the villagers' surprise, and their delight, at his decision.) The truth is, however, that the man is as poor as the day he left the village, and has never been anything else. . . .
   b) The people of a large village, some distance from the main town in that area, are warned through a 'son' who works in the local government headquarters that an inspector is on his way to investigate rumours of bribery and corruption that are circulating about the village. These stories are in fact true, and those guilty of corruption in the village panic when they hear the news. An unknown visitor arrives one day at the village, claiming to be the new schoolteacher who has long been awaited. Someone suggests that he isn't really a schoolteacher but the inspector in disguise. . . .

   As you have already done in the first exercise for Chapter 4, draw up a plot-outline (scenario) for a play on either of these subjects. (Of course, you are free to create a scenario from an idea of your own.) Having settled on what your first scene will contain and which characters appear in it, write that scene, trying to make your dialogue work on several levels at once (i.e. giving necessary information and establishing the basic situation, creating suspense, depicting character and relationships, developing the action as a whole).
   You may need to rewrite the scene several times before you are satisfied with it. When you are, move on to another scene. (It doesn't have to be the next in sequence: if you have a very clear idea of the last scene of the play, for example, you can write the dialogue for that before you work on the intervening scenes.) When you have finished the play read through it carefully, revising the dialogue (and anything else) in the light of reading it as a whole. (Group improvisation may be used instead of, or in conjunction with, this exercise.)

6 The Strong Breed: a dramatic reading

Our main concern so far has been to isolate and analyse the basic elements of drama and to suggest a method for appreciating the dramatic qualities of plays even when they are read rather than enjoyed in the theatre. It cannot be emphasised too strongly that our procedure has been highly artificial. The breaking-down of drama into 'elements' such as character, plot, dialogue and so on, is merely a critical convenience. In reality, in any particular play, there are no such clear-cut compartments, because the various elements are always inter-related parts of a whole. When we visit a theatre, or read a play at home, we never perceive and enjoy the presentation of the characters in isolation from what they say or do, or the situations in which they find themselves. Rather, we receive a steady flow of impressions, of different kinds and varying intensity, from the moment the play begins until the moment it ends. Our enjoyment and understanding of it is the sum total of these impressions.

Having emphasised the elements of drama each in its own right, let us now restore the balance by looking at the way they are brought together to form a continuous, living unity. The best way of doing so is by experiencing this unity in the form of a particular play, and for this purpose I have chosen Wole Soyinka's *The Strong Breed*, first produced on stage in Nigeria in 1966. What follows is not a critical essay which tries to give a comprehensive interpretation of the play's meaning, but a dramatic reading which tries to recreate in the mind's eye and ear the impressions we would receive were we sitting in an auditorium watching a well directed and acted production of it.

After the list of characters the dramatist has inserted a note about the staging of the play, which reads:

> The scenes are described briefly, but very often a darkened stage with lit areas will not only suffice but is necessary. Except for the one indicated place, there can be no break in the action. A distracting scene-change would be ruinous.

We must bear this in mind as we read and imagine, for it indicates that a smooth progression of scenes, without interruptions, is an essential part of the effect Soyinka wishes to achieve. Now we turn to the text proper and read the first stage direction, which indicates a scenic arrangement suggesting a room in a mud house, with a space in front of it which is the street. Three characters are on stage: a man standing beside the window, looking out; a woman, who is in an *'agitated'* way *'clearing the table of what looks like a modest clinic'*; and, crouching just below the window, an idiot-boy, who looks up occasionally, smiling, *'waiting for Eman to notice him'*.

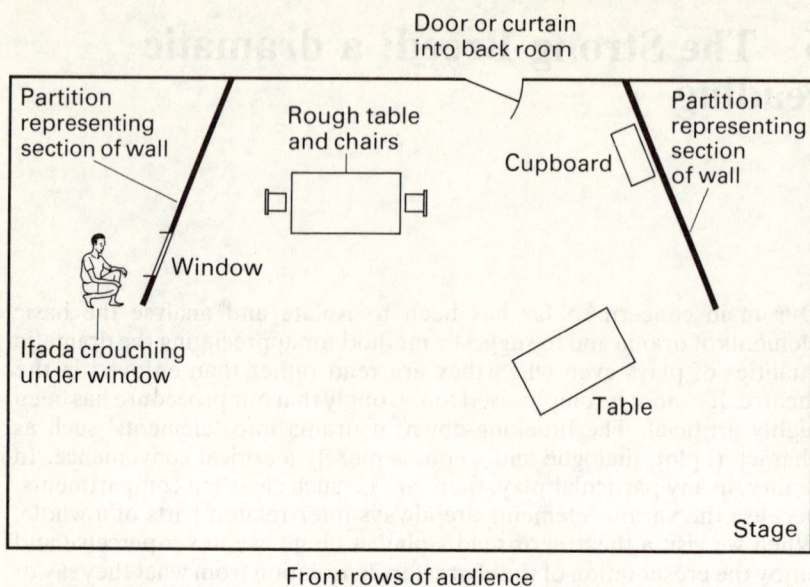

A diagram of the set for a performance of The Strong Breed.

Suspense, in drama and in life, is often caused by waiting for someone to make up his mind about something. The woman's first words create this kind of suspense in relation to the man: 'You will have to make up your mind soon, Eman. The lorry leaves very shortly' (p. 115). The suspense is prolonged by the fact that Eman doesn't reply, and intensified by the hurried passing of two travellers along the street, the man urging the woman to make haste. Clearly, the lorry will leave at any moment. Whatever it is that Eman must decide that has to do with the lorry, it must be decided very soon or he will have missed his opportunity. The woman's next words raise the tension further: 'Eman, are we going or aren't we? You will leave it till too late' (p. 115). The woman, and the audience, now receive Eman's reply to her question: 'There is still time — if you want to go' (p. 115). The verbal emphasis is clearly on the word 'you'. Eman is telling the woman that she is free to leave but that he is not going. His reply prompts a bitter rejoinder from her: 'You never want to go away — even for a minute' (p. 115).

Eman now turns his attention to the idiot-boy, patting him on the head, which so pleases the boy that he brings him some oranges. Eman's response lets us know that it is a day of festival in the locality. The sound of his voice brings the woman back on the stage, asking, 'Did you call me?' (p. 115). We have not been told that she ever left it, and it is puzzling at first what is meant by the stage direction: *'She has gone inside the room. Looks round the door'*. A little thought suggests that we have to imagine a stage which has partitions representing sections of the wall of the house, with a door or perhaps only a curtain at the back of the room indicating the entrance to an inner room, into which the woman has gone (see diagram).

The woman goes back into the inner room and Eman continues talking to Ifada, asking him what part he will play in the festivities. When he discovers that the boy will do nothing, he suggests that he make his own masquerade, and says that Sunma, the woman, will give him the necessary materials. But when she once more enters from the back room we discover that helping Ifada is the last thing Sunma intends to do. Instead, she shouts at him, telling him to get away, and makes it very clear to Eman that she can no longer bear the sight of the idiot-boy. Eman, like the audience, is taken aback at the violence of her outburst: he says, 'You cannot be telling all the truth' (p. 117), which corresponds to our own feeling that there is something more to Sunma's hostility than the mere fact that Ifada is abnormal. Neither Eman nor we are made much the wiser by the woman's 'explanation' that 'it must be the new year . . . I don't want a mis-shape near me. Surely for one day in the year, I may demand some wholesomeness' (p. 117).

Sunma's words, rather than clarifying, serve to deepen the mystery and to stimulate our curiosity. What is making her so nervous and hostile? What is it about her life which makes her so desperate to have some 'wholesomeness', if only for one day? What does this have to do with the earlier point of suspense, still not resolved, about leaving in the lorry? Why does she say in a *'half-pleading'* way to Eman that, if anything, she needs more kindness from him than the idiot-boy? We shall have to wait for the answers to such questions, but Soyinka has certainly made it powerfully apparent that there is considerable tension in the relationship between Eman and Sunma which is being expressed through her irrational behaviour towards Ifada.

As Sunma pleads with Eman, a girl enters, *'dragging an effigy by a rope attached to one of its legs'* (p. 118). Her conversation with Eman, who we now learn is a teacher, is joking but at the same time solemn and unsmiling. She is not going to the festival, even though she has an effigy, which she calls her 'carrier'. She tells Eman that she is sick, which is why no one will play with her, and that her mother has said her carrier will take away her sickness with the old year. If we are alert we will recall at this point that a moment ago Sunma was packing up medicines. Why has the girl not been sent for treatment at Eman's clinic if she is sick? Our question is voiced by Eman, and the girl's curt reply — 'My mother said No' — suggests that some at least of the people in this place have no faith in Eman; and when the girl begins to say, 'I must not stay talking to you. If my mother caught me . . .', we are aware of something worse than lack of faith. We perceive suspicion and perhaps even outright hostility.

It transpires that the girl wants some clothes for her effigy, and Eman is happy to give her a *buba* of his own. Sunma re-enters just as he is about to hand it over, and her reaction is as harsh and as apparently irrational as in the case of Ifada: 'She is not a child. She is as evil as the rest of them' (p. 119). Certainly we note the strangeness of the girl, her possession of what a stage direction has called *'a kind of inscrutability which does not make her hard but unsettling'*. And this is allied to her mysterious sickness and her refusal to be approached, even by Eman, who does not fear catching her disease. But why does Sunma go so far as to call this seemingly innocent child, and indeed the entire community, evil? We are given no answer, and Eman and Sunma go into the inner room.

Our curiosity can only be intensified by what now follows. Lacking anyone better, the girl invites Ifada to play with her. His task is to whip the effigy hard with a big stick and then, under the girl's supervision, to hang it from a tree, where she will set fire to it. There is something sinister about her coldly cruel attitude towards the effigy and this is heightened when we see, in our mind's eye, the object dressed in Eman's *buba*. The effigy is a visual image, communicating to us the suggestion that Eman is now, in a sense, the sacrificial victim, even though this seems to have come about by harmless chance. And the menacing undertones are increased when, with what the stage direction describes as '*surprising venom*', the girl assures Ifada that 'just because you are helping me, don't think it is going to cure you. I am the one who will get well at midnight, do you understand? It is my carrier and it is for me alone' (p. 120).

The stage is empty for some moments, giving the audience a breathing-space in which they can take stock of what has happened so far. We have seen the tension in the relationship between Eman and Sunma; been aware of Sunma's hostility towards Ifada and the girl, whose behaviour certainly has sinister undertones, especially in relation to the effigy now dressed as Eman; and throughout the first few minutes of the play the tension and indefinable air of menace have been linked to the possible departure of Eman and Sunma by lorry. We are brought back to this immediate point of tension and suspense when we hear the lorry's horn, which brings Sunma rushing out from the inner room. In the dialogue that follows we witness the woman's final desperate attempt to make Eman agree to their going. She puts pressure on him by telling him that he is not wanted here, and by repeating her mysterious and frightening assertion that the people, young and old, are nourished in evil and unwholesomeness (p. 121) and that he is consequently wasting his life among them. Sunma's pleas become more intense and desperate as the minutes go by and Eman's resistance remains unyielding: 'Tonight. Only tonight. We will come back tomorrow, as early as you like. But let us go away for this one night' (p. 122). Inevitably, we want to know why she is so frantically concerned to get away from the place on this particular night, and our curiosity is further assured when she tells Eman that 'it is only I who stand between you and contempt. And because of this you have earned their hatred' (p. 123). But we hear the lorry depart: whatever Sunma fears in this community cannot now be averted simply by leaving.

The nature of the suspense now changes. It is no longer a matter of whether or not Sunma can persuade Eman to board the lorry. Our curiosity is directed towards what will happen now that they must stay, and whether Sunma's conviction that the people are evil and hate Eman will have any tangible expression. Eman has remained unshaken by Sunma's pleading, to the point of appearing unfeeling towards her. Why is he like this? We are given a small but striking clue just before we hear the sound of the departing lorry. Sunma realises she cannot change his mind; she is suddenly calm but full of bitterness: 'The whole village may use you as they will but for me there is nothing . . . Sometimes I think you believe that doing anything for me makes you unfaithful to some part of your life. If it was a woman then I pity her for what she must have suffered' (p. 122). Although Sunma doesn't at first notice the effect her words have had on Eman, we do: he *winces and hardens slowly*, according to the stage direction. She goes on to say: 'keeping faith with so much is slowly making you inhuman'; and only then does she notice the change in Eman and is distressfully apologetic: 'I swear I didn't know . . . I would not have said it for all the world' (p. 122).

If Sunma cannot take Eman away then she wants to be together with him on this night. Eman reminds her that she has a part in the festival, but she denies it: 'I have renounced it; I am Jaguna's eldest daughter only in name' (p. 123). Eman's response to this is striking but mysterious: 'Renouncing one's self is not so easy — surely you know that' (p. 123). It indicates that he knows something about the process, and if we put his comment together with his earlier reaction to Sunma's inadvertent remark about his past it suggests that renouncing oneself, in his case, has had something to do with a woman. Sunma doesn't let this line of talk continue ('I don't want to talk about it,' she says). Nor will she have anything to do with Eman's suggestion that they go out and join in the festivities: 'Rejoicing! Is that what it seems to you? No, let us remain here. Whatever happens I must not go out until all this is over' (p. 124).

So far it has been very difficult to decide whether there is more truth in Sunma's view of the people and the nature of the festival or in Eman's. What happens now gives us some external evidence which will reinforce ominously Sunma's opinion and makes us wonder what precisely will happen this night about which she is so nervous. Sunma goes into the inner room to light the lamp, and Eman sits down at the table to play *ayo*. The next stage direction reads:

> *The girl is now seen coming back, still dragging her 'carrier'. Ifada brings up the rear as before. As he comes round the corner of the house two men emerge from the shadows. A sack is thrown over Ifada's head, the rope is pulled tight rendering him instantly helpless. The girl has reached the front of the house before she turns round at the sound of scuffle. She is in time to see Ifada thrown over the shoulders and borne away. Her face betraying no emotion at all, the girl backs slowly away, turns and flees, leaving the 'carrier' behind.*

When Sunma goes out of the house to hang up a lamp above the door she sees the effigy left by the girl and gasps in fear. Eman rushes out, wanting to know what has frightened her. She replies: 'I thought . . . I didn't really see it properly' (p. 124). If she had finished what she was going to say, it would have been something like 'I thought for a moment it was you, Eman'. We have already seen Eman being visually associated with the sacrificial effigy; that connection is now impressed upon us once more as Sunma momentarily mistakes the effigy for Eman. For the audience there is also a further connection, though still vague, of which Sunma and Eman are as yet ignorant: it is the momentary identification Sunma makes between Eman and the effigy in the context of Ifada's kidnapping. We don't yet know why this has happened, or what it has to do with Eman and the effigy or with Sunma's fears about this particular night, but the dramatist has arranged the sequence of events and created an atmosphere which has us waiting expectantly for further illumination.

Eman, in fact, is made to voice our own thought a moment or two after Sunma has been frightened. He says: 'I know there is something more than you've told me. What are you afraid of tonight?' (p. 125), and when she answers evasively he persists with 'What does tonight really mean that it makes you so helpless?' (p. 125). Soyinka knows that we want to know as much as Eman, especially as we now know more than Eman — we know that Ifada has been kidnapped. But Sunma continues to be evasive ('It is only a mood. And your indifference to me . . .') and they go back into the house, she closing and bolting the door. When Eman looks at her with *'questioning'* eyes she explains her action with 'There is a cold wind coming in'; and when he *'keeps his gaze on her'* she defiantly persists: 'It *was* getting cold' (p. 125). Whatever it is she knows about her own people that makes her frightened, it is something that not only makes her refuse to go out but even causes her to bolt the door. As a result, we — with Eman — can only be more curious about the unnamed threat she feels.

They sit together at the table playing *ayo*. Sunma asks him: 'What brought you here at all, Eman? And what makes you stay?' (p. 125). Her question follows naturally from Eman's response to her previous inadvertent comment about his past: she wants to know more about his past, and so do we. But Eman does not reply. Sunma assures him that she knows him too well to expect to share his life, but she feels that she deserves to know a little, having worked with him since he arrived. Eman wants to continue as a stranger, especially to her, for the puzzling reason that 'Love comes to me more easily with strangers' (p. 125). His replies only deepen the mystery of his past, rather than clarifying it. Why, for example, does he smilingly refer to the 'ties of blood' (p. 125), suggesting that he is still tied in some way to his family even though he lives in a distant place? And what does he mean when he goes on to say that 'I am very much my father's son' (p. 126)? The exchange of dialogue intensifies our curiosity to know more about Eman's past life.

Their dialogue is interrupted when Eman hears a noise. He thinks it is the dancers and he wants to invite them in. But the figure who hammers on their door has nothing to do with merrymaking: it is the *'terrified and disordered figure'* of Ifada. Eman's natural reaction is to unbolt the door and let him in, but Sunma tries to persuade him to pay no attention, not to interfere. Her words become increasingly pleading. When Eman asks: 'Do you know something of this then?' (p. 126), she responds with: 'You are a stranger here, Eman. Just leave us alone and go your own way. There is nothing you can do' (p. 126). She *'clings fiercely to him'*, trying to prevent him from letting Ifada in. We can 'hear' her almost screaming her last words before Eman succeeds in opening the door: 'Why won't you listen to me Eman? I tell you it's none of your business. For your own sake do as I say' (p. 126). And she continues to plead even when Ifada is inside, breaking off only to hurl abuse at the poor idiot-boy.

Something, clearly, frightens Sunma a great deal to make her act in so emotional and irrational a manner. We, the audience, having witnessed Ifada's kidnapping, already have some confirmation that Sunma's fear of her own people is not without substance. We notice that Eman re-bolts the door, suggesting that even he is now aware of danger. And as we hear the voices approaching Eman's house, and especially when we hear such comments as 'I hope our friend won't make trouble' and 'He had better not' (p. 127), Sunma's opinion of her people seems more than ever justified. Eman takes the precaution of hiding Ifada in the back room. The villagers, led — we soon learn — by Sunma's own father, come straight to the point. They want the idiot-boy back. When Sunma refuses to help them to persuade Eman, she is more or less forcibly removed from the scene.

Eman is now alone with the people Sunma has warned him against and whom she so much hates, even though they are her own. The village leaders make clear what is happening: Ifada has been chosen as the 'carrier' who will symbolically bear the burden of the community's evil during the past year, thereby cleansing it for the new year. But instead of ending up in the bush, as he should, Ifada has taken refuge in Eman's house. There is more than a hint of menace in the villagers' words: 'We don't want to have to burn down the house you see, but if the word gets around, we would have no choice' (p. 128); and 'A contaminated house should be burnt down' (p. 128). It is made quite clear to Eman that this will happen unless he brings out the reluctant carrier. Eman agrees, but confronts the villagers with a question: ' . . .why did you pick on a helpless boy? Obviously he is not willing' (p. 128). Eman points out that in his own home area the carrier must perform his task willingly, and makes it clear that he knows something about the ritual, confirming an elder's belief that he is 'one of the knowing ones' (p. 129).

So far the discussion between Eman and the two elders has not been openly antagonistic: but it becomes so when Eman bluntly declares that the villagers 'are not behaving like men' (p. 129). 'It is,' he says, 'a simple thing. A village which cannot produce its own carrier contains no men' (p. 129). A villager is ordered inside the house by Jaguna to bring out Ifada. The other elder, who gives the impression of being more restrained and thoughtful than Jaguna, says sadly: 'I am sorry you would not understand, Mister Eman' (p. 129). His words suggest that it is now too late for any kind of understanding between Eman and the villagers. Clearly, the two parties have quite different outlooks and values. For the villagers, a carrier cannot return to the village; strangers must therefore perform the function, since 'it is too much to ask a man to give up his own soil' (p. 129). Mysteriously, Eman replies: 'I know others who have done more' (p. 129), a response which intensifies our curiosity about his past. Ifada is brought out, abject with terror, and pitiably keeps his eyes on Eman as he is carried away. Ominously, we are told that when he is 'prepared' he will be 'the most joyous creature in the festival', a remark to which Eman replies: 'Do you believe the spirit of a new year is so easily fooled?' (p. 129). As they go, Jaguna directs a final derisory comment to Eman:

> You say there are no men in this village because they cannot provide a willing carrier. And yet I heard Oroge tell you we only use strangers. There is only one other stranger in the village, but I have not heard him offer himself [*spits.*] It is so easy to talk is it not?
> (pp. 129–30)

The challenge is all too clear. As the stage lights dim we are left to ask ourselves: will Eman, out of pity for the boy, perhaps from moral conviction, offer himself in Ifada's place as the sacrificial carrier?

There is a black-out '*lasting no more than a minute*'. When the lights come up we see Ifada returning to Eman's house, banging on the window-sill to catch his attention, but getting no response. As he crouches against the wall, the idiot-boy's eyes turn to the girl's effigy which still lies where it was left during his kidnapping. Almost no action has yet taken place, but from the moment we first see Ifada again we can sense that something is wrong: why, we ask ourselves, has Ifada been released after so much trouble was taken to capture him? That there seems to be no one in the house makes us ask: where is Eman? Taken together the two questions, and our tentative replies to them, can indicate only one thing: that Jaguna's challenge has been accepted by Eman, that he is now the carrier in place of Ifada.

But we do not yet know this for certain; our feeling is one of suspense rather than of sure knowledge. As we consciously or unconsciously ponder what has become of Eman, Ifada gets up, goes over to the effigy and, according to the stage direction, *'begins to strip it of the clothing'* (p. 130) — the clothing, of course, being Eman's *buba*. As he does so the girl enters and tells Ifada to leave her effigy alone. But he merely speeds up the stripping of its clothes, which brings about a quite violent struggle for possession of the object.

Why is Ifada taking Eman's clothes from the effigy? And why does the girl resist so strenuously? Our sense of what is happening at this point emerges from the visual dimension of the action rather than from the dialogue. Ifada is stripping the effigy of its acquired 'personality' as Eman. We sense that despite his limited understanding he is aware of the symbolism of the occasion, that he is symbolically protesting against Eman's role as the sacrificial victim for the community. When Sunma enters and breaks up the fight, it is the girl who has possession of the effigy. The suggestion conveyed by the stage picture is that Ifada has 'lost' his symbolic struggle and that Eman, as carrier, has fallen into the hands of the community, represented by the girl. Sunma is about to go into the house when she realises this. We, the audience, have probably only briefly anticipated her in the realisation. She seizes Ifada by the arm, dragging him in the direction that the villagers have taken Eman.

Without any break in the action, there is now a scene change. Using the minimum of stage scenery and maximum lighting effects, the stage should represent *'a narrow passage-way between two mud-houses'* (p. 131). Men are running across the entry to the passage-way, while inside, crouching against a wall half-way down, we see Eman. His eyes have been ringed in a reddish colour, and his body *'whitened with a floury substance. He is naked down to the waist, wears a baggy pair of trousers, calf-length, and around both feet are bangles'* (p. 131). We only have to see him to realise that he has been, or was in the process of being, prepared as the carrier.

Eman's desire to rest is frustrated when a woman recognises him and raises the alarm. We note the contrast between her initial apologies for having accidentally thrown slop on someone she believes to be a neighbour, and her immediate nastiness — she spits and throws her pail at him — when she recognises him as the carrier. Eman flees, pursued by the villagers. In their rear come the two village leaders, Jaguna and Oroge. From their dialogue we learn that Eman has escaped before being fully prepared, and that this process must be completed when they catch him. Jaguna believes that Eman lost his courage when he realised he was being taken round the compounds to be beaten; his verdict is that Eman is a 'woman'. But his colleague disagrees: 'No, no. He took the beating well enough. I think he is the kind who would let himself be beaten from night till dawn and not utter a sound' (p. 132). But he is unable to answer Jaguna's question: 'Then what made him run like a coward?' (p. 132). They go off in pursuit, lamenting that 'our own curses remain hovering over our homes because the carrier refused to take them' (p. 132). And we are left wondering why Eman, despite his courage, recognised even by at least one of his pursuers, should have refused, and for how long he can stay on the run.

The scene changes again: *'Eman is crouching beside some shrubs, torn and bleeding'* (p. 132). He is thirsty, and looks for a stream, but as he looks around his eyes — and ours — encounter a surprising and at first inexplicable scene. The stage direction reads:

> *'An old man, short and vigorous-looking, is seated on a stool. He also is wearing calf-length baggy trousers, white. On his head, a white cap. An attendant is engaged in rubbing his body with oil. Round his eyes two white rings have already been marked'* (p. 132).

What strikes us first is the visual resemblance between Eman and the old man: both are wearing calf-length baggy trousers and both have their eyes ringed. This, for the moment, is the only perceivable link between the two men. The Old Man asks his attendant if his son has been sent for, and goes on to speak of the heaviness of heart with which he is 'carrying . . . the boat' on this occasion. There is now a stage direction which reads: *'Enter Eman, a wrapper round his waist and a "dansiki" over it'*. We are perhaps a little puzzled for a moment. How can Eman enter this scene, wearing this costume, when he is crouching beside some shrubs, dressed as a carrier and being pursued by the villagers? We realise that what we are witnessing is intended as a representation of what is passing in Eman's mind as he rests during the pursuit.

The Old Man, addressing his son, again speaks of his sadness, 'my own grief and yours' (p. 133), which, he says, is eating the strength he so much needs for his 'journey to the river'. He tells Eman that they will never meet again 'on this side of the flesh'. The Old Man wants to know whether Eman will return to take his place. He receives the answer: 'I will never come back' (p. 133). It is made clear through the dialogue that the Old Man has for more than twenty years been serving as the 'carrier' — a function which he says can only be fulfilled by 'a strong breed' — and that he has hoped that his son would follow him. But it seems that Eman's connection with his own people and place died with the death in childbirth of his wife Omae. This, presumably, is the grief that was mentioned a few moments earlier. As we watch and listen we realise that we are now learning something about Eman's past, about which we've been curious ever since Sunma made her remark about pitying any woman in his past for what she must have suffered — a remark which, we recall, visibly affected him.

From their dialogue we discover that Eman was away for twelve years, during which time his father and Omae waited for him, the Old Man living with the terrible knowledge that Omae, like all the mothers

Eman's father receives the boat containing the evils of the old year.

and wives of the 'strong breed', would inevitably die giving birth to Eman's child. As well as these facts, we learn about the characters' feelings. The Old Man is insistent that both he and his son belong to a special line of men. 'Our blood is strong like no other,' he tells Eman (p. 134), and he predicts that although his son may leave home now because of his grief, his own blood will eventually bring him back, to continue the hard task long fulfilled by his father. But Eman is equally insistent that it is not only his grief which is driving him away: he changed much during his twelve-year absence, discovered 'even greater things' (p. 134) of which his father is ignorant. He tells the Old Man that he is 'totally unfitted' for following the vocation of carrier. The exchange ends with Eman leaving the stage, and the Old Man beginning his 'last journey' (as he himself knows) as the carrier of the symbolic boat laden with his community's evils.

Clearly, what we have just witnessed is a scene from Eman's past, played out in his imagination. We may justifiably wonder — Soyinka surely expects us to wonder — why Eman should have imagined this scene at precisely this moment, when he is being pursued as the reluctant 'carrier'. The obvious connection between this episode from the past and the 'here-and-now' of the play is that Eman has become what his father has been. At this point we recall Eman's words to the villagers when he told them that he knew something about being a carrier and upbraided them for not having one who belonged to the village and who performed his function voluntarily. And we may also remember his earlier comment to Sunma, that 'I am very much my father's son' (p. 126). The past is relevant here because it bears directly on Eman's present, and that is why Eman is recalling it now. What is especially interesting, and ironic, is that, although Eman is now fulfilling the same function as his father, the scene from the past shows us his refusal to follow in the Old Man's footsteps. We realise that there was prophetic truth in his father's words: 'Your own blood will betray you, son, because you cannot hold it back' (p. 134).

As Eman's vision of the past disappears, his pursuers arrive on stage. He is 'whipped back to the immediate and flees, Jaguna in pursuit. Three or four others enter and follow him. Oroge remains where he is, thoughtful' (p. 135). Oroge, we learn, realises that Eman was seeing something as they came upon him, and he wonders what it was. Jaguna is more immediately preoccupied with the task in hand, and with the practical implications of Eman's escape. Ominously, he speaks of things having taken 'a bad turn' (p. 135); and declares: 'It is no longer enough to drive him past every house. There is too much contamination about already' (p. 135). We don't yet know what this means, but we can guess when Jaguna tells Oroge that the 'year will demand more from this carrier than we thought' (p. 135). Their conversation is broken up by Sunma's physical attack on her father and his retaliation against her. As Oroge reminds his colleague, this is a night when nothing should be done in anger — a taboo that has now been violated. The ominous atmosphere is intensified by Oroge's closing words: 'This is an unhappy night for us all. I fear what is to come of it' (p. 136). The village leaders go, leaving Ifada to help the sobbing Sunma to her feet.

Eman now enters, as the pursued carrier. But as he stands, or perhaps crouches, on the stage, what we actually see is the side of a round thatched hut and a young girl who runs in and calls Eman's name. We are clearly about to witness another 'vision' which, properly speaking, is taking place in Eman's mind in the here-and-now. The girl turns out to be Omae, as the dialogue soon makes clear. She has come to see the young Eman, who is undergoing his rite of passage into manhood. (Young Eman must, of course, be played by a different actor, of appropriate age, from the mature Eman who is also visible on stage throughout this scene.) Omae teases him in a friendly, flirtatious way, but he is in no mood for her mischievousness. We are struck, in fact, by his serious attitude towards his initiation:

> This is an important period of my life . . . We learn many things, do you understand? And we spend much time just thinking. At least, I do. It is the first time I have had nothing to do except think. Don't you see, I am becoming a man. For the first time, I understand that I have a life to fulfil.
>
> (p. 138)

His seriousness frightens Omae and surprises us, especially when he declares that: 'A man must go on his own, go where no one can help him, and test his strength' (pp. 138–9). The contrast is all the more striking, then, between this seriousness, on the one hand, and his instant decision to disobey his tutor, curtail his initiation and even leave the village, on the other hand. The immediate reason for his action is his refusal to see Omae being sexually intimidated by the lecherous tutor, who has returned earlier than expected and surprised Omae and Eman together. But his

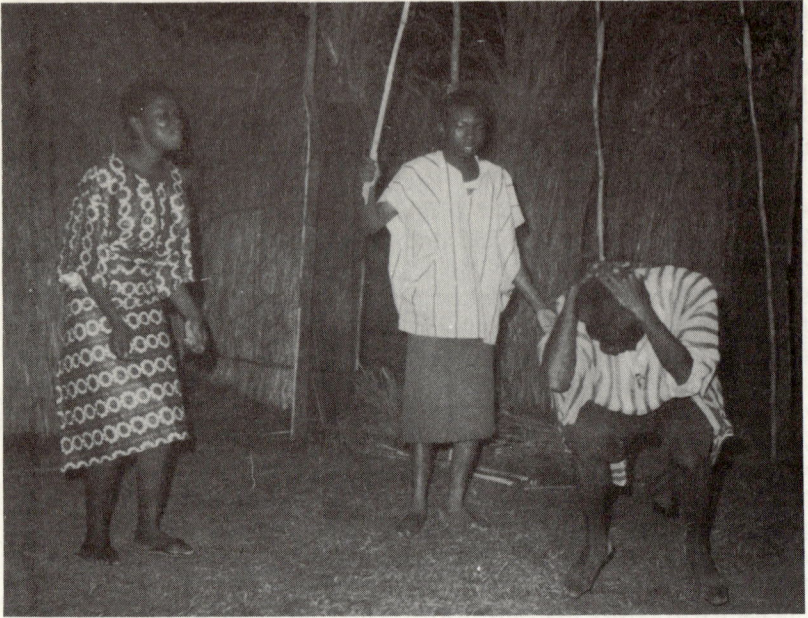

Young Eman attacks the tutor while Omae looks on.

quarrel with the tutor doesn't really account for the far-reaching nature of his decision. In fact, nothing in the dialogue at this point adequately explains why the young Eman decides to forsake Omae, his family and people and to set off alone, presumably to 'test his strength'. All we can say is that he seems to be compelled by a mysterious but extremely powerful force within himself, which makes him as ruthless to the young Omae as we have already seen him being to Sunma in the here-and-now.

This second long 'vision' decisively places the dramatic focus on Eman's past, about which Soyinka has aroused our curiosity earlier in the play. More specifically, the alternation between the past, as seen by Eman, and the reality of the present, forces us to consider the relationship between the two. In other words, we are made to feel that there is some significant connection between past and present in Eman's mind, that his visions of the past occur as he is pursued because in some way they throw light on, or make sense of, his present situation. We want to find out how this is so. We know that Eman's father has been a carrier, one of the 'strong breed', and that Eman has refused to follow in his footsteps, partly because of Omae's death and partly because of what he learned on his long journey. But we also know that the Old Man has predicted that Eman's strong blood will assert itself, despite his conscious desires. As we watch, we wait expectantly to discover the full significance of the connection between past and present.

The action shifts back once again from the past to the present. The girl enters as Eman is staring at the spot where he has 'seen' his younger self and Omae. When Eman asks her to bring him some water from his house she goes off, apparently to do so, but we see her slipping out of the house and running off. Voices approach, and we realise at the same time as Eman that she has betrayed him. As he goes the girl enters, leading Jaguna and Oroge. Although they have once again missed him, they know that he needs water and that they simply need to wait for him in the right place, on the path to the stream. Jaguna and Oroge are themselves aware of the symbolic appropriateness that the village's sacred grove is on this path. If we had not done so before, we now realise what Jaguna meant earlier when he said that the 'year will demand more from this carrier than we thought' (p. 135). Eman is to be sacrificed in the sacred grove.

There is another change of scene, heralding another of Eman's mental journeys into the past. The stage now represents an 'overgrown part of the village' (p. 143). This stage direction makes it clear that a change has come over Eman: he now 'wanders in, aimlessly, seemingly uncaring of discovery'. An area of the stage is lit up, in which stands a group of people with heads bowed. We see one figure move away and stand apart, and then the group disperses, 'coming down and past' Eman as he watches. 'Only three people are left, a man (Eman) whose back is turned, the village priest and the isolated one. They stand on opposite sides of the grave, the man on the mound of earth. The priest walks round to the man's side and lays a hand on his shoulder.'

This stage direction clearly presents a problem of staging: how can the actor playing Eman be both the witness of this scene and a figure in it? The simplest and most effective solution would probably be for the Eman in the vision to be played by the actor who has played him throughout, while the 'witnessing' Eman is played by another actor of similar stature and wearing the costume of the carrier. Since the 'witnessing' Eman can stand with his back to the audience, and in shadow, he can resemble the 'real' Eman sufficiently for the audience to accept the trick. At the end of this scene there is the stage direction: 'Eman, as carrier, walking towards the graveside, the other Eman having gone' (p. 144). At this point the 'real' Eman should replace the 'witnessing' Eman in the darkness at the end of his speech to the Priest.

The scene itself shows Eman talking to the Priest as they stand by Omae's grave. Eman speaks of having been twelve years a pilgrim, 'seeking the vain shrine of secret strength', only for Omae to perish on his return. He tells the Priest that he did not really know for what great meaning he searched, and that, paradoxically, he found what he was seeking in Omae on his return. 'And I threw away my new-gained knowledge. I buried the part of me that was formed in strange places. I made a home in my birthplace' (p. 144). But the 'truth of that' has been destroyed for Eman by Omae's death. Eman recognises, however, that his father's grief is, if anything, even greater than his own: 'He loved Omae like a daughter' (p. 144). The scene ends with Eman, as carrier, walking towards the graveside, falling to his knees and scooping up the sand to pour on his own head. He is living, as it were, more in the past than in the present moment, so powerful is his memory of his own grief and the Old Man's at Omae's burial.

There is a brief black-out, and when the stage lights come up again we see Jaguna and Oroge entering. They speak only a few lines of dialogue but enough for us to be informed that Jaguna has set a trap for Eman in the sacred grove. They leave and Eman re-enters as carrier. As we have now come to expect, he immediately conjures up another scene from the past. The stage direction reads: *'In front of him is a still figure, the old man as he was, carrying the dwarf boat'* (p. 144). In other words, the 'vision' before us is the continuation of the first episode from the past, which ended with Eman's father bearing the symbolic boat on his head and moving towards the river. Eman calls to the Old Man, who tells him to go back. 'We cannot,' he says, 'give the two of us' (meaning that they must not sacrifice themselves together). Eman tells his father that he is also looking for the stream to quench his thirst, but the Old Man tells him that it is the other way: 'I take the longer way, you know how I must do this. It is quicker if you take the other way. Go now' (p. 145). The Old Man breaks into a run; Eman hesitates and then follows: 'Wait, father. I am coming with you … wait … wait for me, father …' (p. 145). The inevitable happens. We hear *'a sound of twigs breaking'* and *'a sudden trembling in the branches'*, followed by silence. Eman has been hanged in the sacred grove.

We have been waiting to discover the full significance of the relation between Eman's past, as revealed in the 'mental flashbacks', and his present as a pursued carrier. This scene has revealed that significance. In his first vision, we saw Eman refusing to follow in his father's footsteps as the carrier. He has left his own community and gone to live as a stranger among people who do not have the 'strength' to provide their own voluntary carrier. But he has taken with him the old man's prophecy that his strong-breed blood will assert itself in any case, even if among 'thieves' who 'take what is ours' (p. 134). In this vision, which ends in Eman's death, we see the prophecy being fulfilled. Literally, as well as symbolically, Eman follows in his father's footsteps, dressed like him as a carrier with the strength to do voluntarily what others need to be forced to do against their will. At the end, Eman has shown himself to be his father's son indeed, even though he never wished to follow his vocation and was only seeking peace among the villagers who finally kill him.

With Eman's death we return once more to the here-and-now, to the original setting: the front of Eman's house. Our eyes first encounter a visual image confirming Eman's fate: the effigy belonging to the girl — which we last saw being fought for, with symbolic implications, by Ifada and the girl — is hanging at the front of the house, just as Eman has been hanged in the sacred grove. Sunma, supported by Ifada, enters and stares *'transfixed'* at the hanging effigy. Ifada, again in spite of his mental limitations demonstrating a capacity for symbolic interpretation, *'rushes at the object and tears it down'* (p. 145), clearly understanding what has happened to Eman. Sunma *'crumbles against the wall'* in final despair. The girl stands by, unnoticed, watching impassively, still representing for us the evil that destroyed Eman. The villagers enter, returning from the pursuit, looking *'subdued and guilty'* (p. 145). Jaguna and Oroge bring up the rear, speaking of the cowardice they have witnessed among their own people. 'One and all they looked up at the man and words died in their throats,' says Jaguna (p. 146). And Oroge points out that it 'was not only him they fled. Do you see how unattended we are?' (p. 146), to which Jaguna responds with a vague but menacing 'There are those who will pay for this night's work!' The light fades slowly on the motionless figures of Sunma, Ifada and the girl.

The final moments of The Strong Breed.

A college professor once wrote to a distinguished American writer, Flannery O'Connor, inquiring about the meaning of one of her stories. In her reply she said:

> The meaning of a story should go on expanding for the reader the more he thinks about it, but meaning cannot be recaptured in an interpretation. . . . Too much interpretation is certainly worse than too little, and where feeling for a story is absent, theory will not supply it.

Miss O'Connor was gently reminding the professor that the interpretation of the meaning of a story must be based on a genuine feeling for it, an appreciation of the effects the story makes on us as we read. She could equally well have been talking about plays. The reading of a play, as of a novel or short story, must involve an imaginative engagement with character and situation, a willingness to accept the reality of the characters, what they say and do, and the situations in which they find themselves. In other words, we must allow ourselves to be imaginatively manipulated by the dramatist so that we recreate as fully as possible what he created originally.

A reading of the kind offered above is an attempt to be as responsive as possible to the effects created by the play. It is not, in the first place, an attempt to interpret what Soyinka means in *The Strong Breed*. It is not an analysis of the play's themes and meaning. But it is the essential precondition for arriving at a well-founded interpretation of theme and meaning. For example, our reading of *The Strong Breed* establishes that Soyinka is much concerned with the relationship between Eman's past and present lives. In the scenes with Sunma in the first part of the play we are made curious about Eman's past and the part it has played in making him the sort of person he is. In the second part, his pursuit as the carrier alternates with scenes showing the decisive moments in Eman's life from his own point of view. Much of the play's suspense, its excitement as drama, is connected with our developing desire to perceive the significance of the relationship between them as two different 'sets' of scenes. Having grasped that this is where the dramatic emphasis lies we will be less inclined to see the play as being, for example, primarily about Eman's relations with the villagers, which a superficial reading might suggest.

The fact is that in such plays as *The Strong Breed* — plays which seriously explore some significant area of experience — it is usually far from easy to decide what the theme and meaning are, at least after a single reading or viewing. As Flannery O'Connor said, the 'meaning of a story [or play] should go on expanding for the reader the more he thinks about it . . .'. With a very simple play the meaning may be immediately apparent; but the richer a dramatist's exploration of life the more difficult it is to encapsulate the meaning in a sentence or two.

This should not cause us even a moment's anxiety, since it is absurd even to think in terms of trying to find such instant meanings. The tendency to do so is sometimes encouraged by the requirements of the classroom and examination hall; but even in an academic setting, where plays are being studied ultimately for examination purposes, the temptation should be resisted, and resistance is stiffened by reading a play in the first place, not with its theme or meaning in mind, but solely with the desire to absorb its impact, to be consciously and willingly manipulated by the dramatist. By doing so, the reader is not only more likely to pass his exam, but actually to enjoy the experience of drama!

Exercises for Chapter 6: *The Strong Breed*: a dramatic reading

1 On the basis of a close reading both of *The Strong Breed* and the 'dramatic reading' of it, write a short essay on what you consider to be the main themes and meaning(s) of the play. Your discussion should suggest what area of experience Soyinka is particularly concerned with in the play. In what way, if at all, is this area of experience especially important in contemporary African life? (In other words, try to relate the play to its time and place.)

2 Taking a play you have particularly enjoyed reading before, or alternatively one of those listed below, try to apply what you have learnt about recreating drama in your imagination as you read. Note the main effects that the play has upon you. (If you feel, after reading a scene, that you have somehow failed to recreate it adequately in your mind's eye and ear, read it again before you continue.) On the basis of your notes (which should always be made *as you read,* not afterwards) write a short essay describing what you think the play is about and what it is saying about the particular experience that it dramatises.

Suggested Plays
J. P. Clark, *The Raft* in *Three Plays,* Three Crowns Series, Oxford University Press, 1964.

Mukotani Rugyendo, *And The Storm Gathers* in *The Barbed Wire and other plays,* Heinemann African Writers Series, 1977.

Any of the plays in Michael Etherton (ed.), *African Plays for Playing,* vol. 1, Heinemann African Writers Series, 1975.

Part Two

Prologue: the kinds of drama

So far, we have been concerned with the basic elements of drama, the 'building bricks' with which all plays are constructed. It is now time to broaden our scope and to consider the *range* of drama that is being written and performed now and that has come down to us from the past.

Certain words are regularly used to describe the different kinds of dramatic experience that make up this range. Readers will already be familiar with at least two — the main two — distinguishing terms: *comedy* and *tragedy*. They may be less familiar with the term *melodrama*, which describes a kind of drama similar in some respects to tragedy. In addition, the word *tragi-comedy* is often used to identify an experience of drama, especially prominent on the modern Western stage, which seems to combine aspects of both comedy and tragedy while modifying both. We shall be concerned with these critical terms for most of the remainder of this book. Before we proceed, however, we need to establish clearly the nature and purpose of our interest in them.

There is a way of 'defining' the dramatic kinds and of using the 'definitions' which, far from stimulating thought and interest in plays, actually impoverishes our understanding of drama. This happens when definition or classification is carried on solely for its own sake, as a kind of 'tidying up' operation. It becomes an end in itself to decide whether a play should be called a comedy, or a tragedy, or whatever. No doubt it is natural for people to wish to be able to name things: this is one of the ways by which we know, and cope with, the world around us. But it is surely misguided for people to devote their intellectual energy to deciding what genre a particular play belongs to if their only concern is in naming for its own sake. 'Pigeon-holing' plays (or anything else) in this way is of no value as a method of analysis and judgment. It is ultimately a sterile activity, which tends to narrow rather than widen our understanding and critical sensitivity.

This does not mean, however, that terms like tragedy and comedy are worthless and can be dispensed with. On the contrary, when properly employed they make a vital contribution to critical enquiry. They do so, I think, when they advance one or all of the following critical objectives:

(i) helping us achieve the fullest possible understanding of individual plays;

(ii) helping us to compare individual plays, even though they might come from very different cultures and historical periods, so that the comparison enriches our appreciation of the forms and meanings of the plays;

(iii) helping us establish a better understanding of the relation between drama and life-experiences, and between drama and other disciplines concerned with the understanding of life — for example, the study of philosophical ideas, or of social phenomena.

Deciding whether a particular play is a comedy or a tragedy for no better reason than to give it a name does not serve any of these functions. Nor is it likely that this kind of definition will enrich our understanding of anything. But if our concern is with considering a particular play or body of plays in relation to some ideas about, say, comedy which we have developed from a close reading of a range of comic drama, then we are surely doing something that is likely to deepen our appreciation of the play or plays, and of comic drama generally, and perhaps — by contrast and comparison — of other kinds of drama also.

Those who read the following pages in the hope of finding neatly-packaged definitions will therefore be disappointed. Readers who believe that each of the main kinds of drama can be 'defined' in a few sentences are in pursuit of an illusion — the 'Idea' of comedy or tragedy, conceived of as a kind of divine being which, when brought down to earth, will reveal all that needs to be known about every comic or tragic play. Comedy does not exist, and neither does Tragedy: what do exist are plays that are called comedies (at least by some people some of the time), and experiences in real life that some people think of as comic, and a number of theories about the nature of these plays and experiences.

Part of the problem is that language and our habits of thought invite us to think of all those things that we describe as comic or tragic or melodramatic as abstract entities. We say things like 'Comedy is such and such' or 'Tragedy is this or that', which creates the impression that Comedy and Tragedy are unified entities with independent existences of their own. What we really mean, but which is too long-winded to write or say all the time, is something like 'The plays and experiences that are generally described as comic because of certain shared characteristics are . . .'. We have to use these 'shorthand' ways of saying things, but even as we do so we must resist the temptation to think of a grand Comic or Tragic Idea.

What may encourage us to do so is the fact that, when they have turned their minds to characterising comedy and tragedy, even the most learned critics have disagreed about almost everything. Consider the following, for example:

(i)   . . . laughter has no greater enemy than emotion . . . it appeals purely to the intellect.

(Henri Bergson, *Laughter,* p. 17)

compared with

the bitterness and sadness that so readily come to the surface in comedy constitute our first, best evidence that in comedy feeling is not only present but abundant.

(Eric Bentley, *The Life of the Drama,* p. 298)

And this:

(ii) For in comedy we must feel that man is free, not fated; if
      anything goes wrong with him, the remedy is in his own hands.

                                        (L. J. Potts, *Comedy,* p. 118)

compared with

Tragedy speaks always of freedom. Comedy will speak of nothing
but limitation.

                            (Walter Kerr, *Tragedy and Comedy,* p. 146)

If it is so hard for such eminent critics to agree on fundamental points, it is
surely useless for us to search for some all-embracing idea of tragedy or
comedy, which embodies the essence of all aspects of the phenomena. It
will not make our critical lives any easier, of course, but such fundamental
disagreements suggest that we shouldn't waste our time searching for a
single key which will unlock the door behind which 'Comedy' or
'Tragedy' lurks. Another method of enquiry is called for.

Our approach in the following chapters will not be to seek
all-embracing definitions but rather to try to identify the recurrent
characteristics and tendencies of the main kinds of drama. Such an
approach is based on the belief that, since certain plays have been
generally called comedies or tragedies by people of different cultures
over many centuries, there is good reason to expect that we may find
certain shared, relatively changeless features in them which sanction the
continuing use of the same descriptive term. By looking at what seem to
be representative plays, which have nevertheless been written in varying
cultures and ages, we should be able to locate these shared features. At
the same time, this approach allows us to take account of the divergences,
the variations in mood, tone, method and purpose which occur within the
same kind of drama. A sense of the relatively permanent characteristics
of a genre goes hand in hand with this awareness of the range and variety
within it. For it is only by appreciating both that we can really grasp how
tragedy and comedy, far from being abstract, changeless entities, are
living, continuously changing experiences which are modified as men
modify their own lives in history.

7 Comedy

We regularly use the words 'comedy', 'comic' and 'funny' (meaning that someone or something has a 'comic' quality) in our normal everyday lives, and it requires only a moment's thought to realise that they are used to mean a wide range of things. A friend tells us a joke or weaves an elaborate, fantastic story full of nonsense, and we think of it as a comic experience. Someone or something presents an absurd appearance, so absurd as to make us spontaneously giggle or smile or laugh right from the belly: for· example, we are sitting in the lecture hall, our elderly, distinguished professor enters, opens his mouth to begin his lecture — and his trousers fall down. We may have the utmost respect and affection for the man, have no intention whatsoever of mocking him, but it would be well-nigh impossible not to laugh at this unfortunate accident. Our motives are not always so pure, however: a surprising, even shocking, amount of our experience of the comic in everyday life involves deliberate mockery, sometimes of the harshest, most cruel kind. We feel justified, no doubt, in making even the most extreme mock of those who are inordinately stupid or evil — the Adolf Hitlers and Idi Amins of this world. But who has not also seen, and perhaps even joined in, the mockery of a handicapped person — someone who is dumb, perhaps, and can only make grunting sounds that are somehow held to be funny?

Our sense of the comic, of what is 'funny', ranges then from the gentlest, most 'neutral' of smiles to the cruellest of mocking laughs. Our appreciation of this fact will help us in our analysis of dramatic comedy, for it disposes us to take account of the variety of comic drama rather than searching for a comic essence or ideal that remains stubbornly elusive. A brief reflection on the everyday experience of comedy can help us in another way, too, by reminding us that comedy is not inherent in things or people: it is by perceiving things or people (or the relation between the two) in a particular way, or combination of ways, that they become comic. This in turn hints at the *relative* nature of comic experience, that a situation which we are willing to describe as comic is so, not in itself, but because it occurs in a particular social context and involves particular social relations. Something which is hilariously funny on one occasion and in certain circumstances may not even raise a smile on another occasion and in different circumstances. And, on a larger scale, something which is felt to be authentically comic by the people of one culture may have no comic associations whatsoever for those of another.

Dramatic comedy

Let us now turn to comedy in drama, bearing in mind that although it is likely to be closely related to our experience of the comic in real life, it is not the same thing. Drama is a conscious and deliberate ordering or patterning of experience, based always on real life but not identical to it. We must therefore expect dramatic comedy to inhabit an artistic world which is distinct from our normal experience.

We first recognise comedy in a play by its *style*, the way its action, characterisation, dialogue, imagery and stage-presentation are combined together to give the drama its unique nature and impact on the audience. Let us now try to identify the main impressions made on us by the first Act of a play which is indubitably a comedy, *The Marriage of Anansewa* by Efua T. Sutherland.

The very first thing we notice, as the actors all appear from one side of the stage, is that there is no attempt to disguise the *theatrical* nature of the play. On the contrary, its theatricality is emphasised by having the actors come on together, not in roles but simply as actors. This is reinforced when the Property Man, instead of being hidden away backstage, hands Ananse the umbrella in full view of the audience. The 'make-believe' effect is further enhanced by the singing of the players, which Ananse joins, and by his direct comments and enquiries to members of the audience, which invite an element of audience participation. The play has only been in progress for a few moments, but the 'joke' of the Property Man handing out the umbrella, and a moment later, the typewriter, and the singing and direct address by Ananse are likely to make the audience feel relaxed and cheerful, and aware that there is more fun in store.

The action continues with Ananse being joined by his daughter Anansewa. She is reluctant to sit down at the typewriter, as her father demands, because she wants to go out. In the dialogue that follows Ananse stresses the wretched poverty of their household, its consequences for her future, and his attempts to do something about their condition. He rhetorically asks his daughter: 'After you have gone out and returned home, here, will my hope for a more comfortable future be any better?' (p. 4); and he begins to enumerate the changes for the better that *won't* take place:

> The mattress on which I try to rest my bones after each day's up-and-down — will it have changed from a straw-stuffed, lumpy mattress to a soft, bouncy Dunlopillo?

He continues:

> . . .will there be a better, leak-proof roof over our heads? Let alone some comfortable chairs to sit in? A 'fridge in the kitchen? A car in the garage? My name on invitation lists for state functions? Embassies' parties? Tell me, tell me. Will I be able to go to memorial services, this week in a fine cloth, next week in a suit or different cloth? Will I be able, if I go, to thrust my hand confidently into my pocket in public and take out a five-guinea donation?

Anansewa pretends to be dead, so that she can marry Chief-Who-Is-Chief.

And so he goes on, rhetorically demanding to know whether he will ever be an affluent churchgoer, or whether at his funeral the mourners will eat 'salad and small chops and drink good whisky, instead of chewing bits of cola and drinking cheap gin and diluted Fanta?' (p. 5).

His speech is all about poverty and its indignities but it doesn't make us sad or depressed as we listen to it. The reason for this, I suggest, is that, though the subject-matter of Ananse's speech *is* depressing, it is contradicted by the liveliness and energetic invention of the *way* he talks about it. We get the sense of a man who cannot and will not be held down for long because he has too much energy, too much 'cheek', to remain in that condition. This comes out in the way Ananse relishes his own words and makes us relish them too, especially when he gives expression to an ever more inflated fantasy of affluence. It is delightful how the things he mentions progress from the very modest Dunlopillo mattress to a 'fridge, a car, to being invited to posh parties and behaving like a 'big man' at church. This is a man with a comic insight into the way society works and with the desire and the inventiveness to make sure that he has an acceptable place in that society. We are not at all surprised when he announces that, following 'a most severe cracking of my brains', he can at last 'see a little hope gleaming in our future . . .' (p. 5).

Similarly we enjoy the ludicrous exaggeration and flattery of the letters that Ananse dictates to his daughter. The fun comes from his adoption of the stance of a praise-singer, and his recital with what the stage direction describes as *'tremendous vigour and at great speed'* of such absurdly extravagant substitutes for 'Dear Sir' as this:

Oh! Fire-Extinguisher!
Fire-Extinguisher,
You have caused flame flashes to darken,
You have caused 'I'm Irreversible'
To come to a full stop.
Blazing-Column-Of-Fire-Who-Says-I
Will-Not-Be-Halted
Has come to a full stop. (pp. 7–8)

And so on. What makes it all the funnier, of course, is that this outrageous flattery is combined with an equally outrageous sense of calculation, for the 'praise songs' introduce exactly the same letter to each of the chiefs.

After the musical 'play-acting' of the trip to the post office, which continues the mood of relaxed make-believe, Anansewa discovers that her father is planning to 'sell' her into marriage. This is certainly the kind of misfortune that could make a girl weep bitter tears and that could serve as the central situation of a 'serious' drama. But even if Anansewa is almost in tears, we are not. Our reaction is partly determined by the mood of cheerful make-believe that has already been firmly established; more specifically, we do not take Anansewa's plight with the seriousness it may seem to deserve because we notice that there is a significant change in her own attitude when she hears that she is intended for 'the finely built, glowing black, large-eyed, handsome as anything, courageous and famous Chief-Who-Is-Chief' (p. 12). It is this, together with the attraction of money which allows her to continue at the Secretarial School, that makes Anansewa agree to collude with her father in his plan, embracing him and calling him 'my loving father' (p. 14). And throughout this little episode, we have continued to enjoy witnessing Ananse's craftiness, both in breaking the news to his daughter only after she has typed and posted the letters and in the scheme by which he hopes to improve their social position.

After a short musical interlude the Storyteller rises to comment on Ananse and his plan. He reinforces the conclusion we have already independently arrived at, that it's 'very clear that he [Ananse] knows the customs more than well' (p. 16). The Storyteller ends his speech with a question:

If negotiations have only reached this stage, is there any law binding him to give his daughter in marriage to any of those four chiefs?

The Players call out that there is no law, and there follows another 'interlude' (*mboguo*) which at first seems to have nothing to do with the action but which we soon realise illustrates the importance of custom, and specifically the fact that there is no obligation until certain agreements have been made and symbolically enacted. After the interlude, the Storyteller returns to voice our own thought, that Ananse's scheme is 'full of snares' from which he might not be able to extricate himself (p. 19). Actually, even at this very early stage in the play, we are quite sure that Ananse will get what he wants for his daughter — that is, marriage to

Chief-Who-Is-Chief — and that he will somehow survive the complications that we suspect await him. Our sense of anticipation has been sharpened: we are now curious to know how Ananse will manage things so that they work out in his favour. And, to remind us of what he has set irretrievably in motion, Act I ends with Ananse receiving a letter containing money from one of his chiefs.

What, then, are the main impressions made on an audience by the first of the four Acts of *The Marriage of Anansewa*? Separating out what in reality would be an inseparable totality of impressions, we can point to the sense of make-believe, the good-humoured recognition that we are involved in a kind of sophisticated game. The good humour is another important element: the songs, the 'jokes' (like the recurrent visual joke of the Property Man handing things to the characters), the tremendous, crafty energy of Ananse which comes tumbling out in his language — these all contribute a festive air to the proceedings. So much so, in fact, that although we know there are problems ahead for Ananse, we have no doubt that the festive mood will be retained to the end, that there is bound to be a happy outcome to our hero's scheming. The cheerful mood and our optimism about the characters' futures thus stands in quite sharp contrast to their present condition and their feelings about it.

These are only impressions, the kind an audience would have watching the play in a theatre. We could analyse this first Act more carefully, bringing out points we haven't even touched on here; and of course there is much more to be said about the comedy of *The Marriage of Anansewa* as a whole. But our brief discussion has at least given us some concrete impressions connected with dramatic comedy which we can now build on. We must tread carefully, however: for, as we have already noticed, the range of comic experience in everyday life is very wide, and this is likely to be true of comedy in drama too. This means that the impact made on us by other comedies may be quite different from that of Efua Sutherland's play. If we are to establish a reliable sense of the main characteristics of comedy, then, we need to widen our scope. And we can begin to do this by comparing our impressions of Act One of *The Marriage of Anansewa* with the popular notion of what constitutes a comedy.

Popular ideas of comedy

There are, I think, two fundamental assumptions about, or expectations of, a comic play. One is that it should make us laugh, or at least smile; and the other is that it should have a happy ending. Most people, I imagine, would hesitate to describe a play as a comedy unless these two basic requirements were fulfilled.

Looked at more closely, however, both ideas present quite serious problems. Let's take the notion that comedy should make us laugh. It is certainly reasonable to expect, both in ordinary life and in the theatre, that whatever deserves the adjective 'comic' should induce in us a certain kind of pleasure which finds physical expression in laughter or smiles. But even a limited experience of comic drama is enough to be aware that there are comedies which, for much of their duration, do not invite laughter from the audience. This is not because they have been badly written or performed, or misunderstood or disliked by their audiences. It is simply because, though they are described by everyone as comedies, they belong to a 'darker', more 'sober' region of the land of comedy which has little or no place for the good-humoured fun of, say, *The Marriage of Anansewa*. Examples of such 'sober' comedy are Shakespeare's *All's Well That Ends Well* and *The Misanthrope* by the great seventeenth-century French dramatist Molière, many of whose comedies for much of their duration are not what most people think of as 'comic'.

We cannot, of course, decide whether a play is or is not a comedy on the basis of the *amount* of laughter it evokes. We do not call a play a comedy because we laugh sometimes during its performance, nor do we think of it as comedy only at those moments when we are laughing. It is a comedy because of its overall nature and effect on us; it is still a comedy even when it is not being funny, which may be most of the time. So, though it's justifiable to expect to be able to laugh at least some of the time at a comic play, it is something more than our laughter and whatever has provoked the laughter which makes it a comedy. It is something about the play *as a whole,* rather than particular 'funny' moments in it. And this is confirmed by the fact that some plays which are commonly called tragedies include moments — sometimes frequent moments — when we are intentionally made to laugh or smile. Reasonable though it is, then, to associate comedy with laughter, we must bear in mind that some comedies are more 'sober' and less productive of laughter than others, and that in any case laughter is not exclusive to plays that we think of as comedies.

The other fundamental belief about comedy is that it should have a happy ending. What do we really mean by this? Probably nothing more than that the characters we have liked and identified with should live happily — or at least not unhappily — ever after, and that the characters we don't like should get their deserved punishments.

One problem about comedies ending happily is that some notable comedies don't. For example, the early seventeenth-century English dramatist Ben Jonson is generally regarded as having been one of the finest European comic dramatists, and *Volpone* is rated as one of his greatest achievements. And yet this play ends with terrible punishments being handed out to the two main characters, Volpone and Mosca, as well as to their foolish and corrupt victims. Volpone and Mosca are not virtuous; Celia and Bonario are the 'moral' hero and heroine: but these two are relatively uninteresting characters, and it is with Volpone and Mosca that an audience identifies, whether Jonson intended this or not.

One could mention other exceptions to the 'rule' that comedies should end happily. What in fact does the happy ending consist of in comedy? How is it that things work out happily for characters with whom we identify — ignoring such irritating exceptions as Volpone and Mosca? It is certainly not true that in real life likeable and virtuous people always emerge happily from their problems, and that comic drama is merely reflecting reality. Comedies end happily — when they do — because we want them to, because we want to believe that likeable and virtuous people are rewarded with happiness ever after. Another way of saying this would be that comedies end happily *because dramatists impose happy endings on them*. More often than one might at first suspect, dramatists contrive happy endings for plots which could just as plausibly, and often far more plausibly, end unhappily. In this sense happy endings are often arbitrary, since the dramatists could just as well have decided to conclude their plays differently.

It even sometimes happens that a dramatist has contrived a conventionally happy ending even though it is apparent to everyone, including the writer, that an *unhappy* ending would have been more appropriate and convincing. Molière's *Tartuffe* has such an ending, in which the apparently inevitable ruination of the foolish Orgon and his family is miraculously averted by the arrival of an officer who proceeds to arrest the villainous Tartuffe on the king's orders. *The Beggar's Opera,* by the early eighteenth-century English dramatist John Gay, has a similarly 'miraculous' conclusion. The Beggar who is the supposed author of the play comes on stage with one of the actors just as Macheath, the 'hero', is about to be executed. He is persuaded that a comedy cannot end with the death of the central character since that doesn't comply with popular taste; the call of 'reprieve' is thereupon raised, and the same character who moments before was to be executed returns to the stage a free man.

Tartuffe and *The Beggar's Opera* are only extreme examples of a common tendency for the endings of comedies to be at ironical variance with real-life probabilities. The happy ending here is a trick, a fraud deliberately practised on an audience which is itself fully aware of the fraudulence involved. We know that in life it would not work out like this, but we agree to be optimistic nevertheless and to pretend that it would. In *The Marriage of Anansewa*, for instance, we liberately disregard the fact that for most people in Ananse's impoverished condition there is no hope of betterment, that if they even attempted to deceive others in the weay Ananse does they would certainly get into serious trouble, and that the daughter of such a man, in real life, would never be able to marry a chief. The happy ending of Efua Sutherland's play is won in the face of impossible odds, at least considered in real-life terms.

Comic plays make us laugh and have happy endings: we can now see that that is not quite a true definition, or at least it is true of most comedies but not all. The real problem, however, is that even when it is true it isn't especially useful because it doesn't help us to gain insights into the nature and functions of comedy. It doesn't tell us, except in the most superficial way, what essential features a comedy like *The Marriage of Anansewa* has in common with other comedies, if indeed it has anything in common. We need another approach to help us look more deeply into the nature of comedy and to see what is essential to it. One possible way is to consider its origins and early forms in the hope of isolating and identifying the seeds from which subsequent comedy has grown.

Comedy and festivity

The earliest surviving comedy comes from the Greek city-state of Athens in the fifth century B.C. We are not exactly sure how this ancient comedy developed, or what it developed from, but it seems certain that it arose out of a religious ritual or group of rituals associated with the celebration and invocation of natural fertility. At some point in its development this ritual celebration was assimilated to the worship of the god Dionysus in his aspect as the god of wine and fertility, when he was known as Bacchus. The word 'comedy' is derived from two Greek words — *comos* and *ode,* meaning 'revel-song'; and the earliest comedy seems to have taken the form of a festive performance in which the revelry was at least in part made up of drinking and sex, and in which the festive participants believed themselves to be aiding the gods in assuring the continued fertility of man and nature.

These rituals may be remote and obscure but the basic impulse animating them seems to be present in rituals familiar to most contemporary Africans. Traditional African festivals, like those in honour of Dionysus, are devoted to the worship of gods and supernatural beings. But their basically religious inspiration in no way implies a concentration on 'otherworldly' matters to the exclusion of the things of this life. On the contrary, the traditional festivals seem to share a common tendency to be celebrations of life and living, and as an African critic has put it, reveal 'a spontaneous and frank preference for this life rather than the life to come'.* Like the Dionysiac festivities, the worship of supernatural forces in African festivals is an assertion of the vitality of human life and a celebration of fecundity in man and nature.

We are helped in understanding how comedy developed out of the celebratory worship of Dionysus by seeing how it forms an important part of African festivity. Lacking dialogue and plot, comic characters are normally established in African festivals through the use of masks and costumes. Just as in early Greek comedy there were certain 'stock' or typical characters who appeared in play after play, so we find a range of comic types tending to recur in contemporary African festival performance. Oyin Ogunba notes that these include

> the masker playing the character of the prostitute, with prominent breasts and hips, moving about the play-ground seductively and sometimes grotesquely; the police officer marching about the arena, officious, cruel and insincere; the foreigner, usually white, authoritarian, his pointed nose high up in the sky.
>
> (p. 23)

Looking at such comic masquerade figures in African festivals today, we can easily imagine how regular comic plays developed out of essentially similar festivities in ancient Greece, and how these plays preserved the mood of celebration underlying the honouring of the god Dionysus.

Fortunately, eleven plays by the finest of Greek comic dramatists, Aristophanes, have survived. Apart from their intrinsic artistic value, Aristophanes' comedies are especially interesting because they are still very close in time to their beginnings in ritual festivity. They can therefore be expected to have preserved to a large extent the characteristics of their origins. By looking at one of these comic plays we can develop our

*Oyin Ogunba, 'Traditional African Festival Drama', in O. Ogunba and A. Irele (eds), *Theatre in Africa*, Ibadan University Press, 1978, p. 7.

enquiry into the nature of comedy. Let us therefore consider Aristophanes' *Lysistrata*, which has kept its popularity on the stage up till the present day.

The basic idea of the play is simple but striking. Athens is at war with Sparta (as it really was at the time the play was written); the women of both city-states, led by Lysistrata, join forces to try to stop the ruinous war, using the most powerful weapon at their disposal — sex. They resolve that they will deprive their soldier-husbands of sexual pleasure until they agree to peace. Their plan, despite the opposition of the menfolk — and even the faintheartedness of some of the women — is successful: a peace is signed and the play ends with a celebratory dance and song.

We've said that the festive rites from which comedy arose in ancient Greece were associated with the celebration of fertility and the erotic impulse. Even from the brief plot outline of *Lysistrata* it is obvious that sex is at the heart of the comedy. The entertainment value of Aristophanes' play depends on the assumption that none of us can do without sex for long. Even when Lysistrata first outlines her plan to the women the response is hardly enthusiastic. She asks:

> Why are you turning away from me? Where are you going? What's all this pursing of lips and shaking of heads mean? You're all going pale — I can see tears! Will you do it or won't you? Answer!
>
> (p. 185)

To which two of the women immediately reply that they won't do it, one of them explaining that 'I'll ... walk through the fire, or anything — but give up sex, never!' (p. 185). Even when Lysistrata gets them to agree to abstain, things do not go smoothly. After five days the sexual deprivation is too much for some of the women, who invent every kind of excuse to slip away and see their husbands for a while. Later, however, the joke is on the men. One of the husbands, Cinesias, arrives looking for his wife, Myrrhine. In the original performance it would have been made perfectly clear, with the help of a large phallus, that Cinesias is suffering from a monstrous erection: as he puts it himself, 'I'm so bloody stretched out I might just as well be on the rack!' (p. 215). He is teased and tantalised by his wife, who runs off at the last moment, leaving him in a state of desperate frustration. Afflicted beyond endurance, the male representatives of Athens and Sparta — all visibly suffering from advanced sex-starvation — come together and, under Lysistrata's guidance, rapidly arrive at a peace agreement.

Lysistrata, like the Dionysiac revels from which it developed, clearly rests on a frank acceptance of the central importance of sex in human life and the pleasure people normally take in it. Of course, sex is not only a form of pleasure but also the means of creating new life, of preserving the species; and it is therefore naturally associated with the larger celebration of life itself, with the fertility of man and his natural environment. *Lysistrata* shows how the basic impulse of the rituals honouring Dionysus — the celebration of fertility, the 'life force' as we may think of it — has been preserved in the literary drama. Sex, in Aristophanes' play, is identified with peace, the preservation of life, and the well-being of Athens and Sparta. And it is sex presented, not in its discreet, romantic guise, but openly and bawdily, in a 'larger than life' way.

Indeed, this 'larger than life' quality, so evident in the comic fantasy of *Lysistrata*, is another characteristic that seems to have been carried over from comedy's festive origins. As we know from traditional festivity in Africa and elsewhere, festive performance tends towards the exaggerated, the fantastic, the licentious and — very often in conjunction — the mocking. Apart from particular episodes in the play, such as the dressing-up of the Athenian Magistrate as a woman, the basic comic idea of *Lysistrata* is outrageous in a way that accords with the general tendency of festive performance. In festivity the social and physical constraints normally obtaining are temporarily placed in abeyance, and a different, more genial mood prevails, in which energies that are normally repressed are given free rein. The original audience of *Lysistrata* watched characters wearing masks with grotesquely exaggerated features and dressed in costumes with a great deal of padding to create a larger than life effect, including a large leather phallus for each male character. The Dionysiac revels also undoubtedly featured such grotesquerie, and incorporated exuberant fantasy and licentious behaviour (drinking, feasting and love-making especially) as part of their festive spirit. Today, in festivals in Africa and many other parts of the world, masks and costumes are similarly used to portray men, animals and spirits, often in a grotesquely exaggerated fashion.

The basic impulse and forms of celebration in the Dionysiac rites were thus carried over into Aristophanes' comedy, and — as far as we can tell — into the earliest Greek literary comedy generally. So also, it seems, was much of the *effect* that the rituals were intended to have. This was essentially to invoke the spirit of fertility and to purify the community of accumulated evil and everything unwholesome and undesirable, leaving it spiritually regenerated. In ritual, this aim is achieved in a primarily *magical* way, whereas in stage drama magic has been replaced by non-magical imaginative identification on the part of the spectators. And yet the effects of Greek ritual and Aristophanic comedy seem to have been similar — a release from the constraints of everyday life, with all that is difficult and stultifying about it, and the exercise of a kind of collective wish-fulfilment in which the community expresses its desire for its future well-being. In *Lysistrata* Aristophanes invokes the 'life force' (sex) to overcome that which is destroying the general well-being (the ruinous war with Sparta) by means of a dramatic action which embodies and imaginatively fulfils the Athenians' wish for peace. If only temporarily, the audience could be released from the troubled realities of contemporary Athens and have their spiritual batteries recharged by contemplating, albeit in fantasy, the return to sanity and peace.

It is worth noting that in ancient Greek festivity for Dionysus, as in much traditional African festive ritual, a double social and spiritual function was served. There was the celebration of what is desirable and at the same time the casting-out of what is evil or undesirable. This dual pattern was preserved in Aristophanes, taking the form of a mixture of joyous celebration on the one hand and denunciation and mockery on the other. In *Lysistrata* the joyous emphasis on sex and the celebration of the restoration of peace co-exist with a good deal of mockery and humiliation, for example of the Athenian Magistrate, of Cinesias, and of the Chorus of old men. (In some of his other comedies, Aristophanes' comic denunciations and mockery are far more virulent and insistent than in *Lysistrata*.) The basic point, however, is that the urge to celebrate and the impulse to ridicule are natural partners, both in festive ritual and in comic drama deriving from it: the celebration of what is most desirable implies a recognition and scourging of its opposite.

Our discussion of *Lysistrata* has concentrated on identifying what early comedy carried through from the ritual festivity out of which it developed. Useful as this may be in giving an indication of what is essential to comedy, we must nevertheless acknowledge that there is no reason why it should not have changed virtually beyond recognition since Aristophanes' time, or at least have grown various 'branches' or traditions which differ greatly from what we find in a play like *Lysistrata*. Moreover, though we've suggested that there are basic affinities between Athenian festivity for Dionysus and much traditional African festive ritual, we must nevertheless recognise that modern Africa and ancient Athens are worlds apart. This being so, it is inevitable that in so far as comedy reflects the nature of the society that produced it the comic drama of modern Africa is bound to be in certain crucial respects very different from Aristophanes'. Similarly, the societies of the West differ markedly from those of Africa, or for that matter of Eastern Europe or the Far East, and therefore are likely to produce quite different kinds of comedy. So we cannot ascertain its main characteristics simply by noting the most striking features of a play or plays written and performed close to the first emergence of comedy from ritual.

What we can do, however, as the next step in our enquiry into the nature of comedy, is to compare what we have found in *Lysistrata* with the comedy of *The Marriage of Anansewa,* and to refer both back to what we know or can reasonably speculate about festival performance, and then identify what is common to all. And if, en route, we take into account everyday comic experience as well as, incidentally, other comedies from different cultures and ages, we may be able to make some useful generalisations about the relatively changeless features of comic drama.

Comic optimism and celebration

We have seen that dramatic comedy developed out of the festive celebration of natural fertility involving a frank acceptance and enjoyment of sexuality. *Lysistrata* and *The Marriage of Anansewa* are both firmly committed to this mood of celebration, though in rather different ways. The ancient Greek and the modern Ghanaian dramatists are alike in inviting their audiences to participate in a festive celebration of life's 'positives', and to take an optimistic view which nevertheless includes recognition of life's problems and hardships.

What are these 'positives' that we're encouraged to celebrate? Sex, not surprisingly, is one. In *Lysistrata* the subject of sex is treated bawdily, bluntly, even obscenely — in very much the same spirit, in fact, that was accorded to sex in Dionysiac rituals and in much festive ritual today. In

Efua Sutherland's play sexuality is a very important presence but a much more discreet one: it is given a romantic cast, being considered not as an enjoyable physical appetite but as a beautiful ideal of love. Sex and love are of course by no means the same thing, even if they are both vital aspects of erotic life generally; and we should make a distinction between 'romantic' comedy, which focuses on the emotional relations between the sexes, and what we might call 'sex' comedy, in which the emphasis is on the physical, appetitive aspect. *Lysistrata* is a good example of this latter kind; in a rather more discreet way Soyinka's *The Lion and the Jewel*, with its portrayal of Baroka's sensuality and his potency in ensnaring the beautiful young Sidi, is another. As examples of comedies celebrating romantic love we may mention several of Shakespeare's plays, including *A Midsummer Night's Dream* and *Twelfth Night*. But romantic comedy doesn't seem to be a favourite genre for modern writers for the stage, either in the West or in Africa. (This is not true of film or television drama, where romantic comedy flourishes.) Though there are several notable non-comic plays in which the love-relationship between a man and a woman is dramatically central (e.g. *Anowa, Wedlock of the Gods, The Burdens*), African drama has not yet produced a body of plays where the love relationship between a man and woman is at the centre of the comic action.

It is obvious enough that sex is being celebrated as the 'life force' that can overcome evil and suffering (the war) in Aristophanes' play. It isn't immediately obvious that love plays an equally important part in *The Marriage of Anansewa*; but it does, and in a way that brings out very powerfully the importance of love in the comic celebration of life.

From the moment that she knows that Chief-Who-Is-Chief may some day be her husband, Anansewa is a firm ally of her father in his plan. We should be clear what sort of plan it is — a sustained and deliberate deception (some might even say a fraud) intended to enrich himself and his family. But Anansewa is content to be a vital part of it because she wants Chief-Who-Is-Chief. Her love for him — note how what begins as sexual attraction (his virility and good looks) so quickly becomes love — is felt to be a sufficient justification for participating in the deception. If the character and her creator feel this, so do we, the audience. We are made to feel that it is right for young love to triumph, for the beautiful girl and the handsome young man to marry and be happy ever after. What begins as a deception by Ananse to acquire wealth becomes a deception to allow a young couple to be happily united.

The love interest reaches a climax in Act Four, when Anansewa pretends to be dead as the messengers from her suitors are brought in. Ananse somehow has to terminate the interest of the other chiefs in his daughter without antagonising them, while still making it possible for her to marry Chief-Who-Is-Chief. In the course of the deception Ananse pretends to go into a trance in which he ritualistically pours a libation of the head-drink sent by Chief-Who-Is-Chief and calls upon the ancestors to return his daughter to life:

> If it is your desire
> As it is ours
> That Chief-Who-Is-Chief

> Should marry Anansewa
> See to it that she returns to life!

(p. 79)

Anansewa awakes — according to Ananse, through the power of love: 'How strong love is. Love has awakened my child' (p. 80). In fact, of course, her miraculous 'resurrection' is a deliberate trick, part of the overall scheme. And yet, in the theatre, it is not just a trick: for if the scene is well acted, and the production as a whole has put the audience in the right frame of mind, most of the audience would be prepared to 'forget' that a deception is being practised and allow themselves to be imaginatively 'carried away' by the 'miracle' they are witnessing. In other words, the audience would experience emotions appropriate to a real 'resurrection', even though at the intellectual level they are aware of the fraud. And when this happens the spectators do indeed feel the 'power of love', which is the subject of the closing song ('Let's relate in love / That we may thrive') and the 'message' of the play. *The Marriage of Anansewa* ends in triumph — for Ananse and his scheming, for Anansewa and her desire for Chief-Who-Is-Chief, and for the audience, who have been persuaded that life's privations and problems can be overcome: and this triumph, this celebration of life, is brought about and symbolised by the power of love.

Sex and love, whether considered separately or together, are not the only positives that comedy invites us to celebrate. In both *Lysistrata* and *The Marriage of Anansewa* we witness a cunning trick which brings about something good. Crucial to human survival and advancement is the 'positive' of intellectual energy, man's capacity for using his brainpower and cunning to overcome life's difficulties. From the earliest times, the roguish trickster has been a central figure of comedy, in whom the celebration of human cunning has been embodied. Ananse is very obviously such a character; Lysistrata performs the essential function of the trickster-rogue, even if we don't think of her as a rogue or her plan as a trick. We find the type in the plays of the Roman comic dramatist Plautus, who died in 184 B.C., and in *Volpone* and *The Alchemist* by Ben Jonson, who lived in the seventeenth century: and the character is common to comic drama of societies as far apart, culturally and geographically, as those of the West, Africa and Japan. The trickster figure is traditional in much African folklore and it is therefore not surprising that his scheming forms the subject of much African comic drama. The influence of the story-telling art of the Akan-speaking people of Ghana (*Anansesem*), in which stories about the spider-trickster Ananse are handed down through the generations, is much in evidence in *The Marriage of Anansewa* and in two other Ghanaian comedies, Martin Owusu's *The Story Ananse Told* and *The Pot of Okro Soup*. And in Prophet Jeroboam of the two Jero plays, Wole Soyinka has created a memorable confidence-trickster whose superior cunning and knowledge of human nature permits him to survive and flourish in a harshly competitive society.

Whether the trickster wins or loses, is a 'goody' or a 'baddy', the audience is invited to identify with and celebrate his cunning and energy as he outwits — or tries to outwit — his victims. This can sometimes lead to moral paradox and even contradiction; for we are sometimes encouraged to view the trickster as the embodiment of the 'life force' even when he is plainly immoral and anti-social. Occasionally, our identification with the immoral trickster is part of a satire on society, the comic hero being the sympathetic agent for the exposure of hypocrisy and the evils beneath the respectable facade. We are on the trickster's side even though he may not be moral or even kind-hearted; and that is because he is nevertheless more likeable than the respectable members of society, whose secret wickedness he exposes. Soyinka's Brother Jero is such a character: we can't help but enjoy and admire his energy and resourcefulness as a schemer, even as we recognise that he's an immoral opportunist in an immoral society.

The celebration of energy — of the fertility of mind and body — seems, then, to be a constant feature of comic drama otherwise very different in cultural origin and kind. Energy is identical with life itself, and with the preservation and generation of life. In celebrating energy, comedy declares itself to be on the side of life, even in its immoral or amoral forms, and even though in particular plays comedy sometimes darkens its mood to include a recognition of the existence and power of suffering and death.

Comic denunciation and cleansing

Celebration of the good things and denunciation of the bad things go hand in hand. If comedy is an optimistic honouring of life's positives (including the supreme positive, life itself), it isn't surprising that it should also be a scourge of life's negative features and representatives (including the supreme negative, death). The two impulses — to celebrate and to scourge — are so closely related that they can very often be found alongside each other in the same play. On the other hand, a dramatist may concentrate on one to the exclusion of the other, or to be more precise it is only by tacit implication that we are aware of the other. For example, in neither *Lysistrata* nor *The Marriage of Anansewa* is there any serious denunciation or scourging of life's negatives as an integral part of the comic drama. It is true that the men, and especially male authority, are ridiculed in Aristophanes' play, but the fundamental emphasis is on the celebration of peace and the sexual urge that brings it about. And there is no place for comic denunciation in the Ghanaian play because it is so much given over to the celebration of Ananse's cunning. It is only in a negative sense, as a kind of unspoken implication, that we are invited to denounce war in *Lysistrata* and poverty in *The Marriage of Anansewa*.

Just as communities have always sought to cast out through magical ritual what is evil or unwholesome, so in comic drama there is often, either openly or by implication, a denunciation and cleansing of what is felt to be negative or 'anti-life'. Sometimes, this is achieved through a character or characters who learn through experience the error of their former ways, so that the optimistic ending characteristic of comedy becomes possible. In such plays we, the audience, are encouraged to take a critical attitude towards the characters concerned, but our awareness of their errors is not so overwhelming that we lose our essential sympathy for them. Retaining our basic sense of identification with them, we are psychologically 'cleansed' ourselves by witnessing the dramatic spectacle of their purification from error.

In *A Midsummer Night's Dream,* for example, we become aware that the confusions which befall the young couples during their night in the wood outside Athens are caused by their own emotional immaturity and lack of rational judgment. But this doesn't mean that we dislike them or regard them as fools. On the contrary, Shakespeare encourages us to be sympathetic, partly because he seems to be suggesting that what the lovers go through is an inevitable and universal experience, part of the common process of achieving maturity and acquiring the right balance between reason and emotion. The lovers awake wiser and more mature, purified of their adolescent follies; and the audience also, by the time they leave the theatre, have had a kind of moral education through their emotional engagement in the play.

The process of purification can be carried out in comedy in quite a different, far harsher, way — through the ridicule and mockery of satire. This tends to happen when the dramatist wishes to show folly or wrongdoing without any sympathy for the characters involved, against whom he may even be directing feelings of great hostility. Instead of gentle criticism followed by reform, we are now presented with scornful mockery which does not reform so much as destroy.

A good example of this kind of comic purification, through satire, is *Who's Afraid of Solarin* by the Nigerian dramatist 'Femi Osofisan. Based on a masterpiece of European comic drama, Gogol's *The Government Inspector,* Osofisan's play was written in honour of Dr Tai Solarin, a well-known and courageous crusader for human rights and formerly the Public Complaints Commissioner for several Western states of Nigeria. It concerns a group of corrupt local government officials, who learn that they are about to be secretly investigated by the Public Complaints Commissioner, presumably Solarin. To their horror, they are informed by their spies that the man they are so fearfully awaiting has already been in town several days, staying with the pastor. In fact, this man is not Solarin but a scoundrel called Isola who has fled Lagos because he's in trouble with the law, and who has only been staying in the town because he was robbed on the road. Knowing this, we take great delight in watching the corrupt officials, desperate to conceal or otherwise neutralise their wrongdoing, as they approach Isola/Solarin with their bribes, which he is of course happy to accept. The Chief Magistrate, the Price Control Officer, the Councillors for Education and Cooperatives, the Chief Medical Officer — all come before him, trying to outdo the others in the size of their 'gifts'. When he has got enough, he disappears, leaving his diary behind. We revel in the characters' discomfiture, in the way they are made to expose their own folly and wickedness, as they read out Isola's opinions of them from the diary. And our satisfaction at the deflation of these characters is complete when one of their spies announces the arrival of a 'gentleman in a grey coat' in an official car bearing the inscription 'Office of the Public Complaints Commissioner'. The real Tai Solarin has arrived!

The satire of *Who's Afraid of Solarin* is directed against recognisable Nigerian types and their corrupt practices. Most dramatic satire, in Africa and elsewhere, assumes this generalised form, in which characters representing social types are exposed for what they really are and scourged. Satire of this kind is not of course encouraged by corrupt or arrogant officialdom or politicians in Africa or anywhere else; and to be performed and read at all it often has to be more indirect and subdued than the author would have liked. In this respect, modern satire is a good deal less personal in its attacks than in some places and times — for example, in Aristophanes, or in the satire of ancient Rome. But the possibilities for merciless and quite personal satire do still exist, provided the dramatist is bold and indignant enough to take a risk. Wole Soyinka has done so in *Opera Wonyosi,* which has recently been published. Never one to be inhibited by censorship or the threat of punishment, Soyinka has satirised the antics of African politicians ever since *Kongi's Harvest,* which was clearly inspired by — if not restricted to — the régime of Kwame Nkrumah in Ghana. In *Opera Wonyosi,* which is an adaptation of Brecht's *The Threepenny Opera* (itself adapted from Gay's *The Beggar's Opera*), the prime personal target for Soyinka's savage satirical denunciation is the former 'emperor', Jean-Claude Bokassa. Alongside this highly personal attack is a fierce condemnation of the Nigerian military and of the materialism of Nigerian society generally, beside which the satire of *Who's Afraid of Solarin* looks quite timid.

Comedy celebrates, but it also denounces, purifying through the more or less ruthless exposure of folly and evil. In this, dramatic comedy can be seen as following the lead of everyday comic experience which, as we noted earlier, involves a surprising amount of mockery and ridicule, often of a very harsh kind. It is also elaborating, in fully dramatic form, the satirical tendency in traditional festivity, in which comic figures with ludicrously exaggerated attributes — often of a socially undesirable kind — are publicly displayed and laughed at. In all these forms — the everyday, the festival and the artistic — comedy seems to be the expression of the desire, by individuals or entire groups, to achieve a 'casting-out' of what is not liked similar to the magical purification of the community at certain seasonal festivals. We need now to look more closely at comedy as the expression of our deepest wishes and desires.

Comic distance and the comic wish

We've seen that the basic situations of both *Lysistrata* and *The Marriage of Anansewa* could be those of non-comic drama; after all, there is nothing obviously comic about war and the desire to end it, or poverty and the struggle to overcome it. But, as we've also seen, it is obvious in the first few minutes that Efua Sutherland's play is a comedy, and that it will continue to be so until its happy ending. Our recognition that it is comedy has a great deal to do with its deliberate emphasis on the element of make-believe, with our sense of the play as a sophisticated, good-humoured game. And this festive, make-believe aspect in turn depends on a sustained *distancing* of the audience from the characters and action. This distancing effect is characteristic of comedy and is closely related to comedy's function as the expression of our wishes, so it needs to be looked at more closely.

What do we mean when we say that an audience has been distanced from a play? It certainly doesn't mean that the spectators are prevented from being interested and engaged in the characters and situations, for if this were so the play — whether tragedy or comedy — would simply be a failure. An audience can be held at a certain distance from the play while still being imaginatively involved in it. In *The Marriage of Anansewa*, for instance, we 'believe in' and identify with Ananse and his daughter even as we remain aware that they are theatrical fictions, part of a theatrical game, the artificiality of which has been deliberately stressed. Ananse and Anansewa exist, but we are reminded that they only exist in the theatre. We engage with them and the situations in which they find themselves, but our involvement is always tempered by the awareness of make-believe.

Rather than concealing the pretence, many comic plays, like *The Marriage of Anansewa,* emphasise their theatricality. Even when they do not, comedies tend to distance their audiences by exaggerating the characters and situations or otherwise stressing, in a laughter-provoking way, their differences from real-life people and events. For example, there is no make-believe element as such in *Lysistrata*; but the outrageous fantasy of its basic premise and its exaggeration of character and action establish its difference from actual reality. It is not always true, of course, that comedies set themselves apart from real life: some are basically realistic or naturalistic, deriving their effects from the audience's recognition of familiar characters and situations. The point is not that *all* comedies advertise their 'otherness' from real life but that this has been a general tendency in comic drama from different cultures over a very long period.

The frequent presence in comedy of deliberate absurdity and exaggeration, of licence and high spirits, the delight in its own make-believe — all these suggest a willingness on the part of the comic dramatist and his audience to connive in the suspension of normal laws and rules, at least for the duration of the performance. This rejection or disregard of life's rules in turn suggests that a very powerful collective wish is at work to enter a realm, however temporarily, where we are no longer imprisoned by the constraints of normality.

We are all apt to fulfil our wishes in our imaginings if we cannot do so in reality: we are all fantasists to some extent. Sometimes, our fantasies are provoked by unhappiness or even despair: we can't bear our real lives or some important aspect of them and so we retreat, for consolation, into an imaginary world in which our problems no longer exist. More often, however, we fantasise simply out of a natural impulse to experience in imagination ways or aspects of life that are inaccessible to us in reality, or to savour certain pleasures in a 'pure', intensely pleasurable way, unhampered by the impediments of reality.

It is not hard to see that both *Lysistrata* and *The Marriage of Anansewa* have been constructed around a wish, and that each can be thought of as a highly-organised imaginary fulfilment of the wish. Aristophanes' play evidently gives public expression to what must have been a desire common to most Athenians — that the disastrous war with Sparta could be brought to a speedy end. In the Ghanaian play, similarly, there is the dramatisation of a wish — that Ananse, the poor but crafty 'common man', should be able to escape hardship, allied to which is the wish that underlies all romantic drama and literature, that the lover (here Anansewa) should be happily united with the beloved (Chief-Who-Is-Chief).

In both our comedies wishes that are commonly held by members of their audiences but which cannot easily be realised in life are fulfilled in the theatre. For a brief while the spectators can 'make their dreams come true', even if in reality they know that sex could never triumph over the politics of war. There is a tacit agreement to indulge in a kind of positive wishful thinking, which knows itself for what it is. The wish in our two comedies happens to be primarily social: peace for Athens and Sparta in *Lysistrata,* the overcoming of poverty in *The Marriage of Anansewa.* But comedy is equally receptive to the fulfilment of more personal wishes — the desire for sexual gratification or a loving relationship, for example.

Does all this mean that comedy is escapist, in that we retreat from the unpleasant aspects of our lives by fantasising a happy fulfilment of our desires? Not necessarily, though it must be admitted that a lot of comedy, especially that devised for primarily commercial purposes, is indeed escapist. There is a difference, however, between escapism and the optimism of comedy which produces the characteristic happy ending. We can 'look on the bright side' and imagine our strongest wishes being realised without escaping from life's realities. Herein lies the essential difference between comic drama of artistic interest and the merely trivial kind: for good comedy always takes into account, and is firmly anchored in, the realities of life — including the unpleasant realities — even as it gives its audience a temporary release from them by showing its wishes being fulfilled; whereas bad comedy, however skilfully crafted, is always apt to turn its back on reality and proceed as if it doesn't exist.

We are generalising, of course, trying to pick out tendencies and general principles; and in doing so there is a temptation to be dogmatic in one's assertions. It may be that there is sometimes an element of pure escapism even in very good comic drama: it is not always easy to judge where a well-founded optimism ends and escapism begins. There will always be room for disagreement in this area since individuals have different life-experiences and ideas that inevitably affect their judgment. It is also important to bear in mind that the endings of comedies, in which the audience's wish is finally fulfilled, are no less make-believe than what has gone before in the play. Aristophanes, for instance, shows the women's sex-strike as triumphing, though we know that in reality this was out of the question when *Lysistrata* was written and performed. Was he then guilty of escapism, as opposed to optimism? Perhaps, though the ending of his play can also be thought of as a piece of make-believe which goes beyond escapism by reminding the audience — and the Athenian authorities in particular — of the essential sanity of peace and the madness of continued war. Behind the apparent escapism of this happy ending there is arguably an impulse which is very firmly and healthily grounded in reality.

The 'distancing' of comedy, then, is closely related to the imaginary assertion and fulfilment of our deepest wishes, which seems to be another of the relatively changeless features of comic drama. When we deal with wishes and their fulfilment we are touching on the emotional aspect of comedy, and the much-debated issue of the relative importance of intellect and emotion in our response to dramatic comedy. Our discussion of comic distancing and wish-fulfilment — and of the comic experience generally — suggests that both intellect and emotion tend to be equally important in our response. As far as our two comedies are concerned, we are encouraged to become emotionally involved *and*, at the same time, to temper our response through our awareness of the distance from actual reality of the comic characters and situations. We are not prevented from experiencing emotions in comedy, as critics occasionally suggest, but rather our response involves a delicate balance between feeling and detachment, between imaginative participation and objective observation and judgment.

It may seem contradictory to speak of the co-existence of feeling and detachment; but even in our normal experience we sometimes have mixed feelings about someone or something, when we feel well-disposed towards a person or thing while having intellectual reservations about him or it. More importantly, though, there is not really such a clear-cut separation of intellect and emotion as our common use of these terms tends to imply. There is a sense in which, most of the time, we think with our feelings, and feel with our thoughts: certain thoughts inevitably arouse particular feelings in us, and our experience of certain emotions may be accompanied by particular ideas. It is, I think, a characteristic tendency of comedy — or at least, of the best comedy — for thought and feeling to be in constant interplay, the one qualifying the other, so that a kind of dual perspective or vision is produced. As an example, we can remind ourselves of how, at the end of *The Marriage of Anansewa,* we are aware *intellectually* that Ananse and his daughter are parties to a deception but nevertheless respond *emotionally* to the 'miracle' of Anansewa's 'resurrection'.

Comedy and social man

The final characteristic tendency of comedy that I want to mention is less immediately visible than the others, and its full significance will only emerge by comparison with tragedy. This has to do with the way comedy tends to depict man in society. As we shall see in the next chapter, the protagonist in tragedy has traditionally been portrayed in his solitary greatness, set apart from others both by his high rank and his unique spiritual capacities and destiny. Even in modern Western tragedy, where the tragic protagonist may take the form of an ordinary salesman like Willy Loman in *Death of a Salesman,* there is still something exceptional, some attribute or vocation or desire, that sets the hero apart from other men and women. In comedy, on the other hand, the characters have traditionally tended to be of more modest social rank — or else, if kings and princes, they've been portrayed in their 'private', 'human', 'unofficial' aspect. What is brought out is not so much their impressive individuality but their *social* nature — those features they have in common with the other members of their society. Modern comedy is in general true to this tradition: the comic hero is a man like ourselves; we look him straight in the eye rather than looking up to someone exceptional, as we tend to do in tragedy.

At certain points in *The Marriage of Anansewa* a screen resembling a spider's web is placed on stage and Ananse appears behind it. The first time this happens is in Act Two, when Ananse receives a telegram from Chief Sapa announcing the arrival of his messengers in two weeks' time to conduct the head-drink ceremony for Anansewa. 'In such a fix,' asks Ananse, 'what am I going to do?' (p. 32). He sits thinking, and there is a stage direction calling on the Property Man to bring the screen and place it in front of Ananse. When he emerges he has decided what to do. At subsequent moments of crisis (see pp. 44–49, 53–54 and 66–82) Ananse similarly moves either behind or beside the screen when he is using his cunning to achieve his aims.

Even a non-Ghanaian audience accepts Efua Sutherland's invitation to associate Ananse's 'spinning out' of his cunning tricks with the spider's clever spinning of its web. But Ghanaian audiences, for whom the play was originally performed, are well acquainted with Ananse from the storytelling art of the *Anansesem* where he figures as the spider-trickster, who is constantly trying to outwit others and advance his own interests through his cunning. The visual image of the screen is a reminder that beneath the human exterior there lurks the spider-trickster of folklore.

And yet, for all his animal associations, Ananse is presented in the play as being very much a recognisable human being in a recognisable human world. Efua Sutherland, in her 'Foreword' to the printed text, has made the point about Ananse's essential humanity as well as it could be put:

> Who is Ananse, and why should so many stories be told about him? Ananse appears to represent a kind of Everyman, artistically exaggerated and distorted to serve society as a medium for self-examination. He has a penetrating awareness of the nature and psychology of human beings and animals. He is also made to mirror in his behaviour fundamental human passions, ambitions and follies as revealed in contemporary situations.
>
> (p. v)

Prominent among these fundamental human qualities is his talent for not only surviving but also for using his wits to prosper. Ananse is a bit of a rogue, but he is a shrewd rogue. His cunning and roguishness are not malicious; we can all sympathise and identify with him because he is striving to eradicate his poverty, to 'better' himself, and this is an aspiration which most of us share in some form. And, as he says himself, 'If the world were not what it is, I would not gamble with such a priceless possession' (i.e. his daughter). Clever and resourceful though he is, Ananse is only human, subject to all the difficulties and constraints imposed upon Everyman:

> But let me tell you this: if you are merely human like me, you'd better make your laughter brief, because in this world, there is nobody who is by-passed by trouble.
>
> (p. 52)

If he achieves success, it is only after a struggle. Ananse is not exempted from the problems and constraints of normal life; he suffers too, but he is better than most of us at turning established customs to his advantage:

> It's very clear that he knows the customs more than well. Notice how he has them at his finger tips, spinning them out, weaving them into a design to suit his purposes.
>
> (p. 16)

The secret of Ananse's success is his knowledge of society and of human nature.

Comedy, then, tends to emphasise the human and social nature of man's life rather than his 'god-like' — or at least aspiringly god-like — nature. Even when the gods are shown, it is in a distinctly human aspect: the gods are made men, and very vulnerable men at that, as the portrayal of Dionysus in Aristophanes' *The Frogs* proves. In comedy no one is so high that he can't be laughed at, and no one so low that he can't rise a little by outwitting his fellows.

Conclusion: comedy and society

It seems that there are certain continuities in comedy, certain characteristic and relatively changeless tendencies that are shared by comic plays widely separated in historical and cultural origin. In conclusion, let us reverse our emphasis and dwell briefly, not on the apparently permanent features of comedy, but on the *variables* and the potential for diversity in the nature and function of comic drama. The points mentioned here will be returned to and examined in greater detail in the final chapter of the book, when the discussion will centre on the making of value-judgments about plays.

Human societies, like everything else, have histories, and these are always histories of change. Drama, including comic drama, obviously cannot remain unaffected by this historical changefulness. And yet we often talk about comedy as if it had an independent existence of its own, like a god in the heavens. This temptation exists, and is 'natural', because to some degree it is justified. After all, as we've just seen, comic plays written as far apart in place and time as Athens in the fifth century B.C. and twentieth-century Ghana do apparently have certain basic features or tendencies in common.

Comedy is not a changeless essence which happens to take somewhat different forms depending on the particular societies in which it is found. Comedy should be seen, first and foremost, as a *social* product, the continuities in which are related to the continuities in human social organisation. By looking at it in this way we can use our awareness of the characteristic tendencies of comedy to go as deeply as possible into its specific nature and function in particular plays. This in turn implies that we look as closely as possible at the social context of particular comedies so that we can discern in what way they are products of their societies.

It is obviously very important, in doing this, to know what we mean when we talk about a society. It is a common view, for example, that comedy serves a social function, and that it is primarily the moral one of exposing and correcting social evils. Dramatists often encourage this idea by claiming that their comedies are intended to reform social behaviour as well as to entertain. We should be clear, however, that such expressions of the social function of comedy are based on a particular view of what society is. In this way of thinking, society tends to be seen as a unified entity, with certain accepted values or 'norms'. But this is not the only possible way of conceiving of societies: instead of emphasising their unity, we can see them as being composed of separable groups and classes which compete with each other in pursuing their interests and viewpoints. In this perspective, comedy is not the unified expression of a single entity, but the product of competing world-views, ultimately based on the material interests of groups and classes.

The nature and function of comedy may vary greatly, then, depending on the specific social contexts of particular plays. It may be that on occasion comedy gives expression to a view or a wish held by an entire society. But bearing in mind what we've just said about social conflict and rivalry, it may also — and more often — be charged with the values of one social group as opposed to those of another. Consciously or unconsciously, a comic play may then be part of the ideological rivalry between competing sections of society. It may even be openly partisan — agitating or criticising on behalf of a particular class and its interests and beliefs against others. As such, comedy may be used as a mouthpiece for those who are in power or as a weapon of subversion by those who are not. Even a comedy as good-natured as *The Marriage of Anansewa,* while obviously not partisan in this way, may be less 'innocent' than it seems: certainly it has quite definite social implications, suggesting as it does that poorer members of Ghanaian society such as Ananse can improve their social position and generally achieve an acceptable life-style without needing to become involved in serious social antagonism. The play says 'Let's relate in love' — not only as private individuals but also in wider social terms; its comedy tries to put us in the mood to do this. Admirable as the sentiment is, it is at least arguable that it is misguided. As we shall see when we discuss the process of judging plays, this is a possibility that can justifiably affect our sense of the overall value of the play.

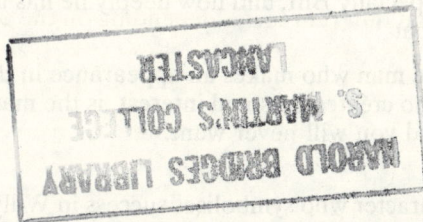

LANCASTER
S. MARTIN'S COLLEGE
HAROLD BRIDGES LIBRARY

8 Tragedy

The words 'tragedy' and 'tragic' occur regularly in the language and situations of everyday life. They are used to describe 'private' events of no great significance for the outside world, for example, the breakdown of a marriage, or, more seriously, the death of a friend or acquaintance in a road accident or by natural causes; 'public' occurrences with wide and unpleasant implications, for example, the assassination of a political leader or a military *coup d'état* ending civilian democracy; and, on the largest scale, natural and human disasters such as an earthquake killing and injuring many thousands, or full-scale war. The fact that 'tragedy', like 'comedy' and 'comic', has such a very wide range of reference alerts us to the likelihood of encountering dramatic tragedy in many different forms or modes.

But it is also reasonable to expect that the continuous use of the term tragedy over a very long period of time implies an underlying similarity between the different forms. Our main concern here will be to suggest the defining characteristics of tragic drama as it has manifested itself in several different cultures over many centuries. We will begin our enquiry with an American play, written in 1948, which Western audiences have accepted as a distinctively modern example of tragedy, featuring a representatively modern tragic hero. The play is *Death of a Salesman* by Arthur Miller.

The first long stage direction tells us that part of the action we are about to witness will be set in the present and involve characters who exist in the 'here-and-now', and part will be the dramatic expression of Willy Loman's imaginings. Throughout the play the scenes enacting the Salesman's imaginings are interlaced with the action happening in the here-and-now. (We are reminded of Soyinka's dramatic method in *The Strong Breed*.) Through them, we see what hopes Willy has invested in his sons, especially Biff, and how deeply he has influenced his boys with his belief that

> the man who makes an appearance in the business world, the man who creates personal interest, is the man who gets ahead. Be liked and you will never want.

> (pp. 25–6)

The character who symbolises success in Willy's mind is his brother Ben, who appears in Willy's second 'memory scene' as the man who 'made it', who walked into the African jungle when he was seventeen and walked out rich when he was twenty-one. Willy idolises Ben, and wishes to imbue his sons with his spirit (p. 41). But we notice that Ben represents a different kind of success from that to which Willy aspires: Ben is presented in Willy's memory of him as a rugged individualist who is associated with the Alaskan forests and the African jungle; but Willy himself believes that success can also be had, not by what you do, but by who you know and 'the smile on your face!':

> It's contacts, Ben, contacts! The whole wealth of Alaska passes over the lunch table at the Commodore Hotel, and that's the wonder, the wonder of this country, that a man can end with diamonds here on the basis of being liked!
>
> (p. 68)

It is, however, apparent that neither Willy nor his sons have succeeded in achieving this kind of commercial eminence. Willy's enacted memories help us to understand why this is so. In the first we see how he condones Biff's theft of the football in the false belief that it shows his son's sense of initiative and is in any case acceptable when one is 'well liked'. At the same time we see his unpleasantness to young Bernard, whom he describes as 'anaemic', and his failure to take seriously the boy's concern over the possibility that Biff will fail maths and be refused admission to the university. We also witness Willy's boastfulness about his prowess as a salesman, even though in this same scene he has to confess to his wife Linda that he is not doing well and has difficulty paying his debts. Being 'well liked', a 'personality' — this is Willy Loman's idea of what matters; and he imbues his sons with the notion, indirectly crippling them for the future.

The falsity and emptiness of his approach to life, and the reason for Biff's failure to do anything worthwhile, are fully revealed in the 'mental flashback' in which the salesman remembers how his son found him in a hotel bedroom with a woman. It is here that Biff discovers his beloved, idolised father to be a pathetic fake, and his world collapses around him. Having come himself to the painful realisation of the phoniness of Willy's dream of success, Biff tries in the here-and-now action to make his father and brother see the error of their ways; but so deeply are they attached to the 'American dream' that they cannot change. The only way Willy can respond to the knowledge that Biff loves him is to commit suicide so that his sons can achieve success with the insurance money. Even at his father's grave Happy still believes that the dream of commercial success is 'the only dream you can have — to come out number-one man' (p. 111).

The intertwining of Willy's imaginings with the action in the present is crucial in bringing out the play's tragic impact and meaning. Miller's dramatic method gives us a special insight into Willy's mind, so that we experience — as he does — his intense hopes and dreams for his sons' success as well as his awareness of guilt and failure. We are able to see Willy Loman, as Biff has come to see him, for what he is: a worn out salesman whose chief commodity — himself — no one any longer wants to buy. But we are also made to see him, at the same time, in another way, as Linda sees him when she says:

> Willy Loman never made a lot of money. His name was never in the paper. He's not the finest character that ever lived. But he's a human being, and a terrible thing is happening to him. So attention

must be paid. He's not to be allowed to fall into his grave like an old dog. Attention, attention must be finally paid to such a person.
(p. 44)

As Linda demands, we must pay attention to Willy; not as a mere failure, to be rather arrogantly pitied as one who didn't have the necessary qualities for success, but with the full sympathy one gives — or at least should give — to a fellow human being to whom something terrible is happening.

It is from this emotional area that the tragic impact of *Death of a Salesman* derives. It is possible to look down on Willy Loman as a misguided failure, a loud-mouthed, hypocritical dreamer; but if we see him *only* in this way the play cannot make what most people think of as a tragic impression upon us. A sense of the tragic, in drama and in everyday life, seems to involve identification with the person(s) suffering. I don't mean by this that we simply put ourselves in the tragic victim's position, that we straightforwardly imagine being him or her. It is more complicated than this, for there is a sense in which we can identify with someone without actually thinking of ourselves as that person. I mentioned earlier that the death of someone we know in a road accident may well be described as a 'tragedy'. Part of our response to such an event may be the fear that the same thing could happen to us, and in our fear we might fantasise being in the dead person's place at the moment of death. But another, and I suspect predominant, part of our reaction would be to feel a sense of loss and waste, a grievous sense of the person having been cut off from life before his time. This is a feeling which comes from our identification with our dead friend, but it is a sense of identity based on an awareness of our common humanity rather than on actually placing oneself in his position. The physical destruction of our friend is felt as a threat to, and diminishment of, our own humanity: we have lost one of our own, and we feel that loss as the loss of part of ourselves, of our common identity.

It is in this way, I suggest, that Arthur Miller encourages us to identify strongly with Willy Loman. We are aware that Willy is inadequate, that he is responsible for the inadequacy of his sons, that he has lived a lie and caused them to do so too. Nevertheless, we identify with him because his yearnings and his failures are common human property: to the extent that we share them, we can't help but feel threatened ourselves as they lead him to his destruction. In committing himself to the dream of commercially-defined success, Willy is representative of many people in modern society. What sets Willy apart is the *intensity* of his desire and commitment, what the dramatist described in the introduction to his collected plays as his 'fanatic insistence upon his self-conceived role . . .'. Willy Loman's ardent attachment to false values is thus only an extreme manifestation of a common enough tendency: when he becomes their victim we surely recognise how we threaten ourselves through our false hopes and dreams, and consequently have a sense of fellow-feeling with him as he heads towards destruction.

This feeling is intensified by Loman's partial awareness of his false position, and also by our appreciation of his reason for committing suicide. Willy is haunted by the consciousness that he has been a failure as a salesman. In his first imagining, for example, we see him exaggerating

Willy Loman and his sons as they appear in Willy's memory of the past.

the commission he has earned, only to be brought down to earth when Linda lists their debts. His imaginings also bring out his awareness, which he cannot openly admit, that he destroyed Biff's life when his son found him with the woman. Despite his enthusiastic propaganda on behalf of the 'American dream' Willy also realises, though obscurely and distortedly, that his values have been mistaken: the figure of Ben, for instance, represents Willy's partial awareness that there is even a notion of commercial success quite different from his own, based not on selling but on rugged, individualistic endeavour in the Alaskan wastes and African jungles. Willy cannot articulate his dim awareness of what is wrong with his life. It finds expression, instead, in the mental disturbance which produces his imaginings — a sort of agonised private conversation with himself — and in his secret thoughts of suicide. Even when Biff makes clear his love for his father, and implores him to 'Take that phony dream and burn it before something happens' (p. 106), Willy cannot break through into a full awareness of his false values. So committed is he to them that his son's love inspires him to pursue his dream to its final, destructive conclusion: he commits suicide, in the heroic but profoundly misguided hope that he will thus help his beloved Biff achieve the American dream of success.

If Willy had had no consciousness of the falseness of his dreams, and had committed suicide solely from self-pity, it would be hard for us to feel for him strongly. But his possession of a degree of self-awareness, however limited, and his suicide, which we recognise as a misguided but genuinely heroic act of love, encourage us to sympathise with him as a fellow human being. Willy is a victim, even if he is partly responsible for his own condition. But we can see how we are also potentially victims, and how we may, like Willy, contribute to our own downfalls. Willy Loman is not impressive, but he is representative — not only of many contemporary Americans, but of all those ordinary people in many different societies who dream, hopelessly, of material success.

Popular ideas of tragedy

Willy Loman's tragedy, then, is that of a common man and of modern urban society, even if it is by no means restricted to America. Presently we shall consider a play from a very different kind of culture which, if it can be described as tragedy — as I shall argue it can — is tragedy in a quite different mode from Arthur Miller's play. Before we move on, which will involve a complication of our discussion as we begin to compare and contrast plays, let us try to clear the critical ground by asking: what do most readers and playgoers expect of a play that they would describe as a tragedy? What, for most people, constitutes a tragic drama?

When Arthur Miller wrote his tragedy of a common man he upset certain traditional notions of what a tragedy should be which have greatly influenced the composition and reception of tragic drama for many centuries, and which continue to influence dramatists and audiences — including African dramatists and audiences — today. The predominant idea of tragedy, I suggest, is something like this: it shows the fall of a great man because of some flaw in his otherwise impressive character, ending usually in the sadness of his death. Witnessing his downfall, and becoming emotionally involved in it, we experience a mixture of pity and fear by means of which emotions we are spiritually 'purged' or 'cleansed'.

This 'definition' of tragedy is largely based on Aristotle's discussion in the *Poetics*, which has had a huge influence through the ages on how tragic plays are written and read. Aristotle's ideas about tragedy were based on his knowledge of the great tragic drama of ancient Greece, but there is no doubt that his characterisation of pity and fear as the tragic emotions accords with many people's response to tragedy written since the Greeks, and plainly brings us close to the heart of tragic experience. The trouble with Aristotle, strange though it may seem to say so, has perhaps been that he was *too* great a critic, and his influence *too* strong. Instead of his great insights into tragedy being creatively questioned, extended, and if need be, modified, they have tended to be slavishly and unquestioningly adopted. The unfortunate result of this has been the dominance of an overly rigid and narrow view of what constitutes tragedy, both in criticism and in playwriting.

Aristotle himself is of course not to blame, especially when his ideas have been distorted by others. Let's take, for example, the popular idea that a tragic hero has a 'flaw' — the 'tragic flaw' — in his character, which causes his downfall. This idea is often thought to have all Aristotle's authority behind it, but this is not so. The word Aristotle himself used in Greek which has come to be popularly rendered by 'tragic flaw' was *hamartia*. It is generally agreed among scholars familiar both with ancient Greek and with Aristotle's writings that this word means an error, or perhaps, an error of judgment, and that it implies a mistaken decision or action caused by ignorance of an important fact or circumstance. There is plainly a big difference between an 'error' and a 'flaw': the former means a single mistake, not necessarily caused by an ingrained fault in character; the latter suggests that the person concerned has some fundamental weakness in his nature. It makes a considerable difference to our view of tragedy whether a tragic hero's downfall is the product of an isolated error, which, like Oedipus, he may have committed unknowingly, or the result of an ingrained weakness in his character.

Apart from such distortion, there is also the problem of knowing just what Aristotle meant when he expressed certain ideas. Take his notion of *catharsis,* which is usually held to mean the audience's emotional purging as they watch tragedy. But what is actually being purged? And what, in any case, do we really mean when we say that emotions can be purged? Is it the emotions of pity and fear themselves that are purged? Or is there supposed to be a painful or morbid element in those emotions that has to be removed? There is a genuine problem in deciding what Aristotle wanted to imply when he used the Greek word *catharsis.* A recent scholar, who has tried to clarify the word by examining how Aristotle uses it in other writings, has suggested that instead of thinking of it as a purging, or removal, of anything, it is more accurate to see it as a kind of exercising and 'training' of the emotions, so that they are in harmony or balance in a way that befits the morally good man.*

Even if there were no difficulties involved in Aristotle's discussion of tragedy, or his ideas had never been oversimplified or misunderstood, it would still be wrong to apply his formulation of tragedy uncritically to our own experience of it. The relevant point has been well made by the author of *Death of a Salesman*:

> It is now many centuries since Aristotle lived. There is no more reason for falling down in a faint before his *Poetics* than before Euclid's geometry, which has been amended numerous times by men with new insights . . . Things do change, and even a genius is limited by his time and the nature of his society.
>
> (Introduction to *Collected Plays*, p. 31)

Miller proceeds to point out that Aristotle's notion that a tragic hero must fall from the social heights has to be understood as a statement by someone living in a society using slave labour. Because he lived in the society he did, Aristotle could not imagine tragedy 'as being possible for any but the higher ranks of society'. In drama reflecting modern societies the stature of a hero or heroine is not necessarily tied to social rank in this way. Audiences can accept that an ordinary 'man in the street' may be as fit, and even a fitter, hero of tragedy than a person of the highest social rank or greatest political power, provided that his life, in Miller's words,

> engages the issues of, for instance, the survival of the race, the relationships of man to God — the questions, in short, whose answers define humanity and the right way to live so that the world is a home . . . .

*See Humphrey House, *Aristotle's Poetics*, Rupert Hart-Davis, 1956, pp. 104–111.

We will return later to Miller's idea of tragedy as being concerned with the world as a home. The point that concerns us here is his insistence that tragedy, like all art and thought, is *social* and *historical* by nature — that it is the product of a particular society at a particular stage in its development. Whatever the relevance of Aristotle's view of tragedy to his own time and place, whatever its continuing relevance may be for us, we cannot use it as a universally applicable 'definition' covering all possible experiences of tragedy, for the simple reason that this would be to ignore the social and historical dimension pointed out by Miller and others. And this suggests that any other 'definition' of tragedy should be treated with equal caution, since by its very nature an approach to tragedy that deals in cut-and-dried 'definitions' is likely to disregard the crucial importance of the social and historical dimension.

We should now be able to see the inadequacies of the popular conception of tragedy summarised above. There is no reason why modern tragedy must show 'great' persons; there is no basis in Aristotle for the concept of the 'tragic flaw', and even if there was, we don't have to accept his word on the matter as gospel; and even though pity and fear may well be emotions we experience as we witness tragedy, it is very doubtful that they involve any kind of emotional 'purgation', or even that Aristotle himself meant such a thing. The only part of the 'definition' of tragedy offered earlier that seems to survive intact is that the hero's fall normally ends in death. We seem to be on firmer ground here, because there is no doubt that most tragedies do end in the protagonist's death, usually after a period of intense suffering. I shall return later to the matter of how tragedies actually do end. For the time being let us consider what Aristotle himself says about how tragic plays should end, and also what we perceive as the relation between death and tragedy in real life.

Aristotle contradicts himself when he discusses how tragedies should end. At one point he praises Euripides for his 'unhappy' endings, which he claims make his plays 'the most truly tragic'. But elsewhere he says something quite different, that 'the best of all' are those endings, like that of *Iphigenia in Tauris*, where there is a happy resolution of the action. Aristotle, then, doesn't say very much about the endings of tragedies, and what he does say is self-contradictory. It would certainly be unjustified on the basis of this to claim that Aristotle thought tragedy should end in death, especially when the tragic plays on which he based his analysis sometimes end in death and sometimes do not, as we shall shortly discover.

But, putting aside the *Poetics,* isn't it reasonable to claim on the basis of everyday experience that suffering and death are essential elements of tragedy? No doubt it is, but my personal feeling — and this is an area where personal feelings cannot be ignored — is that while suffering is indeed an essential aspect of what we call tragedy, death is not, however often it is associated with situations and occurrences we describe as tragic. My reason for saying this is that it is inconceivable that something can be tragic and yet not include human suffering, but that it is perfectly possible to imagine tragic situations that do not involve death. For example, an accident may severely disable someone, damaging not only his body but his life generally: many of us would call such a circumstance tragic, yet it doesn't involve death. To take a different kind of example, we may justifiably describe someone's life as tragic because we recognise that a potentially happy and creative existence has been destroyed by oppressive social and political conditions; again, this does not involve death. We could presumably dramatise these and other kinds of experience in plays that we would be prepared to call tragedies, but they would not necessarily involve death.

The popular idea of tragedy, as I've summarised it, is obviously very inadequate. Not only that, but *any* definition of tragedy which seeks to be universally applicable is likely to be unacceptable because it does not take into account the changing social and historical aspect of tragic experience. It seems that instead of searching for a single, all-embracing description, we need to be more flexible and recognise that the term tragedy can and does include a wide variety of *modes* of tragic experience, even if they share certain characteristic features.

The rest of this chapter will be devoted to identifying some of these modes and their common characteristics. Having begun our enquiry by looking at *Death of a Salesman*, let's now turn to a very different sort of play, from a culture quite unlike that of modern America.

Ozidi

J. P. Clark's *Ozidi* is based on the epic saga of the hero Ozidi, which is narrated and performed among the Ijaw people of the Niger Delta of Nigeria. The play, like the saga, tells the story of how the Council of Orua elects as its king the idiot Temugedege, elder brother of the mighty champion Ozidi, despite the claims of good sense and Ozidi's advice. Having chosen him, they perversely deny their new king the traditional tribute of a human head. Ozidi demands that they pay the proper tribute, and a hunt is arranged, but Ozidi's rivals treacherously ambush and kill him, bringing his head to Temugedege. Ozidi's young wife, Orea, flees to her home town and her mother, the witch Oreame, bearing in her womb Ozidi's son. The rest of the play dramatises the young Ozidi's preparation, under the magical supervision of Oreame, to avenge his father's murder. He kills his father's enemies and other rival champions in a series of epic combats. But in the course of seeking a just revenge, Ozidi oversteps the mark and becomes excessive in his shedding of blood, eventually killing even his beloved grandmother in his blood-lust. He is divinely punished by a visitation from the Smallpox King and his retinue, but is saved by his mother, who acts as if he had merely developed yaws, a common and relatively harmless disease of childhood. Offended at being mistaken for yaws, the Smallpox King and his companions take their leave, and the play ends with a dance of celebration.

As this plot outline suggests, the dramatic world of *Ozidi* is as far removed from that of *Death of a Salesman* as the world of the Ijaw is from that of the average inhabitant of New York City. There is nothing magical or mysterious about Willy Loman's world: his is a representative American life, consumed in acquiring the material accompaniments of commercial success, in his case unsuccessfully. The epic world of *Ozidi*, on the other hand, is populated by heroes and monsters as well as more normal human beings, and is overseen by a variety of supernatural powers which intervene from time to time in human affairs. Willy Loman is an immediately recognisable human character whose imperfections are obvious. The young Ozidi, like his father, is human and imperfect but in an entirely different way from Willy. His is the extraordinary, heroic humanity of the epic champion, of the superman whose power is divinely sanctioned and achieved by supernatural means. And his imperfection is likewise of a different order than Willy's: his excesses are not futile dreams, but the terrible bloodshed of one who is all too well equipped to achieve his desires.

The focus of the two plays is thus quite different. In *Death of a Salesman* the drama centres on Willy's troubled mind and the relationships and conflicts within his family; at the heart of *Ozidi*, on the other hand, is the working-out of a heroic story about a man's treacherous murder and his son's divinely sanctioned quest to gain a just revenge, with its culmination in bloody excess and punishment.

An audience's sense of the tragic in *Death of a Salesman* has to do, as we have seen, with the human waste involved in Willy Loman's intense but deeply misguided attachment to a commercially-based idea of success. If we have a sense of tragedy as we read Clark's play, it is plainly of an altogether different order from that associated with the life and death of Willy Loman. The tragic impact of *Ozidi*, I suggest, emerges from its power *as a story*, a story of epic proportions, and not primarily, as in *Death of a Salesman*, from the dramatization of the characters' psychology and their personal relationships. Of course, the story of Ozidi is not the invention of one man but of an entire people; and it seems safe to assume that it is one of the world's stock of narratives which have a special, deep significance for those who own and love them. To identify the tragic impression of *Ozidi*, then, we need to look closely at the story and try to get a clear idea of its structure and significance.

We are helped in doing this by the dramatist, who has published the original saga and its English translation together with a long introduction in his book *The Ozidi Saga* (Ibadan University Press and Oxford University Press, Nigeria, 1977). In the introduction, Clark outlines the Ijaw world-view, which in its essentials is similar to the traditional world-views of many African (and for that matter, non-African) peoples. There is no sharp dividing line for the Ijaw between the worlds of the living, the dead and the unborn. To die is to be called 'home' by the ancestors, who also regulate the birth of children and oversee the affairs of the living. Those who have lived well and died naturally at a mature age are reserved a place among the ancestors. But someone who has suffered dishonour in life or death must wander in the evil grove until a full rite of purification, usually undertaken by the heir and often taking many years, has been performed. Influencing this constant interchange between the living and the dead are the spirits who inhabit the 'sky, streams, and swamps', as Clark puts it, of the Ijaw homeland: and above all presides the supreme deity, Tamara, 'She Who is the Moulder of All.'

With this in mind, we can see Ozidi's quest to avenge his father as being not just an entertaining story but one that expresses certain essential Ijaw conceptions and beliefs. It is important to see that there is already something wrong in Orua before Ozidi's murder: there is a curse on the city-state which manifests itself in the deaths of six kings in rapid succession. Only Ozidi and his brother are left of their family, and the champion seems to be speaking quite literally when he tells Temugedege that 'having you for a brother I can now see / The curse upon our house' (p. 12). The reason for the curse is known:

> On each mission,
> What message was brought back to Orua except that
> We have enslaved too many,
> Ravished too many lands?
>
> (p. 7)

Ozidi senior has played a crucial part in this sinful onslaught on other peoples (p. 13), and he is generally associated with excess; as a citizen says in connection with his great rage at the absence of tribute to his brother: 'He will not be Ozidi except / He went into excess' (p. 14). His murder should be understood, then, not as an isolated act, but in the context of this general curse: the killing is part of a process, even if we can't yet recognise an overall pattern or meaning in it.

When Ozidi junior seeks out and destroys his father's assassins, he is acting from filial piety and in accordance with the Ijaw moral obligation for a son and heir to seek purification for his dishonoured father, so that he may peacefully join the ancestors. He is aided in his quest for justice by the divine powers through the agency of his grandmother, the witch Oreame. By Act Four, this task has been accomplished: as Orea says to her son: 'Your father is fully avenged, / And after second burial, sleeps well in company / Of his compeers' (p. 90). But Ozidi's rigorous preparation for his mission has marked him in ways he cannot easily throw off. Violence breeds yet more violence: weary with killing, Ozidi must nevertheless murder Tebesonoma's sister and the child for whom she has waited so long because, as Tebesonoma says just before his death, 'except you murder them too, / Twenty years from now, as you did / With your father's assassins, you shall be called to account . . .' (p. 101). The cycle of violence seems destined to be eternally renewed. Like his father before him, Ozidi is now associated with excess, destroying indiscriminately wherever he goes.

The search for justice has thus, with terrible irony, become identified with the evil bloodshed it was meant to redress. The irony extends to Oreame's destruction at the hands of the one she trained in violence. The avenger is now himself to be punished: Tamara withdraws her protection and sends the Smallpox King apparently to destroy the young hero. But help comes to Ozidi from an unexpected source: Orea, who unlike her son and mother has no supernatural powers and no hint of daemonic energies, tends him lovingly and recognises the need for purification of the house now polluted by the wrongful shedding of blood. In keeping with her simple and human nature, she washes her son with common soap and water (p. 120). The Smallpox King withdraws, vowing never to 'Set foot again on this shore' where people have no respect for status. Ozidi, his house and his land have finally been cleansed: after the malice and violence there is now peace and purity, gained through the ordinary love of a mother for her son under the benign supervision of the supreme deity.*

We can now, I think, perceive a basic structure in the story of Ozidi. A general curse is punished by violence and treachery amongst those who have sinned: the son who must take revenge for the sin against his father renews his characteristic sin of excess, thus continuing the cycle of violence and perpetuating the curse. When he is himself about to be punished he is saved by the intervention of simple human love, embodied in his mother and her act of purification, which finally expels evil from the land. There are various subsidiary parallels and contrasts within this overall pattern: our present purpose, however, is not to analyse *Ozidi* exhaustively but to consider it as tragedy. Having established its basic structure, we can now try to answer the question: in what way does it contribute to *Ozidi*'s tragic impact?

Ozidi and the Oresteia

J. P. Clark nowhere describes *Ozidi* as a tragedy; and his discussion of the Ozidi story in *The Ozidi Saga* stresses its epic and heroic qualities. In at least one important respect, moreover, *Ozidi* does not conform to our expectations of tragedy — it ends happily, without the hero dying or even suffering misfortune. I will now suggest in what way J. P. Clark's dramatisation of the Ozidi story is tragic; but to do so we must return to the ancient Greek conception of tragedy — not, however, as it appears in Aristotle but as it emerges from the drama itself.

We have seen that Aristotle contradicted himself about how tragic plays should end. His comments reflect the 'contradictory' nature of the endings of the tragedies he knew and had in mind when he wrote the *Poetics*. It would be a serious mistake to think that all Greek tragedies end unhappily, in death and sorrow. Aristotle praised the happy ending of Euripides' *Iphigenia in Tauris*; he might equally well have drawn attention to the endings of several of Sophocles' plays, such as *Philoctetes*, which ends in the reconciliation of enemies, and *Electra*, in which a son with his sister's help murders his mother and stepfather but which nevertheless, after all this bloody horror, concludes in unambiguous happiness for the murderers. Of course, there are Greek tragedies with quite different endings: no one could possibly describe the conclusion of Sophocles' *King Oedipus*, discussed in Chapter 4 (see pp. 38–46), as 'happy'; Oedipus has discovered his crimes against nature, his mother-wife has committed suicide, he has plucked out his own eyes and is about to be cast out of Thebes. But even in this case it is worth noting that Sophocles wrote a sequel, *Oedipus at Colonus*, in which Oedipus's death is described by a messenger as 'a passing more wonderful than that of any other man': the gods have taken him, and his end is regarded as a miraculous blessing.

There is a saying that the night is darkest just before dawn. Even

---

* It should be noted that Clark's play departs from some versions of the saga in having Oreame killed without being miraculously revived and Ozidi unambiguously cleansed of sin by his mother at the end of the story.

when a tragic play ends in deep darkness, there is usually a counterbalancing anticipation of the dawn, of the light that heralds a new beginning after the long night of suffering. To move away from Greek tragedy for a moment, there is no doubt that Shakespeare's *King Lear* presents extreme suffering and the 'dark' side of human nature in its most terrible form. At the end, Lear and Cordelia are dead, and the state has almost been destroyed. But the forces of evil have also been vanquished, and there has been a kind of affirmation of the power of love in the reunion between the purified Lear and the daughter he so unjustly banished. Bleak as it is, there is a kind of restoration or purification — a light in the darkness — at the end of *King Lear*.

We have seen that tragic experience in real life need not involve death. We have now also seen that there are plays commonly called tragedies which even end happily, and that in others, like *King Lear*, the bleakness may be tempered by an affirmative note, a hint — even if it is only a hint — of restoration. We will now explore further this affirmative quality and its implications for our understanding of tragedy by concentrating attention briefly on one Greek play — or, more accurately, one long drama comprised of three linked plays (a trilogy). This is the *Oresteia* by Aeschylus, one of the earliest Greek tragedies and the only surviving example of the tragic trilogy, the form in which the Greeks originally conceived tragedy. More than any other play, the *Oresteia* permits us a view of the tragic pattern in its fullest, most detailed form, as one of the greatest Greek tragic dramatists conceived it. What is especially interesting for us is that in its subject matter and — more importantly — in the essential shape of the story there are striking similarities between the *Oresteia* and *Ozidi*.

The first play of the trilogy, *Agamemnon*, shows the murder by Queen Clytemnestra and her lover Aegisthus of her husband, King Agamemnon, on his return from the Trojan War. In the second play, *The Libation-Bearers*, Orestes, the son of Agamemnon and Clytemnestra, who had been smuggled out of Argos as a child by his sister, returns to fulfil the god Apollo's command that he should avenge his father by murdering his mother and Aegisthus, who together now rule the city-state. Orestes is reunited with his sister Electra, who has continued to defy her mother and stepfather, and with the help of the Chorus they plot, and Orestes performs, the murders. The final play of the trilogy, *The Eumenides*, opens with a priestess at Apollo's temple discovering with horror the blood-stained Orestes crouching at the altar surrounded by his fiendish pursuers, the Furies. Apollo sends Orestes to Athens, while the ghost of Clytemnestra reproaches the Furies for letting their prey escape. Apollo drives them away, telling them that Orestes has gone to Athens to seek judgment from the goddess Athene at her temple. Athene hears the pleas of both Orestes and the Furies and summons a court of the wisest citizens. The jury votes, but there is a deadlock. Athene casts her deciding vote in favour of Orestes and he leaves the court a free man. Athene persuades the Furies to relent, and the play ends in a great procession.

There is an obvious similarity in subject between the *Oresteia* and *Ozidi*. Both are stories of a son's divinely-ordained revenge for a father's treacherous murder, and of the suffering and punishment which he must endure as a consequence. But the similarity goes beyond the subject matter, extending to the basic shape or pattern of the dramatic plots. In both there is an intial curse, associated in Aeschylus with a crime of Agamemnon's father and in *Ozidi* with the excessive violence by the people of Orua against their neighbours, in which Ozidi has prominently figured. Treacherous and sinful though their murders are, Agamemnon and Ozidi senior are themselves implicated in sin and the spilling of blood, and their deaths can be interpreted as punishments for actions offending the divine powers. The sons, in both plays, grow to manhood acutely conscious of their mission to avenge their fathers: both do so, fulfilling their filial obligations and their functions as agents of divine justice. But there is in both cases the same terrible irony. The purifier himself comes to be in need of purification. Both Orestes and Ozidi, in the course of observing the 'law' of revenge, contravene another, equally grave 'law': Orestes commits the terrible crime of matricide and Ozidi kills excessively, even murdering his own grandmother. Both are visited by a terrible avenger (the Furies and the Smallpox King and his retinue), and both are made to suffer. But before the ultimate punishment can be extracted both are pardoned, the curse is finally expiated and the cycle of violence concluded. Both plays end with a celebratory procession.

We are now, by a rather roundabout route, in a position to begin answering the question asked earlier: in what way does the structure of the Ozidi story as dramatised by J. P. Clark contribute to its tragic impact? It does so in essentially the same way as the story of Orestes creates a tragic impression, by presenting an action in which a cycle of evil, violence and suffering is eventually concluded and an act of purification marks a new beginning. Never mind that both plays end happily. If the *Oresteia* does not deserve the name tragedy then no play does. *Ozidi* is a tragedy in that it dramatises the same fundamental pattern of evil, suffering and purification that we find in Aeschylus's tragic trilogy.

We are only beginning to answer our question, of course: we must now go further, both in bringing out the affinities between the ancient Greek play and the modern African one, and in showing the bearing this resemblance has on our search for an adequate conception of tragedy.

The tragic dilemma

We have identified a common pattern of action in our two plays. A crucial part of this pattern has to do with the dilemma in which the hero finds himself. All.drama presents conflicts and dilemmas of some kind. What is so distinctive about the dilemmas experienced by Orestes and Ozidi? It has to do, I think, with the fact that, in the course of correcting a wrong, they both inevitably commit another wrong. Orestes cannot help but commit matricide if he is to avenge his father's murder; and Ozidi cannot help but become excessively violent after being trained in violence from his earliest youth. This suggests that there are certain conflicts or dilemmas which are unresolvable except through severe suffering, even though the suffering may eventually lead to purification and peace, as happens in both our plays.

It is this kind of dilemma which I suggest characteristically faces the tragic hero. It can be contrasted with the sort of dilemma that we usually find in comedies, which can normally be resolved in a clear-cut way. For example, Ananse has the dilemma of making his plan work without being found out in *The Marriage of Anansewa*. He succeeds in doing so through the device of Anansewa's mock-death, and thus advances himself socially and marries off his daughter to the man she wants. There is no question, in this or most other comedies, of the protagonist becoming entangled in a dilemma that cannot be resolved except through the endurance of severe suffering.

In societies where religion is a living force the resolution of the tragic dilemma is frequently associated with, and depends to a large degree upon, the will of the gods. Orestes is finally released from his dilemma by the goddess Athene; Ozidi is saved by his gentle and very human mother, but under the benevolent auspices of the supreme deity, Tamara. But what about tragedies written in cultures where religion is no longer so powerful a force? This brings us back to *Death of a Salesman*, which was written by a dramatist and for an audience for whom the supernatural is not a living reality as it was for Aeschylus and for J. P. Clark's Ijaw people. Isn't *Death of a Salesman* fundamentally different from the other two plays — in having an unhappy rather than a happy ending, in being non-religious whereas the others have a religious underpinning, in being more 'psychological' in its interest than either the *Oresteia* or *Ozidi*, in not having the triumphant and 'heroic' hero of the Greek and African plays? Despite their evident differences I believe it is possible to detect an underlying similarity between the three plays. And that similarity has to do with the nature of the tragic dilemma faced by our three protagonists.

Willy Loman is caught in a terrible trap ultimately of his own making. He cannot achieve the kind of self-awareness that would permit him to cast off his false dreams and values. But his consciousness of failure is sufficiently strong for him to be capable of a desperate last effort to fulfil his aspirations. Allowing for the very different nature of the characters, and the very different situations in which they find themselves, there is a basic resemblance between Willy's dilemma and those of Orestes and Ozidi. Each is like a man at a crossroads, who does not know which way to turn and for whom, being who and what he is, any direction would somehow be wrong. To do what he considers 'good' Willy — being the kind of man he is — cannot help but be destructive, just as Orestes couldn't help but kill his mother to avenge his father and Ozidi couldn't help but become an indiscriminate murderer despite originally being the agent of divine justice.

Different as they are, then, in their subjects and in the historical and cultural realities and values they reflect, our three plays can be seen to have an underlying similarity in the kind of dilemma or conflict they dramatize. This involves a stalemate or deadlock, in which a 'good' action inevitably — and we must stress the inevitability — has 'bad' consequences; or, as in the case of Willy Loman, the admirable qualities of a man, such as his love for his children, cause suffering and destruction. Nothing is simple or straightforward in this dilemma: the tragic hero lives in a world of often terrifying complexity, being acted upon by powers — or himself producing forces — which he can barely understand, let alone control. The 'good' and the 'bad' are inextricably linked, so that it is a problem even telling one from the other; and what, from one point of view, is admirable in a man may from another be a crime for which he cannot escape guilt.

The scope of tragedy

We have now formulated what seems to be a defining characteristic of tragic drama, linking plays which are otherwise very different. Keeping this concept of the tragic dilemma in mind, let us now try to elaborate and extend our ideas about tragedy, and in the process get a sense of the scope of tragic drama, especially in Africa.

I have just said that what can make a man admirable from one point of view can make him a guilty criminal from another. Guilt seems, in fact, to be a condition characteristic of the tragic hero. To be guilty, of course, there must be responsibility; and for a person to be responsible for what he does, he must have had the freedom to choose between at least two distinct courses of action. The fact that of the two courses both are 'evil' (or at least involve what is felt to be an evil), or equally compounded of 'good' and 'evil', makes no difference. The tragic hero must still choose and he is held responsible for his decision. Willy Loman is a victim of his society and its general moral failure; but he is an *active* rather than a merely passive victim, who has contributed to his terrible dilemma and his sons' failure. Willy is ultimately responsible, for he has all along been free to reject the false values dominant in his society. J. P. Clark merely confirms our dramatic awareness of Ozidi's responsibility for his crimes of excess when he remarks that 'characters, though aided by oracles and gods and other supernatural forces, remain complete agents of themselves' (*The Ozidi Saga*, p. xxxiv). This insistence in tragic drama on the hero's responsibility and guilt can be baffling, for it is sometimes hard to see in what way the character was ever free to choose.

This is especially true of Greek tragedy. It is significant, for example, that Orestes is actually put on trial, and not simply let off by Athene. This suggests that the goddess who here embodies justice does indeed believe he has a case to answer, and that he has been responsible for his actions. Orestes is finally freed: not so Oedipus in Sophocles' *King Oedipus*, though it is difficult to appreciate what the Greeks evidently felt was that character's personal responsibility for his terrible deeds. When he adapted the Oedipus story into a Nigerian setting in *The Gods Are Not To Blame*, Ola Rotimi made his Oedipus-figure, King Odewale, a hero with a much more obvious 'flaw' than he has in Sophocles — his quickness to rash anger. In doing so he created a more straightforward and perhaps more comprehensible tragic impact; but one may also feel that in following so closely an explicitly 'Aristotelian' notion of tragedy, he weakened the *mysterious* nature of Oedipus's guilt, which is so important a part of the Greek play's lasting appeal.

We said earlier, in relation to Willy Loman, that we are made to sympathise and identify with the tragic protagonist, not necessarily by straightforwardly putting ourselves in his position but by experiencing his sufferings as a threat to our shared humanity. This is true, I suggest, even though we are made to feel that the tragic hero is a guilty man. And this in turn seems to indicate that his guilt is of such a kind that the audience can imaginatively participate in it, that we can feel that we are at least potentially guilty in the same way. Extreme as Oedipus's dilemma is, and however obscure the issue of his moral responsibility, there is no doubt that he accepts fully his personal guilt; and in identifying with him in his guilt we seem to be tacitly acknowledging that what has befallen Oedipus could befall us all.

Our sense of the pervasive guilt of the tragic hero brings us to the relationship between the human world and the supernatural in tragedy. For in much tragic drama the hero's dilemma and his guilt exist in relation to the obligations he owes his god or gods. It was, after all, the gods who doomed Oedipus to do what he did, and it was the god Apollo who commanded Orestes to avenge his father by murdering his mother and stepfather. Divine power is less readily discernible by either the characters or the audiences of Shakespeare's tragic plays, but Hamlet's observation that 'There's a divinity that shapes our ends, Rough-hew them how we will' (V.ii.10–11) can be applied to Shakespearean tragedy generally. In *Doctor Faustus*, by Shakespeare's contemporary Christopher Marlowe, the tragic conflict within Faustus is specifically between his worldly ambitions, which have caused him to sell his soul to the Devil, and his awareness of the inevitable divine retribution that will come if he pursues these ambitions. In Greek tragedy, especially, the relationship between the worlds of the human and the divine is further intensified by the fact that in many cases the central characters are gods or, when human, semi-divine, so that their power goes beyond that of mere mortals. Even in Christian tragedy the hero's powers are characteristically beyond common reach. The protagonists of tragedy tend to be, literally, extraordinary in their capacities, aspirations and sufferings. We have a sense of man's great, even terrible energies, which allow him to be both immensely creative and destructive, sometimes at the same time. Even that 'common' tragic hero, Willy Loman, is exceptional: how many ordinary men or women pursue their dreams and hopes with his kind of fanaticism?

During the last hundred years or so in the West active faith in the divine has greatly diminished, and as we shall soon see this process has contributed to the development of a new mode or modes of tragedy. In Africa, however, belief in the spirit world and its crucial influence on every aspect of everyday human life continues to be of the greatest significance, and this is reflected in the subjects, themes and ideological perspectives of much African tragedy. As we have seen, Ozidi, though he has free will, performs his actions under the gaze of Tamara, the supreme goddess of the Ijaw, who controls the distribution of reward and punishment as she sees fit. Like some of the heroes of Greek tragedy both Ozidis are godlike men: they are extraordinarily strong, a strength made even greater by magical powers; and like their Greek counterparts they seem to embody both the highest point of human aspiration and capability and the greatest potential for failure and suffering. The same great range of human potentiality, presented in a context which embraces both the human and divine, is apparent in the tragedies of Clark's

fellow-Nigerian, Wole Soyinka. More than any other African dramatist
Soyinka in his tragic drama explores the passages connecting the human
and the spirit worlds. And central to the highly personal adaptation of
traditional Yoruba mythology which Soyinka employs in his exploration
is the figure of the god Ogun. Like the god-heroes of Greek tragedy and
Ozidi in Clark's play, Ogun embodies that great energy which permits
both awesome creativity *and* destructiveness; and like them also, he
unites the human and supernatural realms in his person, for it was Ogun,
in Soyinka's poetic mythology, who led the other gods down to earth to be
reunited with man. Such characters as Eman in *The Strong Breed*, which
we looked at in detail earlier (see Chapter 6), and Olunde in *Death and the
King's Horseman* can be seen as Ogun-figures, whose tragic function it is
to bridge the 'gulf of transition' between the different areas of experience,
the worlds of the living, the dead and the unborn.

The importance of man's relationship with the spirit world in
African tragedy is illustrated in a rather different way in *Kinjeketile*, by
the Tanzanian dramatist Ebrahim Hussein. Based on the historical reality
of the Maji Maji rising, the action of the play shows how a peasant,
Kinjeketile, unites the divided and antagonistic tribes through his
declaration that the spirit Hongo has given them blessed water (*maji*)
which will make them invulnerable in their rebellion against the German
colonisers. The tragic dilemma lies in the fact that, though it is only
because of Kinjeketile's mystically-inspired 'word' that there can be
sufficient unity to combat the colonialists effectively, the 'word' itself may
be unreliable and could lead to destruction. Kinjeketile suffers agonies
of uncertainty about it and wants to postpone the uprising until he is
certain: but he has given birth to a word, and it has grown 'bigger than the
man who gave it birth' (p. 30). And even when the rebellion ends in
disaster, with thousands of his followers dead, Kinjeketile refuses to say
that the water was a lie:

> The moment I say that, people in the north, south, east and west will
> stop fighting. They will fall into hopeless despair — they will give up.
> I will not say that! A word has been born. Our children will tell their
> children about this word. Our great grand-children will hear of it.
> One day the word will cease to be a dream, it will be a reality!
> (p. 53)

In *Kinjeketile* man's relation with the spirit world has been
thematically interwoven with another, equally crucial, African reality —
the struggle for political freedom and national liberation. For some
dramatists writing in Africa today, tragedy can exist without the gods or
God, in the form of the struggle of ordinary men and women to make
their world a better one. In defence of his conception of tragedy in *Death
of a Salesman* Arthur Miller remarked that the most ordinary 'man in the
street' can 'outdistance' the President of the U.S.A. as a tragic figure,
provided that his life engages those questions 'whose answers define
humanity'. The aspiration towards political freedom is surely one of these
humanity-defining issues, and the clear and deep connections between
tragedy and revolution in the modern world are nowhere more apparent
than in Africa. In *Kinjeketile* the lives of ordinary Africans are seen to be
engaged with the struggle for freedom, with the overwhelming desire, as

Miller puts it, to 'live so that the world is a home. . . .'.

The same is true of another East African play, *The Trial of Dedan Kimathi*, by Ngugi wa Thiong'o and Micere Mugo. Hostile to religion, this play nevertheless makes extensive use as we have seen, of religious imagery (see Chapter 5, pp. 71–73), and presents Dedan Kimathi himself as a kind of political Christ-figure, the saviour of the Kenyan people. Considered as a tragedy (it will be viewed in a different perspective, as melodrama, in the next chapter), the play dramatises the as yet unresolved conflict between the national liberation movement and the forces of colonialism and neo-colonialism. The great suffering which accompanies this conflict is dramatically concentrated in the person of Dedan Kimathi. He is presented as a tragic martyr, torn between his humane desire to be merciful to his nearest and dearest, despite their shortcomings, and the demands of revolutionary discipline; and we are shown him being subjected to a series of temptations intended to nullify his influence over the revolutionary struggle. Again, the tragic hero's life is perceived as being inseparably linked to a momentous issue; and though it is in a quite different way from, say, Ozidi, we also witness the godlike nature and powers of Dedan Kimathi. If tragedy emphasises the extraordinary powers of its heroes, so also does it dramatise them in extreme situations, which epitomise issues of the greatest significance. The situations of *Ozidi*, for example, are conceived as reflecting permanent and universal aspects of human existence, whereas in *Kinjeketile* and *The Trial of Dedan Kimathi* they are historical and political. Kimathi's trial, for instance, is presented as a kind of summation of the historical confrontation between imperialism and its enemies.

The conflict between colonialism and imperialism on the one hand and the movement for national liberation on the other has been at its most intense and tragic in South Africa. In such plays as *Sizwe Bansi Is Dead*, Athol Fugard and his collaborators John Kani and Winston Ntshona have dramatised the sufferings of individuals in a society tragically deformed by racial oppression. The black South African writer Lewis Nkosi, in his play *The Rhythm of Violence*, aspires to show how the violence of the white régime inevitably spawns a violent reaction. Caught in an intractable dilemma, torn between his personal feelings and the demands of violent political struggle, Tula is physically destroyed while his white friend, the innocent Sarie, is arrested by the South African police for sedition.

But the tragic treatment of social conflict is not restricted, in African drama, to the struggle between Africans and their white colonisers. In *The Black Hermit*, for example, Ngugi wa Thiong'o (James Ngugi) anticipates his denunciation of neo-colonialism, and black collusion in it, in *The Trial of Dedan Kimathi*. He shows his hero caught, in the post-Independence period, between the allegiance he is expected — and in some ways believes himself — to owe to his group and his personal loyalty to a national vision. Remi comes back from his self-imposed exile in the city 'to break Tribe and Custom', but he is himself broken and so is his innocent wife Thoni. And in plays otherwise as dissimilar as Ama Ata Aidoo's *Anowa*, Efua Sutherland's *Edufa*, and John Ruganda's *The Burdens*, the various ways in which people can be destroyed by the pressures of their society are tragically presented.

But our purpose here is not to survey exhaustively the entire field of African tragic drama. Enough has been said to establish the main point, that African tragedy displays a wide range of subject, form and underlying world-view, just as tragedy has always tended to do in other cultures and ages. And yet, within this variety (and of course the varied degrees of success with which tragedy has been realised in particular plays), it is both possible and useful to discern certain underlying characteristics which tend to recur in some form or other in virtually every play that has some claim to belong to the genre of tragedy.

Tragedy, comedy and tragi-comedy

It is common to think of tragedy and comedy as opposites. Tragedy is supposed to be everything comedy is not: serious, full of pain and suffering, concerned with violence and death, displaying the human potential for weakness and error but also its capacity to be heroic, even in defeat.

The fact is, however, that these supposedly characteristic features of tragedy are also essential features of comedy. For comedy, as we have seen, is also concerned, in its own way, with the 'dark' side of life: we witness suffering, weakness, violence in tragedy and we experience the tragic emotions; we witness them in comedy and we laugh. This is surely sufficient proof that tragedy and comedy stand in the closest possible relationship to each other. And if further proof were required, it could be drawn from the circumstances of their birth and early development. Dramatic tragedy and comedy came into being in ancient Athens within a very short time of each other — close enough, in fact, for us to be able to think of them as twins, even if, as sometimes happens, there was a short wait before the second twin emerged. And we also know that the performance of the early tragic trilogies was habitually followed by the performance of a comic play, the 'satyr' play, which was apparently regarded as an essential complement to the tragedy.

Instead of regarding them as mutually exclusive, as separate kinds of drama, we would do better to see comedy and tragedy as complementary. Nor need it surprise us to discover features associated with both genres co-existing within the same play. Shakespeare's *King Lear* includes the comedy of the Fool as well as the anguish of Lear; and the comedy is not separate but part of an overall tragic effect of great power and complexity. There is a difference, however, between this traditional coexistence of the tragic and the comic within a single play and the kind of modern drama known as tragi-comedy. Let us conclude our discussion in this chapter by looking a little more closely at this drama which seems to combine tragedy and comedy in a distinctively new way.

Tragic and comic elements are blended in a play like *Waiting For Godot*, written soon after the Second World War by the Irish dramatist Samuel Beckett, so as to produce a quite different effect from the co-existence of tragedy and comedy in *King Lear* or the porter scene of *Macbeth*. To state it as succinctly as possible, the comedy of *Waiting For Godot* does not contribute to a total effect that is immediately recognisable as tragic in any of its traditional or established modes. Rather, it *modifies*, and more specifically *undercuts*, a recognisably tragic impression. It is as though the tragic impulse of Beckett's play were being subverted by its comic impulse. And the result is a play that we hesitate to name either as a tragedy or as a comedy since it departs too radically from the traditional impression created by either.

We can illustrate the point from the end of *Waiting For Godot*. Two tramps, Vladimir and Estragon (whose nicknames for each other are Didi and Gogo), have been waiting throughout the play for the arrival of a character named Godot. Neither has ever met Godot, nor are they sure that they will recognise him when, and if, he shows up. But he doesn't come, though a boy claiming to be from Godot twice appears to promise his impending arrival. The two tramps seem to be doomed to go on waiting for Godot, who they think will somehow change their lives for the better, though they have no idea how or why this should be so. Here are the final moments of the play:

> *Estragon draws Vladimir towards the tree. They stand motionless before it. Silence.*

ESTRAGON: Why don't we hang ourselves?
VLADIMIR: With what?
ESTRAGON: You haven't got a bit of rope?
VLADIMIR: No.
ESTRAGON: Then we can't.
VLADIMIR: Let's go.
ESTRAGON: Wait, there's my belt.
VLADIMIR: It's too short.
ESTRAGON: You could hang on to my legs.
VLADIMIR: And who'd hang on to mine?
ESTRAGON: True.
VLADIMIR: Show all the same. [*Estragon loosens the cord that holds up his trousers which, much too big for him, fall about his ankles. They look at the cord.*] That might do at a pinch. But is it strong enough?
ESTRAGON: We'll soon see. Here.
They each take an end of the cord and pull. It breaks. They almost fall.
VLADIMIR: Not worth a curse.
Silence.
ESTRAGON: You say we have to come back tomorrow?
VLADIMIR: Yes.
ESTRAGON: Then we can bring a good bit of rope.
VLADIMIR: Yes.
Silence.
ESTRAGON: Didi.
VLADIMIR: Yes.
ESTRAGON: I can't go on like this.
VLADIMIR: That's what you think.
ESTRAGON: If we parted? That might be better for us.
VLADIMIR: We'll hang ourselves tomorrow. [*Pause.*] Unless Godot comes.

ESTRAGON:	And if he comes?
VLADIMIR:	We'll be saved.

Vladimir takes off his hat (Lucky's) peers inside it, feels about inside it, shakes it, knocks on the crown, puts it on again.

ESTRAGON:	Well? Shall we go?
VLADIMIR:	Pull on your trousers.
ESTRAGON:	What?
VLADIMIR:	Pull on your trousers.
ESTRAGON:	You want me to pull off my trousers?
VLADIMIR:	Pull ON your trousers.
ESTRAGON:	[*realizing his trousers are down.*] True.

He pulls up his trousers. Silence.

VLADIMIR:	Well? Shall we go?
ESTRAGON:	Yes, let's go.

They do not move.

CURTAIN

The dialogue is mainly about suicide. Underlying it is the deep despair that makes Estragon cry out: 'I can't go on like this.' For the tramps to kill themselves now would presumably be felt by many spectators to be an appropriate ending for a tragedy, though for a reason I shall mention in a moment it is doubtful whether their deaths would be enough to persuade the audience that they were involved in a genuinely tragic experience. But in any event their suicides do not transpire, not because they weaken in their intention but because the actual mechanics of the operation defeat them. Instead of being shocked at witnessing a despair so total that the characters calculatingly commit suicide, we witness their ludicrous attempt to find a suitable rope, culminating in Estragon losing his trousers. They promise that they will hang themselves tomorrow – as if this was a consolation, a hope of something better – but in the meantime Vladimir has to remind his companion to pull up his trousers, which he has forgotten are still around his ankles.

It is not that tragic experience is simply giving way to comedy in this episode. What most of us would be prepared to call tragedy is there, in the terrible despair of the characters, and in their desperate yearning for someone who never comes. But this tragic aspect is made to co-exist with 'low' comedy, the tramps' inadvertent clowning. We witness suffering without recognisable heroism, pain without nobility of the kind we expect from the traditional hero of tragedy. And even if Beckett had shown the tramps suicide it would probably not have made any essential difference to our response, because this blend of comedy and tragedy, of suffering and clowning, has characterised the entire play.

The particular kind of tragi-comic effect Beckett achieves in *Waiting For Godot* and his other plays is of course peculiar to him. But there is no doubt that a great deal of modern Western drama might be described as tragi-comedy, and that to a greater or lesser extent the characteristically modern tragi-comic effect is produced by the portrayal of pain and suffering without an accompanying sense of the heroism of those afflicted, and without a sense of the ultimate significance of their affliction. No purification, no regeneration occur; there may not even be

The South African actors John Kani and Winston Ntshona as the tramps in Waiting For Godot.

the sense of hopelessly misguided heroism of the sort we find in Willy Loman. Rather, there is a consciousness of futility without end, of a tomorrow no better than today and possibly even worse.

It is tempting, but dangerous, to generalise. But one final point is worth making. I mentioned earlier that active religious faith has diminished, especially among educated people, in the West during the past century or so. For many Western intellectuals and writers, God is dead — or was never alive. This loss of faith is, arguably, the single most influential factor in the development of tragi-comedy. The feeling that, since there is no God, there is no inherent meaning in existence or the suffering that is part of it; the feeling that it is virtually impossible for there to be heroism in the modern world — these are characteristic qualities of much modern Western thought and art. The decline of religion does not necessarily produce a view of life like Samuel Beckett's: it may lead, for example, to the humanistic Marxism of Bertolt Brecht in such plays as *The Good Woman of Setzuan* and *The Caucasian Chalk Circle*.

This means that modern tragi-comedy has taken a variety of forms, the world-views underlying which differ considerably and may even be in conflict with each other. It may even be time to stop using the term tragi-comedy for this variegated drama, and to recognise that, different though it is from traditional tragic modes, it constitutes the ways in which modern Western man perceives and articulates his sense of tragedy. Tragi-comedy, in other words, is merely the dominant modern form — or more correctly, forms — of tragedy. It will be interesting in the years ahead to see whether African dramatists are influenced by Western

141

tragi-comedy and develop their own forms of it, which they have so far shown little or no inclination to do; or whether, as African societies change, new and distinctive forms of African tragedy will emerge.

9 Melodrama

'Melodrama' and its adjective 'melodramatic' are terms not nearly so widely used in ordinary life as 'tragedy' and 'tragic', 'comedy' and 'comic'. There is not the same general sense of melodrama as a type of drama certain basic features of which are also evident in the non-dramatic situations, persons and attitudes of real life. Nor is the term so commonly used by playgoers and readers to designate a distinct sort of play. This suggests that melodrama is not as prominent or distinctive a kind of drama as tragedy and comedy. But it would be entirely wrong to draw such a conclusion. For melodrama is actually the dominant, most popular dramatic form of our time, in Africa as elsewhere, and it reflects a most distinctive and pervasive view of life. We need to identify the characteristic effects of melodrama; to do so let us look again at a play we have already discussed in other contexts, *The Trial of Dedan Kimathi*, by Ngugi wa Thiong'o and Micere Mugo.

Identifying melodrama

When we considered the importance of stage directions earlier (see Ch. 2, pp. 13–20), we examined the first few moments of *The Trial of Dedan Kimathi* and saw that it opens with a series of enactments or *tableaux* depicting the history of oppression of black people. There is the sound of drums and singing in the darkness, then a shot rings out followed by screams, groans and the crack of whips. In the twilight we watch the selling of blacks into slavery, their transportation across the sea, their toiling on the plantation. Then the mood changes: an *'angry procession of defiant blacks'* chants slogans and sings of freedom. The sound of machine-gun fire interrupts, and as the stage lights come up we see running figures, and specifically two Mau Mau guerillas carrying machine guns. The 'darkness' of slavery and oppression has now given way to the 'dawn' of the liberation struggle, which we are reminded has not yet ended. This opening sets the rest of the action in a specific historical perspective and also helps determine our attitude to the drama of Dedan Kimathi: we will see it, in short, as part of a long struggle by black people for freedom. At the end, there is a return to, and continuation of, the opening enactment: once more there is darkness, a loud shot is heard, and then the stage lights come up to reveal a large crowd of workers and peasants thunderously singing their freedom song.

Skilfully performed, the end of *The Trial of Dedan Kimathi* would doubtless be an emotional experience for most members of an African audience. If we look a little more closely at the play's final moments we can see what emotions are likely to be involved and how they are aroused. The final scene is set in the courtroom. On one side are the blacks, on the other the whites and their black collaborators, the betrayers of Dedan Kimathi, who stands in chains before the white judge. The woman guerilla, whose attempts to free Dedan we have been following during the play, enters the court; but she is recognised and led out, though as she goes she fills the courtroom with her rendering of the freedom song. The Boy and Girl take their places, watched by Kimathi, who in reply to the court's verdict of guilty makes a long, defiant speech rejecting its legality and asserting that the anti-imperialist struggle will continue until freedom is achieved. The judge pronounces the death sentence on Kimathi and as everyone rises the Boy and Girl come forward, break the loaf of bread and bring forth the gun concealed inside. It is at this moment that darkness falls, the shot rings out and then the lights come up to reveal the crowd singing the song of freedom.

There are at least three very powerful emotions likely to be stimulated in an attentive, engaged audience by this scene. One is great indignation, amounting to hatred, for the white representatives of imperialism and their black stooges; this is a feeling which is likely to be felt most strongly when the judge sentences Kimathi to death. Another is an equally powerful feeling of compassion and admiration as we watch Kimathi standing before the judge in his chains, the heroic martyr betrayed by his own people. And thirdly, there are the stirring emotions of rebellion and defiance, created by the scene —indeed the play —as a whole and specifically brought out by the woman's singing of the freedom song, by Dedan's speeches of defiance and exhortation, and by the intervention of the Boy and Girl and the closing, thunderously sung, hymn to freedom. These emotional reactions, which have been developing through the play, reach a powerful climax in this final scene, and culminate in the feeling of victorious defiance and the celebration of hard-won freedom.

The audience's emotional response is a vital element in comedy and tragedy. At the end of *The Marriage of Anansewa* we are — or at least are supposed to be — in a joyful, celebratory mood: the revelation of the full truth about King Oedipus and its aftermath make the final moments of Sophocles' play a richly emotional experience. There is nothing out of the ordinary, then, about the Kenyan play arousing emotions in its audience, or even about those emotions being so strong. What does set *The Trial of Dedan Kimathi* somewhat apart from the other two plays just mentioned is the way the dramatists emphasise the emotional aspect of their subject, encouraging us — indeed, manipulating us — into reacting in an emotionally extreme manner. It is this element of calculated manipulation, and manipulation of very specific emotions, which distinguishes Ngugi and Mugo's play. The difference should not be exaggerated — it is one of emphasis rather than of kind. But it is there, and it suggests that the dramatists' main aim was to make the audience leave the theatre in the grip of certain very strong emotions.

It is not only the conclusion of *The Trial of Dedan Kimathi* that is so emotive, though it is the point where the emotional impact is deliberately at its most heightened. From beginning to end, the play is full of situations, dialogue and images that arouse strong feelings in the audience. The opening *tableaux* constitute one example, arousing an African audience's feelings about slavery and the exploitation of black people. The betrayal of Dedan Kimathi is another. And we have already seen how the dramatists deliberately use religious imagery to reinforce the meaning and emotional impact of their portrayal of Kimathi's career.

The emotionalism of *The Trial of Dedan Kimathi* — the recognition that its striking impact on our feelings is a dramatic end in itself — is a first step to understanding the nature of melodrama. For it is characteristic of melodrama that it strives to create as strong an emotional impression as possible on its audience. But it is only a beginning, not sufficient in itself to mark off melodrama as a distinct genre from comedy and tragedy. We need to go further in identifying the characteristic tendencies of melodramatic plays. We can do so by asking: what is the purpose of the emotionalism of *The Trial of Dedan Kimathi?*

It is not too difficult to see what Ngugi and Mugo were trying to do when they wrote their play. They evidently wished to rekindle the spirit of revolutionary struggle, which they see as being embodied in Dedan Kimathi, among their audience. Through the prominence of Kimathi's betrayers and the 'temptations' offered him by his fellow blacks, the writers make it apparent that they believe the Kenyan bourgeoisie to be serving the interests of imperialism and oppressing the masses. The play is saying that the Kenyan masses have achieved nationhood but not genuine national liberation. The emotionalism of the drama is closely connected with this message, and the dramatists' aim in stating it. They want to influence the social and political thinking of their audiences; and the stimulus to do so is to make them feel, very strongly, their continuing exploitation and the heroism of Dedan Kimathi in fighting against it.

The manipulation of the audience's emotions in *The Trial of Dedan Kimathi* is linked, then, with its social and political function. More specifically, it supports the writers' desire to show the struggle between the forces of good and evil in Kenyan society. There can be no mistake about it: Kimathi and his followers represent goodness, and the allies of imperialism, white and black, represent evil. We are made to feel admiration and compassion for Kimathi; and, equally strongly, we are encouraged to feel contempt and hatred for his enemies. The play's emotionalism and its dramatisation of a clear-cut conflict between good and evil are inseparably connected.

The emotional impact of the Kenyan play —even the elements of manipulation and 'extremism' in its emotional effects —are not enough to set it definitively apart as belonging to a distinct *kind* of drama. What does, I suggest, is the way its intense emotionalism is related to the depiction of the struggle between a clearly identifiable good and an equally clearly defined evil. Melodrama makes us feel, and typically we feel sympathy and admiration for the hero or heroine and contempt and fear for the villain(s). The battle between good and evil is always fiercely waged in melodrama, and it is always embodied in characters who are unambiguously virtuous or wicked, like Kimathi on the one hand and Shaw Henderson on the other in our play. When characters are ethically so easily identifiable, virtue and vice are presented as being real and immediately recognisable forces in human existence. We see Virtue before our very eyes as it is persecuted by Vice, in the unmistakable form of the villain. And we are invited to experience a number of simple but deep emotions as we witness goodness in adversity and its eventual recovery and triumph over evil.

Having identified the characteristic combination of intense emotional feeling and clear-cut moral antagonism in melodrama, we can now proceed to look in more detail at its distinctive features, and to consider the variety of forms and functions associated with it. Before we do so, however, let us relate what has so far been said about melodrama on the stage to our everyday experience and our usual ways of perceiving reality. This should contribute further to our understanding of the basic nature of melodrama, and will help us appreciate its importance and popularity as a kind of drama.

The melodramatic vision

Much of our routine existence and our perception of it belongs to the realm of melodrama. How, and why, is this the case?

Here is a day in the life of Mr A, who is a clerk in the offices of a private company. On this particular day, Mr A has decided, he will ask his boss for a pay increase: rent, food, clothes and life's other essentials have been getting dearer all the time, so that he is now beginning to get into debt whereas he could once even save a little out of his wage. As he waits at the bus stop he is in a bad mood. He strongly suspects that his boss will deny him any increase. He is also irritated because, as usual, the bus is late, which will make him late in arriving at the office — and this will no doubt be noticed and used by his boss as a reason for not giving him more money. 'This country's going from bad to worse,' he thinks. 'Where will it end? Nothing works any more and everything is dearer. They [he is thinking of his boss and everyone else who is better off than himself, all of whom he groups together and calls 'they' or 'them'] — they are all right with their big salaries and fancy cars. But what about the rest of us? How are we going to survive?' He eventually gets to his office, where his lateness is indeed noticed; and after an hour or two Mr A summons up the courage to go to the manager and make his request. To his surprise, his boss hears him out and then, instead of immediately saying no, tells Mr A to come back just before closing time, when he will have thought about it and made his decision.

Mr A spends the rest of the day in a state of growing agitation. Why did his boss not turn him down straightaway? Why does he need all day to think about it? Mr A becomes increasingly convinced than an unpleasant surprise awaits him at the end of the day — that not only will he not get his pay increase, but that he is going to be sacked. He is not sure why he thinks this; it is merely a terrible feeling he has in his bones. He imagines his boss's words: 'I'm sorry, but these are hard times for us all. We can no longer afford you. And to be quite frank, we can do without you. You regularly arrive late for work — even this morning, after which you had the cheek to come to me asking for more money. And when you're here you're a notorious time-waster. And you can't deny that you're also much too careless, always making silly little mistakes in the book-keeping.

You'll have to go.' Mr A begins to sweat. 'How dare that toad do this to me', he thinks. 'I've always done my best for this company, and I've never had any thanks. Even the most conscientious clerk can make the occasional mistake, and it's not my fault if the bus is always late. The toad obviously hates me. But I won't let him get away with this. Just let him dare, and then he'll see what. . . .'

At this moment Mr A's reverie is interrupted by the gruff voice of the manager calling him into his office. There is a silence as he finishes writing something ('My letter of dismissal', thinks Mr A, now drenched in sweat). The boss finally looks up. 'You want more money. These are difficult times for us all, you know.' He sighs. 'Still, if we want to keep you we'll have to pay you more, I suppose. From next week you'll get a 5 per cent increase on your present salary. That's all, close the door as you go. And Mr A, please try to be a bit more punctual, won't you?' Mr A scampers out of the office, hardly believing his ears. By the time he reaches the bus-stop he has calmed down a little. He thinks how silly he was for believing that he might be sacked, how unfair to have thought his boss capable of being so nasty. And as the bus finally appears, late as usual, Mr A says to himself: 'Maybe life's not so bad after all, despite its ups and downs.'

Mr A's is obviously not a very exciting life, and this is not an especially exciting story of a day in it. Not for us, that is. But for Mr A himself it has been a quite exhaustingly animated day. Never mind the fact that nothing in the least bit 'dramatic' has happened; for Mr A the day has been packed with action, even if it has all been restricted to his own mind. He has been the hero of a drama — specifically, a melodrama — in which he has been threatened by a villain, his boss. As hero, Mr A has seen himself as the virtuous representative of all the oppressed and his manager as the embodiment of 'them', all those who hold down the poor, all those who are 'against' Mr A, all those who make buses late and cause prices to rise. Into this stark mental encounter between Good and Evil, Right and Wrong, Mr A has infused a rich emotional content, compounded of —among other things — social resentment (because his boss is better off), fear (of being sacked), guilt (at sometimes being late and making mistakes), and — most strongly of all — righteous indignation. He has been ready to take a terrible revenge, as the representative of Good, on the Evil which is persecuting him —even if he wasn't quite sure what form it would take. Indeed, who knows how Mr A's mental drama may have developed had he not been brought back to reality by the summons of the manager.

Mr A, like most of us, is a natural melodramatist, who happened on this day to create a little drama of the kind we are all apt to invent from time to time. In this drama morality and emotion are both considerably heightened and fantasy has been given free rein, even if it is fantasy which has been inspired by solid realities. Our fantasies, like Mr A's, are in fact characteristically melodramatic; and not only our fantasies, for even when we are thinking, saying and doing things in reality (as opposed to imagining that we are doing them) we very often perceive that reality in the terms of melodrama.

This is as true of the collective, public sphere as of individuals in their private lives. Politics, for example, are conducted in countries the world over in almost exclusively melodramatic terms. Politicians habitually suggest, either overtly or tacitly, that their particular party or system has a monopoly of political virtue and that its rivals possess almost every conceivable political vice. Frequently, the rival party is projected as being a villainous threat to the country, whose policies will bring it to ruin. Religious belief, especially in its fundamentalist forms, is also typically, and intensely, melodramatic: one does right and is saved; one does wrong and courts eternal damnation.

All of this suggests that the melodramatic tendency is not a temporary aberration or extravagance in individuals, but a universal and permanent way of apprehending reality. And at the root of the melodramatic vision seems to be the desire to affirm that there is a fundamental distinction between good and evil, that they can be recognised as operative in the world, and that one is oneself firmly identified with the force of goodness. Closely associated with these desires is the urge to be assured that good (which happens to include ourselves) will ultimately triumph over evil. And as we saw in the case of Mr A, the melodramatic way of looking at life includes the projection of our dreams, fears and desires — the unconscious, irrational side of our natures — in a vivid, very concrete way. Within an intensely moralistic framework we give our deepest anxieties and hopes free rein, especially our anxieties and fears about the things that we feel threaten us. When our Mr A fantasises as he waits to see his boss, he indulges his guilt feelings and anxieties about making mistakes and being late, and generally exploits his latent capacity for feeling resentful of, and threatened by, 'them', represented by his boss. Similarly, when a politician catalogues all the dreadful things that will happen if his rivals gain power he is attempting to exploit our fears, our capacity to feel threatened.

If melodrama is, as I'm suggesting, a permanent way of seeing things —a permanent vision of life —which is deeply ingrained in our private and public existence, then we need not be surprised to discover that it is the most genuinely popular type of drama. In the twentieth century drama is not of course restricted to the stage: it flourishes, and is seen by many millions of people every day, on television and in the cinema. And a vast amount of this drama — certainly the kind enjoyed by most people — is melodrama. Kung Fu films from Hong Kong; romantic love films from India; the wide variety of film drama produced in Hollywood: in all these the underlying dramatic structure is a struggle between good and evil in which, despite being temporarily defeated and persecuted, good is finally triumphant.

The same is true of the most popular television serials, usually of American origin, which are shown around the world: 'Hawaii Five-O', 'Starsky and Hutch' — this is the dominant drama of our times, and it is firmly within the mould of melodrama. And where a genuinely popular indigenous stage-drama exists in Africa — for example in the form of the Yoruba travelling companies of Hubert Ogunde and Baba Sala in Nigeria — the entertainment provided normally combines bold emotional effects with a strong moralistic framework typical of melodrama.

From what has been said above, it is clear that a great deal of melodrama is of no intellectual or artistic significance, merely providing entertainment on a mass commercial scale. But the fact that we began the process of identifying its characteristic effects by looking at *The Trial of Dedan Kimathi* confirms that it is not restricted to commercialism or escapist entertainment, but that it can be an intensely serious type of drama. Melodrama evidently covers a broad range of dramatic forms and subject matter, and varies widely in quality and function. It is now time to get an idea of its scope, and to deepen and extend our understanding of its characteristic features.

The forms and features of melodrama

'Zulu Sofola, the Nigerian authoress of *Wedlock of the Gods*, describes her play as 'a tragedy which finds its roots in the ritual of death and mourning' (p. 1, 'Production Note'). It is both possible and illuminating to consider some plays from more than one point of view — as both tragedy and melodrama, for example. Here, I want to discuss *Wedlock of the Gods* as a melodrama, and specifically as an example of a very popular and appealing form of melodrama, that which centres on the passionate but doomed love of a man and a woman.

Ogwoma, a young widow, has been forced by her parents to marry a man she hated solely because they needed her bridewealth. To make matters worse, Ogwoma was passionately in love with another man, Uloko. When her loathed husband, Adigwu, dies, she resumes her relationship with Uloko, even refusing to complete the period of mourning required by custom. She becomes pregnant by Uloko, causing both of them to incur the wrath of the families involved and the disapproval of the community as a whole. The dead man's mother, Odibei, who hates her daughter-in-law, practises witchcraft on Ogwoma to gain revenge for her dead son: she puts her into a trance and directs Ogwoma to drink poison, which kills her. Uloko, on discovering this, kills Odibei and then also drinks the poison and dies alongside his beloved.

Even this brief plot outline suggests the emotional intensity of the characters and situations, and the powerful feelings they are intended to awake in the audience. There is no emotional moderation among the main characters, who are presented as being caught up in feelings so strong that they cannot be tempered or even controlled. Dominating everything is the passionate love between Uloko and Ogwoma, which is so overwhelming that neither is prepared to observe the short period of mourning before they continue their relationship, even though this would have prevented them from breaking the crucial tribal taboos. Passion, in this play, exists as as a kind of elemental force: Ogwoma and Uloko love each other passionately; Ogwoma hated Adigwu with the same strength that she loved the man she was denied; Odibei hates Ogwoma and Uloko with the same unqualified, irrational force with which she reveres the memory of her dead son. Even the lovers' mothers, Nneka and Ogoli, hate each other with a passion.

The intensity of feeling experienced by the characters is revealed through what they say to, and about, each other. Listen to Ogwoma explaining her feelings about her relationship with Uloko to her friend Anwasia:

I prayed for the past three years for my God to deliver me from this marriage. My prayers were answered and nothing can stop me this time. Let the moon turn into blood; let the rain become fire; Ogwoma loves and Ogwoma will do it again!

(pp. 9–10)

And when Anwasia remarks that she has been blinded by love for Uloko, she willingly, even rhapsodically, agrees:

> Oh God, Uloko has blinded me.
> I go to the market,
> It is Uloko I see in every stall;
> I go to the farm,
> It is Uloko in every tree;
> The wind blows,
> It is his hands that touch me;
> The birds sing,
> It is his voice I hear;
> Oh God, his child moves in me.

(p. 10)

And here is Neka, Ogwoma's mother, telling Uloko what she thinks of him:

> You are evil. A man who visits the house of a woman in ashes hides so that the people will not see his face. He hides because what he goes to touch has not been cleansed. A man who does such things says nothing about it for others to hear because it is a word that cuts the tongue. But you have said it and said it loudly. And your life will see nothing but misery. That bastard which you have planted in her will not see your face, nor will he taste his mother's milk. You will walk on your head and talk with your anus . . .

(p. 38)

Nothing is hidden in these speeches. Extreme emotional states (e.g. Ogwoma's love) and moral judgments (Nneka's 'You are evil') are openly and fully expressed. In this, *Wedlock of the Gods* is exemplary of most melodramatic plays, in which characters typically give voice, whenever and wherever possible, to their deepest feelings.

The passionate rhetoric of melodrama, its tendency towards inflated and extravagant expression, is matched by the sensationalism of its action. Consider the hectic, sensational activity of the final scene (Act 3, scene 2) of *Wedlock of the Gods*. Odibei performs her magical ceremony which brings Ogwoma onto the stage in a trance. She drinks the poison, stumbles and falls, a few moments after which Uloko rushes in. Ogwoma dies, and Uloko dashes out. A few seconds later Ogwoma's friend Anwasia enters and finds her dead: she falls on her friend's corpse, sobbing. Nneka, Ogwoma's mother, now arrives on the scene, and also falls on her daughter's body, weeping, which commotion brings Ogwoma's father, Ibekwe, running into the house. He at least, we are told in a stage direction, tries *'to control his emotions like a man'* (p. 55), but presumably has great difficulty in doing so when, a moment later, Uloko re-enters with a bloodstained cutlass in his hand. Nneka dashes across to him and beats him hysterically, accusing him of killing her child. In fact, he has just come from killing Odibei; having confessed to her murder, he *'searches frantically for something, knocking everything over as he does so'* (p. 55). He finds what he's looking for — the poison that killed Ogwoma — and drinks it himself, finally dying beside his beloved as the others rush around in confusion.

Admittedly, the action of melodrama is not always as frenetic as this, but there is an undeniable tendency for such plays to be packed with tense situations — often confrontations between the representatives of good and evil — and marked by spectacular occurrences and reversals. And this is the case for essentially the same reason that we find so much extravagant rhetoric — because in melodrama everything must be brought out into the open, made ummistakably clear and direct. Characters say exactly what is on their minds, and they also do precisely what their strong feelings urge them to do.

The characterisation itself conforms to this basic demand that everything should be brought out into the open. Characters in melodrama are rarely complex and many-sided: they tend, rather, to have a few simple but plainly observable traits that unambiguously signal their natures and the attitudes that we should adopt towards them. For example, Uloko is the passionate lover of Ogwoma, and Ogwoma of Uloko: their characters are defined by, and restricted to, their mutual passion; they don't have any other sides to their personalities, or any other aspects to their lives. If Ogwoma and Uloko are Passionate Lovers, Odibei is the Hateful Mother-in-law: she is completely defined by her love for her dead son and her desire for revenge on Ogwoma. Because of their one-dimensional nature there is no psychological depth in the portrayal of the characters of melodrama, at least as a general tendency. We are not invited to look into their minds and see there a complex network of ideas, emotions and desires. On the contrary, everything being apparent on the 'outside', these are characters who have no 'inside'; and if we try to probe too deeply it is usually to discover that, despite their surface clarity, the reasons why they behave as they do are obscure or unconvincing. We must simply accept that Ogwoma and Uloko are as they are, with no questions asked.

In its language, action and characterisation, then, melodrama tends towards essentially simple but bold and powerful effects. This is true also of the vaguer but important quality that we might call mood or atmosphere. The 'melo-' of melodrama comes from the Greek word *melos*, meaning a song. And this form of drama got its name from the fact that, towards the end of the eighteenth century, plays in which the action and dialogue had a musical background became very popular. The music was used to heighten the emotional effects, as it still is in most melodrama on television and in the cinema. This suggests the importance of mood or atmosphere in melodramatic plays, and the way it is achieved.

'Zulu Sofola, in her production note to *Wedlock of the Gods*, stresses the importance of music and lighting — the other main technical means of creating mood-effects — in her play:

> Slow, mournful music to create a sad atmosphere may be played at
> the beginning and end of each scene, during intervals and in the

death scene while Ibekwe and Nneka cover the corpses. The lights should fade gradually in this scene as the music also grows more solemn and funereal. (p. 4)

The technical effects of sound and lighting are often used in melodrama to heighten a sense of menace and threat, which is naturally an important and pervasive feature of a type of drama which regularly shows virtue afflicted at the hands of evil. The atmosphere of menace, and the suspense created by it, are exemplified in the scene where Odibei performs her rites of witchcraft and puts Ogwoma into a trance, causing her to drink the poison.

The elements of drama are thus brought together in *Wedlock of the Gods* to create strong emotional effects in the audience. As we saw in *The Trial of Dedan Kimathi*, this emotional impact is in support of the drama's aim of presenting as strikingly as possible the struggle between the forces of good and evil. There is no doubt, in *Wedlock of the Gods*, where our moral, as well as our emotional, sympathies are encouraged to lie: we are on the side of the young lovers and their passionate love. Ogwoma and Uloko stand for the right of the individual to live according to his or her deepest needs and desires rather than as the slaves of custom and social convenience. But they are finally defeated and destroyed by the forces that oppose them, which seems to contradict what has been said about melodrama's tendency to show the ultimate triumph of the forces of good. Actually, the defeat is more apparent than real: the villainess of the play, Odibei, is killed, so that the evil which she represents can be seen to have been destroyed; and in their deaths the lovers assert the undying strength and beauty of their love. Their triumph-in-defeat is poetically expressed by Uloko in his dying speech:

> Ours is the wedlock of the gods.
> Together we shall forever be lightning
> and thunder — inseparable!
> Our love shall live forever;
> Your light to keep it aglow,
> My thunder to demolish all obstacles.
> We shall leave this cursed place;
> We shall ride on the cotton of the heavens;
> We shall ride to where there is peace!
> The rain shall cool our sweats and pains;
> The sun shall dry our tears;
> The stars shall crown our heads;
> The night shall hide and protect us.
> Over and around we shall together roam;
> Beautifying as we impress!
>
> (pp. 55–6)

Mukotani Rugyendo's play, *The Barbed Wire*, is very different from *Wedlock of the Gods* in its subject, theme and purpose. The latter is one of many melodramas that dramatise in a very emotive way the pains of passionate love, often culminating in the death of one or both of the lovers. The spectators of 'Zulu Sofola's play, if they feel so inclined, can live out in imagination their own fantasies of passion through the characters and participate, in an entirely safe way, in an individualistic rebellion against constraining social custom. *The Barbed Wire*, on the other hand, deals with the struggle of a peasant community in Uganda to prevent a wealthy businessman and farmer from taking traditionally common land and enclosing it for his own use. Rugyendo's play certainly does not invite the kind of intense emotional identification with a passionate personal relationship such as we find in *Wedlock of the Gods*. Our feelings and moral judgments are directed, in the Ugandan play, to social and political issues, and they contribute to Rugyendo's *didactic* aim of educating his audience —presumably intended to be an audience of peasants and workers —in the most effective way to take action when presented with the problem of land-grabbing.

And yet, for all their differences, the two plays exhibit the same basic melodramatic features. *The Barbed Wire*, perhaps even more clearly than the Nigerian play, is structured around the struggle between the readily recognisable forces of good and evil. The peasants, led by Birakwate and Nyamuganya, are innocent victims; the businessman-farmer, Rwambura, is the embodiment of pride, arrogance and greed, which makes him totally indifferent to the well-being of others. Rugyendo's play is also typically melodramatic in the way that it introduces early on the threat to the representatives of goodness, and for the greater part of the action shows them in a situation of peril as the force of evil appears to go from strength to strength. The difference between *Wedlock of the Gods* and *The Barbed Wire*, in this respect, is that in the latter goodness is visibly triumphant in the end, whereas the hero and heroine of the former are defeated in body, if not in spirit. In both plays, however, the ultimate power of goodness is resolutely affirmed, though in quite different social and dramatic contexts.

As in *Wedlock of the Gods* and *The Trial of Dedan Kimathi*, Rugyendo enlists our emotional support for what he presents as the force of goodness in his play. We are encouraged to feel sympathy for the peasants and indignation against Rwambura and those who side with him. These feelings are especially strong in scenes 4 and 5 when the police use physical force against the peasant farmers. The situation dramatised here will be familiar, if only as a possibility, to many African audiences: the oppression of the poor and defenceless by figures of authority who are in league with the wealthy and influential. And it will undoubtedly arouse strong feelings of resentment and a desire to see such an unjust state of affairs redressed.

Though *The Barbed Wire* is emotive, it is probably true to say that it is less arousing at a purely emotional level than *Wedlock of the Gods*. This is not the result of a failure on Rugyendo's part, but has to do with the didactic or socially educative aim of his play. 'Zulu Sofola's play is not concerned with teaching anything: its emotionalism and moralism are at the service of pure entertainment. This is plainly not so in the Ugandan play. It is easy to see how *The Barbed Wire* could be performed for rural audiences who may well face comparable problems to those of the peasant characters, and how it would communicate the unmistakeable message that men like Rwambura should be resisted. Not only this; it also suggests *how* to resist, at least in the context of the political structures of one-party East African states. Instead of conducting a hopeless fight with their sticks and pangas, ending in their inevitable arrest, the peasants should try to make their grievances known through the party: if enough people protest the party must act, and can use its power to correct abuses in government. *The Barbed Wire*, then, belongs to that kind of melodrama which puts its emotional and moral impact at the service of ethical or social education. There is nothing new in this: we can find a similar employment of melodrama (long before the genre acquired this name) as far back as the medieval morality play, *Everyman*, which also presents a striking contrast between good and evil to show right behaviour.

Sharing the same essential features of melodrama, our plays can thus be seen to diverge widely in their concerns and purposes. Combining protest and inspirational example, both *The Trial of Dedan Kimathi* and *The Barbed Wire* belong to a type of socially-orientated melodrama which is likely to make an increasing impact in Africa as social and political conflicts and awareness sharpen. (Rugyendo has also used melodrama effectively in *The Contest*, which uses the traditional performance form of a heroic contest to show the ideological superiority of socialism over capitalism.) But at the same time melodramatic plays like *Wedlock of the Gods*, by African dramatists, and primarily intended to entertain, will doubtless retain and extend their popularity, as will imported forms on television and in the cinema. The two forms of melodrama we have concentrated on do not exhaust the range of melodramatic drama found in Africa — or, to put it another way, the range of drama which can be fruitfully considered from the viewpoint of melodrama. They suggest, rather, the great variety possible in subject, theme and purpose in plays of this genre, even as they share certain recurrent characteristic features.

Comedy, tragedy and melodrama

As in our discussion of comedy and tragedy, we have been concerned to isolate and analyse those characteristic qualities which make it possible to think of melodrama as a distinct dramatic kind. But it has probably become apparent to most readers that, just as comedy and tragedy are closely related, so melodrama has elements in common with both. Let's conclude by briefly considering the links between them.

The most obvious resemblance is between melodrama and tragedy. We have seen, for instance, that *Wedlock of the Gods*, which its author describes as a tragedy, has lent itself quite naturally to discussion as melodrama. It is worth stressing that our main aim is certainly not to decide at all costs which type of drama 'Zulu Sofola's play belongs to: we can consider this and comparable plays from both viewpoints, without even bothering ourselves with the fruitless question of which it should 'rightly' be attached to. Melodrama and tragedy have several crucial features in common. They share a similar kind of 'seriousness' which is distinct from the seriousness of comedy. Plays of both kinds invite us to witness the spectacle of pain, sometimes in its most extreme forms, and to identify ourselves emotionally with the character(s) experiencing it. We thus often feel emotions of a sorrowful kind, combined with admiration — even awe — for the protagonists, as we watch both tragedy and melodrama. There is also a resemblance in the kind of ethical experience we have in watching plays belonging to the two genres, for in both there is a sense of coming into close and painful contact with the reality of good and evil as forces operating in our lives.

The crucial difference between tragedy and melodrama lies in their respective conceptions of the nature of the dilemma they both dramatise. In tragedy, as we've seen, the dilemma experienced by the hero is not resolvable in any clear-cut way. I suggested earlier that Orestes, Ozidi and Willy Loman can all be likened to men standing at a crossroads, from which any path they choose is bound to lead to suffering and perhaps death. For one reason or another, there is no clear course of action that they can take which is 'good', and which is wholly free of consequences or implications that are 'evil'. This ethical complexity, together with the complicated emotional and intellectual response it is likely to arouse in an audience, are not present in the conflicts and dilemmas of melodrama. Conflict in plays like *Wedlock of the Gods* and *The Barbed Wire*, and the dilemmas it creates for its protagonists, are purely external, in the sense that the characters are not torn by opposing forces between which it is difficult or impossible to choose, or entangled in moral complexities beyond a clear-cut confrontation between good and evil. In melodrama conflict tends not to be *within* characters but *between* them, with one (or one group) embodying evident virtue and innocence and the other, equally clearly, embodying evil.

We therefore do not usually find in melodramatic plays those *divided* characters of tragedy, who are caught in the dilemma of being pulled in opposing directions by equally powerful forces. The division is outside the characters, in the separation of good from evil. In tragedy, on the other hand, there is rarely, if ever, such a strict separation: tragic protagonists tend to be entangled in moral forces which combine both good and evil, depending on how they are viewed, and which in any case are often ethically obscure, so that it is difficult to make definite judgments as to their goodness or badness.

If melodrama can be closely allied to tragedy, and even sometimes seem indistinguishable from it, so there is a strong affinity between melodrama and comedy in the form of their joint attachment to wish-fulfilment. We saw how *Lysistrata* and *The Marriage of Anansewa* both fulfilled in imaginary but vivid form the wishes doubtless entertained by most people in their audiences. *The Trial of Dedan Kimathi* and *The Barbed Wire*, provided they are performed before suitable audiences, do the same, though the former play devotes much of its dramatic energy to imbuing the audience with the wish. In both, as in our two comedies, the final scene presents us with the victory of good over evil and invites us to participate in the appropriate kind of celebration. Even where the representatives of goodness have failed to endure the menace of evil, as in *Wedlock of the Gods*, and where there is consequently no scene of joyous triumph, the audience's wish for the lovers to be permanently united is conveyed in Uloko's death speech, when he says that they will live on inseparably as the thunder and the lightning.

Melodrama, then, like comic drama, tends to bring out the fantasist in us all. As we watch innocence and goodness being threatened by evil we live out in a potent imaginary form our own anxieties and fears; and when evil is finally, and against all the odds, defeated — which it usually is — we obtain a welcome, if temporary, release from those fears. To what extent, then, is the appeal to our fantasy-life proof of the essentially escapist nature of melodrama? Certainly, the term is often used pejoratively, to connote an inferior kind of drama which self-indulgently turns its back on reality. But we will reserve our discussion of this question for the next chapter, in which we consider the process of making value judgments not only on melodramas but also on plays belonging to the other genres.

10 Judging plays

This has not been, like a critical study, a book full of value judgments about plays. In Part I we were concerned with the elements common to drama generally, and with reading plays so that we can appreciate their dramatic qualities as fully as possible. Part II extended this approach, moving outwards from the individual play to consider the characteristic features of the main kinds of drama. In all this there have been no value judgments of plays, nor has much been said about the actual process of judging individual plays. But this is evidently a vital and inevitable part of dramatic criticism, whether it is practised academically by students and their teachers in the classroom, or by professional critics and reviewers, or more casually by people who simply enjoy reading or watching plays occasionally in their spare time. Most of us expect to form an opinion of a play, even if it goes no further than pronouncing it 'good', 'bad' or 'all right'. I will conclude by looking a little more closely in this chapter at the business of forming critical opinions about drama. In the process we cannot avoid touching on some theoretical issues, but we will do so only as part of offering essentially practical, and I hope helpful, guidance about judging plays.

It may seem unnecessary to ask what a value judgment or critical opinion of a play actually consists of. After all, we spend a good deal of our everyday lives making judgments of one kind or another, and it seems reasonable to believe that judgments about drama are not essentially different from these day-to-day kinds. When we judge, say, whether to buy a Honda or a Suzuki, or whether to apply for this college or that, our main concern is to decide which is 'better', at least for us: which motor-bike will be the most reliable mechanically, or will go the fastest, or will be the cheapest to run and maintain. Shopping around for a motor-bike, we look at the various models available and try to place each of them on a scale going from the least desirable to the most desirable, from 'bad' to 'good'. Judging a play is arguably no different in nature from making such judgments in normal life: it is primarily a matter of deciding whether the drama is good or very good, bad or very bad, or somewhere in the middle.

'What did you think of the play?' you ask a friend as you leave the theatre. 'Oh, I thought it was good,' is the reply. 'So did I,' you say. And off you go, having established quite satisfactorily what you both think, and being in all probability quite sure what you both mean. But what *do* you mean? Do you mean that it was good in relation to other plays you are acquainted with? Or that it was good in relation to what you know of real life? Or both? And if you are tacitly judging it against other plays, what particular features of the other plays are you comparing your play with?

There is another point, which has to do with personal subjectivity. Someone shopping around for a motor-bike, as we have seen, might be particularly concerned with one or more of several factors: its mechanical reliability, its speed, cost, and so forth. In other words, motor-bikes will be judged differently depending on different personal needs and desires, on what people are looking for. This subjective element is likely to affect the judgment of plays in a similar way. For example, it may be that when your friend said the play was good he was thinking primarily, or even exclusively, of the dramatist's skill in handling characterisation, plot and so forth, while you were thinking mainly of what it was communicating.

We may reasonably suspect, then, that people mean all sorts of different things — and sometimes next to nothing at all — by the common run of summary and essentially uninformative judgments like 'It was good' or 'It was bad' and the possible variations upon them. For a judgment of a play to be of any real interest or value it must obviously have access to a more sophisticated critical vocabulary, which in turn requires the aspiring critic to have a fairly clear understanding of what he is actually doing as he makes his judgment. So it seems that we do have to enquire into what a value judgment in drama consists of: what is it, first and foremost, a judgment about?

I suggested above that of two people who judge a play to be good, one may be basing his opinion on the skill with which the drama has been made while the other is making a critical comment on its success in saying something which he considers interesting. This suggests that critical judgments are commonly applied to two related but distinguishable aspects of a play: the technical skill with which the dramatist handles such dramatic elements as characterisation, plot, dialogue and imagery — the things we looked at in Part I; and, on the other hand, the interest or otherwise of the statement or insight that is offered by it. It is important to see that these two dimensions *are* related, for what is actually communicated cannot help being deeply affected by the playwright's skill in communicating, which depends on his ability to handle the basic elements of drama. But that they are distinguishable is proved by the fact that a play which has been incompetently conceived and written may still, for all its imperfections, say something interesting about life, while a skilfully composed play may have nothing worthwhile to communicate.

An adequate critical judgment must take both aspects into account. To consider only the technical skill with which a dramatist puts together his play — unless the critical context specifically sanctions a discussion of this limited kind — is to be guilty of the failure to see that art, including the art of drama, is always vitally related to life, and that this relation is crucially important in making critical judgments. Similarly, to concentrate exclusively on this relation, and hence to form an opinion solely in terms of what is believed to be the interest or rightness of its preceptions of reality, represents a failure to take account of the independent artistic life of the drama. As we shall see, a lack of concern with the artistic or aesthetic aspect often prevents the reader or playgoer making a proper judgment about what a play is communicating. Neither aspect is more important than the other, nor can criticism concentrate satisfactorily on one without concerning itself with the other.

This said, it must be stressed that the starting-point of all good dramatic criticism is a willingness to submit oneself as imaginatively as possible to the experience of the play. We have to allow the play to work on us in whatever way it does. For all plays — and especially good plays — make a special claim on us: they insist that we enter their worlds, that we give ourselves over for a time to their imaginary but persuasive realities. In a theatre, watching a good performance, this is relatively easy: much of the imaginative work is, so to speak, done for us. It requires a much greater effort of the imagination, at least initially, when we have only the play-text in front of us. Part I of this book was concerned with suggesting a profitable approach to the problem of reading plays so that their dramatic qualities are brought out, and I do not propose to go over this ground again, even in summary. But one or two general remarks, specifically related to the process of making value judgments, are in order.

It is probably only after a person has had considerable experiene of reading plays of various kinds that he or she acquires sufficient confidence and sensitivity to be able to get the most out of playreading. It is especially hard, particularly for the inexperienced reader, to sustain a genuinely dramatic reading of a play whose formal qualities are unfamiliar, either because it is from a foreign culture or because its author, though perhaps from one's own culture, is an experimentalist who is trying to do something new and different. By 'formal qualities' I mean the impressions made on us by the way the dramatic elements of characterisation, plot, dialogue and so forth have been arranged and presented within the framework of certain conventions. These conventions, as we saw earlier (Ch. 2, pp 7–9), are the tacit agreements between the participants in a play — its author, director, designer, performers and audience — about how it is to be conducted. Now, it is through their formal qualities that plays bring us into their fictional worlds and sustain our attention for a time. It is through them that a certain representation of reality is achieved in theatrical performance; they are, so to speak, the fictional moulds into which the writer's and performers' perceptions of life are poured and allowed to become firm, so that we are left with something which, while being its own thing, also has real life in it. The problem, when unfamiliar with the style and conventions of a play, is how to make a meaningful connection between the formal qualities and the reality which they portray.

There is no easy solution to the problem; but one can at least make a suggestion which may be useful to readers who find themselves facing this difficulty. We've seen that each of the main kinds of drama share certain characteristic tendencies or features, which seem to recur even in plays whose formal qualities in other respects differ widely. What this means, to be more concrete, is that we can read two comedies which create quite different impressions and yet know that they are both comedies, that they have in common certain characteristic tendencies of comedy. It may help, in reading a play whose formal qualities are unfamiliar, to keep comparing one's impressions — however confused they might be — with those made by other plays one has read or seen, and thus to try to 'place' that play in relation to others. We can do this in the reasonable expectation that the play is virtually certain to have some resemblance to other plays we know in displaying the basic characteristics of one or other of the main kinds of drama. If, then, the unfamiliar play seems to lend itself to fruitful comparison and contrast with, say, other comedies of our acquaintance, at least in certain of its characteristics, we are then in possession of a kind of mental compass which should help give us some sense of the nature of the dramatic landscape.

In doing this, of course, we are only making conscious a process that occurs unconsciously, or semi-consciously, in all reading. Even when we read a play that is very familiar in its basic characteristics we are constantly 'situating' it in relation to others, both of the same essential kind and perhaps also of other kinds. It is in this way that we get a sense both of genre, of what the play has in common with others, and of its uniqueness, its own special, distinctive quality. At its best, the process of making a judgment on a play involves a very wide range of conscious comparison and contrast with many other plays of different kinds, thus allowing the critic to situate his play as precisely as possible both in terms of its affinities and its distinctiveness. Criticism such as this obviously implies a considerable experience of drama, but the basic principle of the process stands for inexperienced readers and playgoers as well. If the discussion of the main kinds of drama in Part II helps its readers in this process, then it will have served its purpose.

The enjoyment of drama, then, and our understanding of it as a meaningful representation of reality, depends on our appreciation of its formal qualities, on giving due imaginative and critical recognition to the impressions it makes on us and the means by which these are achieved. We have said that the willingness to let a play work its effects on us is the necessary starting-point of all good dramatic criticism. But it is only the starting-point and not the entire process. For we expect to recognise, *through* and *in* our response to the play, some kind of 'statement' about life, some kind of insight into our common reality. That this is so is evidenced by the disappointment or even annoyance that most readers feel when they cannot abstract from the dramatic experience some meaning in relation to a recognisable reality. We enter the world of the play and let it work its effects on us; but we expect this imaginary world, however self-sufficient it may seem, to throw a new and revealing light on the world we have left and will re-enter when the play is over.

There is a mistaken but very widespread notion of how a play should illuminate real life. This can be stated as the belief that a play is only any good when it is 'true to life', meaning that what we see and hear is as much like real life as possible. In this view drama is at its most serious — or only serious at all — when its conventions make for the greatest possible degree of realism. Put like this, it is fairly easy to see where this 'naive realist' approach (as I shall call it) goes wrong: it fails to take sufficient account of the relative independence of the formal qualities of drama and hence expects art to be indistinguishable from the appearance of real life. (Naive realists cannot see that the conventions of naturalism or realism are just as artificial as those of non-naturalistic plays.)

But in practice the temptation of naive realism can be hard to resist, especially for the relatively inexperienced play-reader. For example, it is understandable why some readers, in the West as well as in Africa, judge Samuel Beckett's *Waiting For Godot* to be a 'trivial' and 'meaningless' play, with nothing to say about or do with real life. True, Beckett's tramps, and the other two characters, Pozzo and Lucky, do not talk or behave as tramps usually do in real life. True, they don't inhabit a recognisable social environment, or indeed even what could be called a society. Nor, admittedly, is there usually any evident point or 'meaning' (in the sense most people have of that word) in what they say, which can easily lead us to believe that there is no point or meaning to the play as a whole, either. For the naive realist, then, *Waiting For Godot* is simply not 'true to life' and therefore essentially 'unserious', in spite of actually being one of the most serious of modern plays, which offers a weighty and sombre, if also entertaining, statement about how so many people spend their lives in futile waiting for something that never comes.

There is another common misconception, often committed by — but certainly not restricted to — our naive realists, which can greatly distort the judgment of plays. This, like naive realism, also involves a misunderstanding of the proper relation between drama and life. It is that a good play must communicate a readily comprehensible meaning or 'message'; that plays which do not, have something wrong with them; and that, of plays which do make recognisable statements about reality, the degree of success is to be measured in proportion to the 'truth' of what is communicated.

This is a more complicated, and I think more dangerous, kind of misconception about how plays are to be valued than the problem of naive realism. I can perhaps best illustrate the point by reference to my personal experience. I have found that many of my students, over several years, have admired *The Trial of Dedan Kimathi* very often more than plays that I consider more interesting. My disagreement with their opinion has usually been met with the assertion that the Kenyan play has, first, the great merit of communicating a clear statement in a forceful way; and second, that, it is a true statement which is highly relevant to the political realities of contemporary Africa, which makes its merit all the greater. These two points are doubtless correct; what I cannot accept, however, is that they justify the view of *The Trial of Dedan Kimathi* as an outstanding play.

The problem involved here is more complex than the temptation to believe that drama should always be 'true to life' in a naturalistic way. This is because it involves a consideration of the nature of dramatic meaning, which in turn raises the whole issue of the relationship between drama and reality. It would be possible at this point to embark upon a theoretical analysis of this relationship and its implications for our particular problem, embracing in its scope issues of great interest and importance which are much, and often hotly, debated among modern critics. But to keep our discussion within manageable proportions let us consider specifically what is meant when a play is said, as it often is, to 'make a statement' about life or reality, or, more simply, that a play 'says' something.

The Trial of Dedan Kimathi makes a statement about life, at least about Kenyan life, which can be paraphrased as: 'the revolutionary struggle for the emancipation of the masses is not yet over: look to the heroic example of Dedan Kimathi and continue that struggle by all possible means until victory, which is certain, is achieved'. This summary of the play's 'statement' could be elaborated, or phrased rather differently, but I think it adequately conveys the essential dramatic 'message' or meaning. Now, it is possible, and in criticism often necessary, to extract statements of this kind from plays generally. Are all plays, then, like *The Trial of Dedan Kimathi* in the way they 'say' things to their audiences? I think not, for this reason: that in some plays, though it is undoubtedly possible to give a useful summary of their 'statements', the meaning is not exhausted, or even adequately conveyed, by the summary, whereas in the Kenyan play (for example) the meaning is satisfactorily communicated by the summary statement. (In this case, what is not and cannot be adequately conveyed in summary is the *emotive impact* of the play, which is part of its effect but not part of its meaning.) To put it rather too bluntly, the meanings of some plays can be boiled down to a sentence or two, while with other plays this is not possible. I do not think one could convey adequately the meaning of Soyinka's *The Strong Breed*, for example, in the way I have done for Ngugi and Mugo's play. It *is* possible to offer a few sentences indicating what one takes to be the area of experience with which Soyinka is dealing in that play; but this would not, in my view, be more than a helpful starting-point for a consideration of its meaning.

This does not mean that *The Trial of Dedan Kimathi* is a bad play and *The Strong Breed* a good one. I can only agree with my students when they point to the Kenyan dramatists' effective use of drama to make a political statement of considerable force and relevance. The Kenyan play is doubtless in its way a success: the point is that it is a different, and far *simpler*, way than that of, say, *The Strong Breed*. However we judge Soyinka's play, it must be as a *richer*, more *complex*, statement about life than *The Trial of Dedan Kimathi*. (This does not mean that it is necessarily *truer*: again, we have to say that their 'truth to life' are of quite different kinds.) If we agree that this is so, it cannot but affect our ultimate valuation of the interest and worth of the two, even if we can agree that both are successful plays.

Judgements about the comparative richness and complexity of specific plays are necessarily subjective. I mention these two plays, not because they are especially comparable or because I have particularly strong feelings about either, but merely because they are convenient examples. The important point is this: that although we commonly talk of plays 'making statements' or 'being statements' or 'saying' something about life, if the validity of my example above is accepted, then we must accept that these 'statements', these things that are 'said', vary in their nature or essential quality; and that this is a fact which inevitably influences our judgment of the ultimate value of plays. Some dramatic statements are 'simple', in the sense that they can be readily paraphrased or summarised; others are 'complex' and do not yield their full meaning except by exhaustive analysis and commentary. It is perhaps unfortunate that we so often use phrases like 'what the play says' or 'the statement of the play' in relation to drama like *The Strong Breed*; the subtly persuasive way in which such plays draw us into certain kinds of experience, and spin their webs of meaning, does not accord with the connotations of cut-and-dried assertion carried by words like 'statement' or 'message'.

It can now be seen, I hope, why it is a mistake, if an understandable one, to judge plays according to how easily comprehensible or direct their meanings are. However much we may find ourselves in agreement with them, and however convenient they may be when it comes to writing answers on them in exams, we must surely value dramatic complexity over such relative simplicity. This does not mean, of course, that a play is better the more obscure the dramatist contrives to make it. Obscurity is not to be confused with complexity; and a play which is hopelessly obscure is not *too* rich in meaning but altogether devoid of meaning, at least for most readers.

We have stressed throughout this book that words like 'drama', 'tragedy', 'comedy' and their adjectives are regularly used in ordinary life in and about non-theatrical contexts. Let's conclude by briefly noting how the way plays 'say' or mean things can be usefully compared with the way people say and mean things in everyday life. And our perception and judgment of dramatic 'saying' can also be related to the way we perceive and judge what people say in everyday speech. Plays 'say' things which may be simple or complex, just as, in real-life speech, things said sometimes have direct and straightforward meanings and sometimes have elaborate meanings which may not even be fully comprehended at once. For example, people sometimes speak ironically, so that they mean the opposite of their literal statement. Irony can operate in a more subtle and complex way, however, by qualifying or adding to the literal statement rather than indicating its direct opposite. This can be done through tone of voice, or through facial and bodily gestures, or even through the 'significant' use of pauses and emphasis. Even more elaborately, the words that a person uses, as well as the way they are said and the gestures accompanying them, can produce a very complex statement. A well-placed proverb, for example, said in the appropriate tone of voice and with the appropriate manner, can 'say' more than a hundred sentences and mean things at a number of different levels. In speech of this kind, the face value of the words spoken constitutes only one dimension of their meaning: beneath them, there is a whole 'subtext' of meaning. The existence of such 'subtext' is apparent, for example, when one has the experience of reporting a conversation to someone who wasn't there and of being aware that the 'flavour' of the talk, all the things that were going on in it, are not coming through in one's report.

In drama, as in life, meaning can range from the simple and straightforward to the indirect, the highly ironical and complex. As we have seen, plays like *The Trial of Dedan Kimathi* or *The Barbed Wire* which make direct, powerfully relevant statements to their audiences have their place in a flourishing drama. But having overcome the temptation to judge plays by the accessibility of their meaning, the way is open to explore with pleasure drama which speaks in a subtler, richer voice. I say 'with pleasure' because the prospect of making sense of a play which seems to have no clear or definite meaning can be, for many readers, a far from pleasurable one.

There is a psychological problem here, I think, and also, to some degree, an institutional one. To go ever deeper into a play, to tease out ever more intricate meanings and hints of meaning, can instil something akin to fear and depression in many readers. It seems that one may never emerge with an overall sense of the play's meaning. The desire to be able to state in a reasonably concise form what a play means is natural and very strong, and not in itself a bad one. It becomes bad when the reader refuses to be an explorer and hangs on for dear life to some formulation or other of the meaning which is quite inadequate. And unfortunately, educational institutions, and the essays and exams associated with them, often reinforce the natural temptation to turn back rather than perhaps get lost. But to get lost in a play, or at least to go so deeply into it that one isn't sure whether one is lost or not, is part of the pleasure that the best drama offers. The depth and resonance of the best plays invite such exploration, and not once but repeatedly.

Finally, we can extend the idea that plays speak to us in ways comparable with those of ordinary speech by noting that, just as we judge what people say by referring it to our personal experience of life, so we can and should judge what plays 'say' by the same criteria. Drama is not to be judged, ultimately, by values separate from those of ordinary life: we rightly demand of plays that their insights, their assertions — whether simple or complex — should be testable against real-life experience, and valued according to how 'true' they are in relation to reality.

I suggested, in the conclusion to the discussion of comedy, that it's at least arguable that the 'message' of *The Marriage of Anansewa* is misguided, and that this can justifiably affect our judgment of the value of Efua Sutherland's play. Considering that its message is 'Let's relate in love/That we may thrive', this may seem a harsh and perverse idea. But let us consider this exhortation in relation to the play as a whole. It concerns a poor man's successful scheme to improve himself socially, which he does by exploiting his only asset, his daughter, and the customs of his society, to his advantage. The comedy of the play endorses, in a genial, light-hearted way, Ananse's clever scheming. In other words, a social attitude is embodied in the apparently neutral, and certainly good-humoured, comedy: and this attitude involves the idea that poverty can be successfully overcome through personal resourcefulness, the use of one's wits. This attitude is further linked with the idea that, provided we all 'relate in love', we will all thrive. But is this borne out by general experience in Ghana or in societies like it? The reader can decide for himself, but I think it should at least be clear how doubtful, and even perhaps undesirable, the propositions embodied in *The Marriage of Anansewa* actually are.

The point is that in judging Efua Sutherland's play we rightly demand that its meaning or 'message' should be measurable against real experience, and that our sense of its value will in large measure be governed by whether or not we believe it to be 'saying' something true. One may wish to argue that it is actually saying something false, or, less harshly, something which doesn't accord with reality; and consequently, though one can confidently declare it to be a skilfully written and charming play, one may also wish to suggest that it doesn't make a 'truthful' exploration of life in the way that some comedies do. The same criteria apply to every other play, whether it be tragedy, tragi-comedy or melodrama. However skilfully it may have been contrived, however impressive it is in its theatrical effects, our judgment of it must ultimately be based on values which are drawn from, and operate within, our everyday experience of life.

This is a subject that could be pursued at greater length, but this is not the place for it. Our main purpose in mentioning it here was not to explore all its theoretical implications but to help the reader in judging plays by stressing that the process of judgment cannot be divorced from the critical, judging sense in life. In this, as in other things, there are the closest connections between drama and the activities of life. As a last word, I offer the hope that this book may make a small contribution to the process of making these connections even stronger for its African readers by encouraging them not only to read but to make drama, individually or collectively, as words on a page or through improvisation, and to take it wherever an audience can be found.

Further reading

On drama generally

BENTLEY, ERIC, *The Life of the Drama*, Methuen, 1965.
ESSLIN, MARTIN, *An Antomy of Drama*, Abacus, 1978.
STYAN, J. L., *The Elements of Drama*, Cambridge University Press, 1960.

On comedy, tragedy and melodrama

DRAPER, R. P. (ed.), *Tragedy: Developments in Criticism*, Casebook Series, gen. ed. A. E. Dyson, Macmillan, 1980.
HOWARTH, W. D. (ed.), *Comic Drama: The European Heritage*, Methuen, 1978.
KERR, WALTER, *Tragedy and Comedy*, The Bodley Head, 1968.
SMITH, JAMES L., *Melodrama*, Critical Idiom Series 28, gen. ed. John D. Jump, Methuen, 1973.
STYAN, J. L., *The Dark Comedy: The Development of Modern Comic Tragedy*, Cambridge University Press, 2nd ed., 1968.
WILLIAMS, RAYMOND, *Modern Tragedy*, rev. ed., Verso Editions, 1979.

On African theatre

ETHERTON, MICHAEL, *The Development of African Drama*, Hutchinson, 1982.
OGUNBA, OYIN and IRELE, ABIOLA, (eds.), *Theatre in Africa*, Ibadan University Press, 1978.

Other works cited

BERGSON, H. and MEREDITH, G., *Laughter, Essay on Comedy*, Ed. W. Sypher, John Hopkins University Press, 1980.
BRECHT, B., *The Good Woman of Setzuan*, in *Parables for the Theatre*, ed. Eric Bentley, Oxford University Press, 1965.
HUSSEIN, EBRAHIM, *Kinjeketile*, New Drama for Africa, Oxford University Press, 1970.
KIBWANA, J. M., *Utisi*, Comb Books, Nairobi, 1974.

LADIPO, DURO, *Moremi*, in *Three Nigerian Plays*, ed. Ulli Beier, Longman, 1970.

MILLER, A., *Collected Plays*, Viking, 1957.

POTTS, L. J., *Comedy*, Hutchinson, 1949.

SHAKESPEARE, W., *As You Like It*.

SOYINKA, W., *The Road,* in *Collected Plays 1*, Oxford University Press, 1973.

Index